Pisemsky
———
A Provincial Realist

Pisemsky

A Provincial Realist

Charles A. Moser

Harvard University Press
Cambridge, Massachusetts
1969

© Copyright 1969 by the President and Fellows of Harvard College
All rights reserved
Distributed in Great Britain by Oxford University Press, London
Printed in the United States of America
Library of Congresss Catalog Card Number 78-78521
SBN 674-66975-4

Preface

The fate of Aleksey Feofilaktovich Pisemsky in the historiography of nineteenth-century Russian literature has been unenviable. Though hailed by some during the 1850's and early 1860's as a major figure in Russian letters, long before his death in 1881 he had been thrust into oblivion, from which he has only begun to emerge. In the final accounting it is hoped that his work will receive a more judicious evaluation and that he will be granted a higher place in the ranks of nineteenth century authors than he has heretofore been assigned.

A sound reappraisal would hardly result in Pisemsky's being proclaimed a "classic," in the same sense in which the term is applied to Dostoevsky, Tolstoy, Turgenev, Gogol, Goncharov, and other great figures of the last century in Russia. His total achievement as a writer fell short of such stature, although his masterworks—the novel *One Thousand Souls* and the play *A Bitter Fate*—certainly approach it.

Pisemsky owed his success in literature to a natural endowment, which he failed to cultivate properly. Though actively involved in the intellectual and journalistic battles of that period of immense ferment bracketing the liberation of the serfs on February 19, 1861, he was not a powerful thinker. He made up for this failure by applying a pitiless honesty to his analyses of human relations and social affairs. The fact that he did not conduct his personal life with similar honesty did not lessen the indignation aroused in him by public immorality. Moreover, his intellectual candor led him to dissect contemporary radical movements as mercilessly as he investigated established society. This forthrightness proved costly, for the anathema of the radicals has lain heavy upon him since 1863, the year of publication of his anti-radical novel *Vzbalamuchennoe more* (Troubled Seas).

The political animosity generated by *Troubled Seas* would not in itself have been sufficient to suppress the remembrance of Pisemsky so thoroughly. The writer's own lack of staying power was an important factor. Though he produced and published for more than thirty years, the period of his highest literary accomplishment lasted for little over half a decade, roughly from early 1858 to 1863. Afterward Pisemsky's talents and energies waned, although some of his later writings are worthy of literary note.

Pisemsky's biographers have not been kind to him. The best known account of his life is that written some eighty years ago by S. A. Vengerov, originally commissioned to accompany the first complete posthumous edition of Pisemsky's works. Vengerov was a meticulous scholar, but the animus he bore to his subject was so obvious in the finished product that the publishers, aghast, rejected it and substituted an extensive memoir by Pavel Annenkov. Vengerov's study contains some interesting materials, even though many of its judgments and interpretations are open to dispute.

Pisemsky's second major biographer, the radical critic A. M. Skabichevsky, who published a booklet on him in 1894, was for political reasons even more violently prejudiced against him than Vengerov. One might have expected Pisemsky to find a more sympathetic interpreter in I. I. Ivanov, who issued a verbose study of him in 1896, but Ivanov's treatment was so replete with personal views and so short on Pisemsky as to be nearly worthless for scholarly purposes. At this same period, however, the writer's fortunes improved with publication of a lengthy and reasonably objective article by V. V. Zelinsky, written as a preface to the second complete edition of Pisemsky's works.

During the final two decades of the nineteenth century and the first years of the twentieth, articles dealing with specific facets of Pisemsky's career appeared now and again, but for fifteen years following the revolution of 1917 his work was virtually ignored as a subject of scholarly investigation, and it did not come into its own once more until after the Second World War. Despite general neglect, two important books on Pisemsky did appear in the 1930's. The first was an edition of his selected works, published in 1932 under the editorship of P. N. Berkov and M. K. Kleman, containing an interesting if doctrinaire foreword, notes, and a bibliography of all editions of Pisemsky's individual or collected works in Russian to date. This edition, the first of any size to appear for twenty years, evidently stirred interest in Pisemsky, for in 1933 the Soviet writer Konstantin Fedin considered composing a full biography of him, although evidently nothing came of this intention. The second and even more significant book was a large tome issued in 1936 under the editorship of M. K. Kleman and A. P. Mogilyansky, containing the texts of all Pisemsky's letters available to date, copious notes, and extensive materials bearing upon the writer's life and work. This collection is indispensable for any discussion of his career.

One might have expected that a serious biography based on the collection of 1936 would have been written long before now, but in fact no such work has been published. In 1945 a study in pamphlet form was printed in Russia. Other studies have taken the form of longer or shorter general articles appended to editions of his writings. None of these has been comprehensive, and all of them apply the orthodox Soviet line to the interpretation of Pisemsky's career. Since 1950, however, Soviet scholars have been more attentive, and numerous editions of Pisemsky's fiction have been offered the public. The most significant are a selected edition in three volumes of 1956 and a collected edition in nine volumes of 1959, the second being equipped with valuable notes and commentaries. A relative profusion of articles has also been published on aspects of Pisemsky's life and work. In 1964 a volume of *Literaturnoe nasledstvo* (Literary Heritage) was issued containing materials from Ivan Turgenev's Parisian archive, among which were included forty-seven previously unpublished letters from Pisemsky to Turgenev. Most of these are lengthy and of great aid in interpreting the writer's outlook. In the past decade or so western Slavists have also arrived at a fuller comprehension of Pisemsky's importance for nineteenth-century Russian literature. Claude Backvis printed a stimulating article in 1955, and since then a smattering of articles and dissertations dealing with one or another facet of his career have been completed.

In the present study I have utilized the extensive materials on Pisemsky that have appeared in recent decades to construct a full-length literary and intellectual biography. Designed around a chronological account of Pisemsky's life, the book traces the history of his relationships with fellow writers and his contributions to the intellectual life of his time, his views on contemporary literary and political problems as well as his personal characteristics. In treating his fiction, I have paid close attention to the genesis of his works, their links with his own life, and the reception they were accorded by his contemporaries, both in the public press and in private correspondence and comment. My object has been to present a factual analysis of Pisemsky's life and works that may stimulate interest in him and serve as a basis for future research into his writing. Thus, though I devote a number of pages to discussion of his literary works proper, including the neglected post-1863 writings, my book remains primarily an essay in literary history. There is no doubt that Pisemsky's fiction deserves a thorough critical investigation, but this task I leave to others.

Before 1918 in Russia the Julian (Old Style) calendar, which ran twelve days behind the western calendar, was used. Accordingly, dates given singly in this text are Old Style. All translations are my own.

I should like to express my gratitude to Professor A. P. Mogilyansky of the Institute of Russian Literature in Leningrad for his invaluable assistance with the bibliography; and to Mrs. Harris Coulter of Washington, D. C., for her close scrutiny of the manuscript.

C. A. M.

Washington, D. C.
January 1969

Contents

Frontispiece. Aleksey Pisemsky, 1880.
Portrait by Ilya Repin.

Pisemsky

———

A Provincial Realist

I

The Provincial in the Provinces

Aleksey Feofilaktovich Pisemsky boasted of few illustrious fore-bears. He himself, apparently drawing upon family tradition, traced his ancestors back to the fifteenth century, to a saint Makary Unzhen-sky, who died no later than 1444. Makary was connected with the Makarev Unzha monastery, located in Pisemsky's native Kostroma Province on the Unzha River, and it was in this monastery that his remains were preserved. However, the historical sources on Makary indicate that he was originally from Nizhny-Novgorod rather than Kostroma, and provide no hint that he belonged to any branch of the Pisemsky family.[1] A more probable ancestor was a ''dyak Pisem-sky'' entrusted by Ivan the Terrible with the delicate task of visiting England to interview Mary Hastings, whom the Czar was thinking of marrying. Pisemsky departed in 1582 at the head of a small dele-gation and returned by the late summer of 1583, when he submitted a noncommittal report on the lady.[2]

Later Pisemskys did not rise to the level of either the saint or the envoy. Apparently several of them were moderately wealthy, but the branch from which Aleksey was directly descended included none of these. In fact, Pisemsky's grandfather had sunk so low in the social scale that he was ''illiterate, went around in bast shoes, and worked the land himself'' (I, 3).[3] Pisemsky's father, Feofilakt Gavril-ovich Pisemsky (1781-1843), raised the family prestige to a some-what higher level, even if he did not become rich. Entering military service, he attained the rank of lieutenant-colonel (*podpolkovnik*).

He actively participated in such undertakings as the Persian campaign, eventually returning to Kostroma Province after a lengthy period of service. Since he had joined the military at the age of fifteen, however, he was still reasonably young when he resolved to marry and settle down. His bride, Avdotya Alekseevna Shipova (1787-1857), who was no longer young herself, brought along her two maiden sisters to live in her new home. These sisters later doted on the young Aleksey to such an extent that the neighbors joked that he had three mothers instead of one.[4]

Aleksey Feofilaktovich Pisemsky was born on the eleventh of March 1821[5] at the family estate of Ramene in the remote Chukhloma district of Kostroma Province. The fifth child in the family, he had a total of nine brothers and sisters, but the others all died in childhood, leaving him alone. With his parents' love concentrated exclusively upon him as the sole survivor among so many offspring, he became for them something of an "idol" (*bozhok*), to be pampered and spoiled. Pisemsky remembered his father as a strict disciplinarian but also a good-hearted man and a model of honesty. His mother, he recalled, was "nervous and dreamy," a person of considerable spiritual endowments.

The young Aleksey grew up in the midst of an affectionate family circle. His childhood was spent in the city of Vetluga, of which his father was mayor in the early 1830's. In later life Pisemsky's most vivid remembrance of this portion of his childhood was one of "clear, bright days and the large river which my nurse would never let me go near" (I, 5). Thereafter the Pisemsky family moved back to Ramene, where Aleksey romped in the open and led the carefree country life that he would later describe in the second chapter of his novel *Lyudi sorokovykh godov* (Men of the 1840's). Pisemsky's upbringing seems to have been as happy as may reasonably be expected, and it would be pointless to dig for the roots of his later bilious attitude toward society in a twisted childhood.

As befitted a member of the gentry class, Pisemsky's formal education was initially entrusted to tutors, first in Vetluga and later at Ramene. Pisemsky recalled especially his old tutor Nikolay Ivanovich Bekenev, who spent more time constructing amusing things out of paper than instructing his charge. At the age of fourteen Pisemsky left his tutors' care to attend the gymnasium in Kostroma. There he was regularly promoted with his class, although he attributed his advancement more to native ability than to any diligence.[6] He evidently found the reading of novels more appealing than memorizing Latin conjugations and declensions. In his youth he spent a great

deal of time devouring foreign and domestic adventure stories, including nearly everything of Sir Walter Scott's, *Don Quixote,* Hoff-
mann, Pushkin, and the now utterly forgotten A. Churovsky, author
of such thrillers as *Vedma, ili Strashnye nochi za Dneprom* (The
Witch, or, Dreadful Nights Beyond the Dnieper, 1834) and *Chernoy
Koshchey, ili Zadneprovsky khutor u Lunnoy gory* (Black Koshchey,
or, The Farm Beyond the Dnieper Near the Moon Mountain, 1834).
Pisemsky's interest in academic matters waned even further when
he first conceived a passion for the stage. For a while he was content
merely to attend the local theater faithfully; then he began or-
ganizing his own presentations, initially a puppet theater and later
a genuine one. He played mostly comic roles, achieving his greatest
success in the part of Prudius from A. A. Shakhovskoy's *Kazak-
stikhotvorets* (The Cossack Poet).

Just as he had switched from play-going to play-acting, before
long Pisemsky effected a transfer from fiction-reading to fiction-
writing. At the age of about seventeen, encouraged by his literature
teacher, Aleksandr Fedorovich Okatov, in the fifth class of the
Kostroma gymnasium, he wrote a story entitled "Cherkeshenka"
(The Cherkessian Woman). Even in the sixth and seventh classes,
when he was studying more seriously in the hope of gaining ad-
mittance to the university, he found time to compose another story,
"Chugunnoe koltso" (The Iron Ring). These early experiments in
prose have not survived, and we know nothing about them except
their titles.

In 1840 Pisemsky graduated from the Kostroma gymnasium and
promptly applied for admission to Moscow University. Though he
had wanted to enter the literary faculty (*slovesny fakultet*), he was
prevented by his ignorance of Greek and was admitted instead to
the mathematical faculty. The idea of Pisemsky as mathematician
is rather incongruous, for in later life he never displayed any particular mathematical bent, and his mathematical training left little
impress upon his character or interests. He apparently selected the
mathematical faculty solely in order to gain entrance to the university, for once there, he devoted much of his study time to literary
subjects. In particular, during his first year he attended the lectures
on literature given by Stepan Petrovich Shevyrev (1806-1864), a
prominent poet, literary critic, and journalist. Encouraged by Shevyrev, as he had earlier been by Okatov, Pisemsky composed a work
entitled "Smert Olgi" (The Death of Olga), which Shevyrev read
and praised. His warm words brought tears of ecstasy to Pisemsky's
eyes, in the best tradition of the 1840's, and induced him to continue

his literary efforts. As a consequence he received very poor marks in mathematics for his first year.

Over the next three years, according to Pisemsky's recollection, he did become absorbed in his major subject, because the sciences suddenly "made sense of nature, which up to that time had seemed to me to be just a collection of various haphazard phenomena."[7] It is nevertheless doubtful that he ever cast himself wholeheartedly into his mathematical studies at the university, for he was too much attracted by the bohemian student life, an existence that laid little emphasis upon study. The poet Yakov Petrovich Polonsky has left the following vignette of Pisemsky in his student days: "He was a short young man with a haggard face and dark, penetrating eyes. I saw him for the last time as I was passing through someone's courtyard: he was sitting by an open window among some card-playing students. It was probably his apartment, since he was wearing a sort of *tulup* [coat], his hair was all tousled, and he was holding a long chibouk."[8]

Evidently, Pisemsky did not waste all his time at the university, for later on he claimed that while there he had read widely in the classics of world literature, such as Shakespeare, Schiller, Corneille, Racine, Rousseau, Voltaire, Hugo, George Sand, and Goethe (I, 6). Of all these foreign authors, Goethe seems to have impressed him most. In a letter of 1877 to the scholar F. I. Buslaev, Pisemsky recalled reading *Wilhelm Meister* as a student, which had aroused within him a feeling of "reverent rapture." The theory of dramatic art expounded in the heroes' conversations "illuminated as if by an electric spark" the vague, chaotic ideas about the theater that had been floating around in his head. The emotionalism of Pisemsky's response to Goethe emerged even more vividly in the one-sentence summary of his feelings about the German poet: " 'Goethe,' I exclaimed, 'makes it seem as though all my innards (*nutro*) were turned inside out.' "[9] The exclamation was characteristically inelegant and imprecise. Despite the ardor of Pisemsky's reaction to Goethe, the poet left few traces on his work.

Such enthusiasm as Pisemsky displayed for acquiring a general literary education was largely confined to his university years. Later on he worried little about culture. He apparently possessed a minuscule library: in his last years he still did not own a copy of Shakespeare or even of his native Pushkin.[10] He rarely mentioned any current reading in his letters. His attitude toward the life of the mind and cultural pursuits found reflection in his fiction in such characters as Elchaninov from *Boyarshchina* (a place name).

Elchaninov entered Moscow University at the age of eighteen, with every intention of becoming a scholar. He bought textbooks and registered in various libraries but soon discovered that both the university lectures and private study bored him immensely. When he found that he could pass his course with almost no studying, he allowed the university to slip into the background and let "life breathe upon him with its charm." "Life," of course, consisted of going to the theater, gadding about, carousing at night with other students, writing verse, and making love (II, 72). Pavel Beshmetev, the hero of *The Simpleton,* is a scholar *manqué,* capable only of dreaming of becoming a famous professor (I, 440). Through him Pisemsky revealed a certain disdain for the scholarly profession, by causing a man who was utterly unequipped for coping with real life to yearn for scholarly renown.

Even if Pisemsky did in fact devote much of his time between 1841 and 1843 to mathematical studies and the reading of literary classics, the theater remained one of his great loves. In April 1844 he and several other students organized a presentation of Gogol's *The Marriage,* in which Pisemsky played the lead role of Podkolesin, a part that remained one of his favorites. He did so well that some claimed seriously that Pisemsky surpassed the famous actor Mikhail Shchepkin in the role.[11] Although this was surely an exaggeration, Pisemsky always regarded himself as a gifted actor and apparently possessed some talent.

Pisemsky managed to complete his university course in the usual four-year period despite his extracurricular activities. His satisfaction at graduating on schedule in 1844 must have been diminished by the knowledge that his father had died the previous year and that his mother was seriously ill. As he himself was short of funds, there was no alternative but to return to Kostroma. After a period of illness, in January 1845 he obtained a position as a civil servant in the Kostroma Chamber of State Properties (Palata gosudarstvennykh imushchestv), where he worked until August. At that point he was able to return to Moscow for a year and a half, as an employee in the Moscow Chamber of State Properties. In February 1847 he returned to Kostroma once more because of ill health and domestic difficulties.

It must have been during these interrupted residences in Kostroma that Pisemsky came into contact with that representative of a belated classicism, the poet Pavel Aleksandrovich Katenin (1792-1853), who lived out the last fifteen years of his life at his Kostroma estate, passing for a "freethinker and atheist" among the neighboring gentry.[12] According to Pisemsky's close friend Boris Almazov (1827-1876), each tried to convert the other to his own brand of literature: Katenin promoted the French pseudo-classicists, while Pisemsky made propaganda for Gogol.[13] Yet in a literary sense Katenin seems to have had as little influence upon Pisemsky as did Goethe. He merely served as mentor to the budding author and may also have helped to sustain his interest in the theater, although that never required much encouragement. Pisemsky was evidently not overawed by his literary advisor, for later he created a pompous character in "Komik" (The Comic Actor) who claimed to be a disciple of Katenin's in the technique of dramatic readings (III, 28).

Beginnings of a Literary Career

Russian literary and intellectual life of the 1840's—that "remarkable decade," as the critic and memoirist Pavel Annenkov termed it, and which Pisemsky was to remember fondly for the rest of his life—was concentrated primarily in the country's political capital, St. Petersburg. Moscow was in the process of losing its eminence as an intellectual center, which had drawn to its university a number of exceptional men, including Lermontov, Herzen, Ogarev, Goncharov, Konstantin Aksakov, and Stankevich. By the beginning of the 1840's, during Pisemsky's tenure at Moscow University, most of these men were either dead or departed from the city. Moscow unquestionably remained a major cultural center, but the field was largely abandoned to the Slavophiles. This group emphasized what they considered to be Russia's unique path of historical development and the special quality of Russian society, which in their view was cemented by Christian love rather than, as in the West, by force or the threat of force. Their opponents, the "Westernizers," who expected western Europe to furnish models for Russian progress, tended to gather in St. Petersburg. Among the leaders of the Westernizers was the single most influential figure of the decade, the critic Vissarion Belinsky (1811-1848). Years later, upon rereading early Belinsky articles, Pisemsky exclaimed that he had been a "great man," endowed with "astonishing sensitivity, extraordinary intellectual honesty, and knightly bravery" as well as a burning love for Russian literature that most of the critics of a later age had lost.[14] Belinsky's unusual feel for literature and spiritual purity placed their stamp upon this era of high-minded discussion of philosophical and aesthetic problems. The decade was the seed-time of the Russian intelligentsia.

If Belinsky was the chief critical influence upon the literature of the 1840's, its main creative impulse came from the work of Nikolay Gogol, especially his novel *Dead Souls* (1842) and his short story "The Overcoat" (1842). Gogol's genius was too individual to attract any direct imitators of worth, but his themes—especially his attention to the "little man," including the "impoverished civil servant"—and what could be transmitted of his peculiar realism were central factors in the literature of the 1840's. The Gogolian influence was noticeable in the appearance of the so-called "natural school," which undertook to depict types from the common people, usually from urban settings, such as organ-grinders, janitors, and petty clerks. Sketches of this kind were gathered in the collection *Fiziologiya Peterburga* (Physiology of St. Petersburg), published under the editorship of the poet Nikolay Nekrasov in 1844. These sketches were designed to be objective if somewhat sentimentalized portraits of typical representatives of social classes that had been too long ignored in literature. But the urban lower classes could not lay exclusive claim to the writer's attention, and in a short time the peasantry was also being described in a more or less "realistic" way, as by Dmitry Grigorovich in "Derevnya" (The Village, 1847) and Ivan Turgenev in *A Sportman's Sketches*, which began to appear in 1847.

The middle years of the 1840's witnessed the debuts of several impressive literary talents. Turgenev had appeared upon the scene as a writer of verse in the early years of the 1840's. Fedor Dostoevsky published his first work, *Poor Folk*, in early 1846 and was welcomed with prophetic enthusiasm by Belinsky, as was Ivan Goncharov a year later when he issued his first novel, *A Common Story*. Nekrasov was building a reputation as poet, editor, and literary entrepreneur. The playwright Aleksandr Ostrovsky published his first work in 1847, and Aleksandr Herzen printed his problem novel *Who Is To Blame?* in 1846. The years that saw the emergence of these names were bound to be stimulating for an aspiring literary man, and Pisemsky, even though located at a remove from St. Petersburg, where most of these writers lived, could not avoid being affected by the ferment. The "remarkable decade" came to an abrupt end, however, in 1848.

The reign of Nicholas I (1825-1855), although recorded in Russian history as an oppressive one, had up until 1848 witnessed an unquestioned outburst of intellectual creative energy. After the European revolutions broke out this state of affairs was suddenly and drastically altered. Determined to ensure that the Russian Empire would remain a bastion of stability amid revolutionary upheaval, the state imposed strict restraints upon literary and intellectual life. Thus began the *mrachnoe semiletie* or "epoch of censorship terror," which lasted from 1848 to Nicholas' death in 1855. The name of Belinsky, who had died prematurely in 1848, could not be mentioned in print. Herzen, sensing the oncoming storm, had in 1847 entered voluntary exile abroad, from which he never returned. Gogol developed into a religious maniac and died an agonizing death in 1852, although long before he had spiritually ceased to exist in the eyes of the progressive intelligentsia. Dostoevsky was arrested in 1849 for participating in the allegedly subversive activities of the Petrashevsky circle and dispatched into Siberian exile after a terrifying mock execution. The satirist Mikhail Saltykov-Shchedrin was exiled from 1848 to 1856, and even the mild-mannered Turgenev was forced to retire to his estate for a short time in 1852-1853. The censors maintained a vigilant watch for anything that could possibly be interpreted as undermining the foundations of the state. It was an unpropitious period for writers, particularly beginning ones, and on several occasions Pisemsky was to encounter censorship difficulties. Nevertheless, Russian literature was not totally transformed into a desert over these seven years, for the energies released in the 1840's were too powerful to be utterly repressed by the measures of the czarist regime, and despite all obstacles, by the mid-1850's Pisemsky would have established a reputation as a voice from the provinces.

Inspired by the surge of literary enthusiasm in the mid-1840's, Pisemsky resolved to set about writing in good earnest. While residing in Moscow in 1846, he put in much effort on his novelette *Vinovata li ona?* (Is She To Blame?), a work given the question-title then in vogue. According to Pisemsky, it was through this story that he first made the acquaintance of Ostrovsky, who was then just beginning his successful playwriting career and who was to be a friend until Pisemsky's death. After leaving Moscow in February 1847 and returning to Kostroma, Pisemsky wrote a short story entitled "Nina." On March 13, 1847, he sent it to his former professor Stepan Shevyrev, along with a letter requesting that it be placed in a journal and reporting on the reworking of *Is She To Blame?* which he had undertaken at Shevyrev's behest. Since his own name was completely unknown, Pisemsky thought that he would have a better chance of breaking into print if Shevyrev acted as his agent. His understandable hesitation about publishing is apparent in the following passage from the letter: "I have been writing for a long time, writing while giving short shrift to my practical obligations, but my labors have been for the desk drawer and have never been crowned with success, and thus I still do not know whether this is my genuine calling, even though I am sacrificing nearly everything for it."[15]

Unhappily, *Is She To Blame?* was blocked by the censorship, and the manuscript was returned to the author in the fall of 1850. Some time elapsed before it was published, in mutilated form. On the other hand, Shevyrev succeeded in placing "Nina" in the journal *Syn Otechestva* (Son of the Fatherland) for July 1848, and thus for the first time the signature "A. Pisemsky" appeared in print.

"Nina" is an ordinary story about a young man who falls in love with a girl who appears to him to embody all the romantic ideals of the 1840's. To his dismay, the hero realizes that he has no chance of winning the lady because of a rival, Mazurin. After Mazurin departs from the town, leaving behind a temporarily broken-hearted Nina, the hero himself is obliged to go away for some years. On his return he discovers that his ethereal Nina has been transformed into a thoroughly commonplace woman, married to an equally uninteresting husband. Nevertheless, the hero refuses to part with his illusions. "Is it possible that she could have changed so much?" he ruminates at the story's conclusion. "No, she was evidently always that way, I just attributed to her what I wanted to see in her and clothed the live Nina in the form of my dreams. God grant that I may always make such mistakes and see man better than he actually is! . . . I did not see Nina any more, I left the town of M. and forgot her; but I remember another Nina, the Nina of my dream!" (I, 285-286).[16]

"Nina" went completely unnoticed in the periodical press: apparently no reviews or comments upon it were printed. Not for another two years did Pisemsky begin to publish in quantity. In the meantime he settled down to provincial life for a seven-year period coinciding almost precisely with the censorship terror, supporting himself through civil service employment. On October 6, 1848, he was appointed a special agent (*chinovnik osobykh porucheniy*) attached to the military governor of the Kostroma Province, a post he retained until July 4, 1850. In this capacity he was available to be sent on specific missions that gave him an opportunity to gain first-hand acquaintance with the life of the common people instead of sitting in an office shuffling documents. One permanent post he is known to have held was that of secretary to a secret advisory committee on the affairs of the Old Believers, or religious schismatics. In this capacity he personally had to attend to persecutions of the Old Believers, including the destruction of some of their chapels. His heart may not have been in assignments of this sort, but he carried them out, all the while gathering material that would later be useful in his writings.

At the age of twenty-seven Pisemsky decided that the time had come to establish a family, and on October 11, 1848, he was married to Ekaterina Pavlovna Svinina (1829-1891), who had not yet reached her nineteenth birthday. Ekaterina Pavlovna had excellent literary connections. Her father was Pavel Petrovich Svinin (1787-1839), a minor writer and founder of the journal *Otechestvennye zapiski* (Notes of the Fatherland), which became the major intellectual organ of the 1840's.[17] Ekaterina Pavlovna's mother, Nadezhda Apollonovna Svinina (1803-1857), had been born a Maykova and thus belonged to the family that for 150 years, from the mid-eighteenth to the late nineteenth century, produced some of Russia's most brilliant and cultured individuals. In particular, Apollon Nikolaevich Maykov, a confidant of Dostoevsky's and a leading poet, thus became related to Pisemsky by marriage. Vital as were Ekaterina Pavlovna's family connections, her sterling character was of greater immediate significance. In view of Pisemsky's numerous weaknesses, especially his alcoholism, it is probably no exaggeration to say that his wife alone kept him on course through many difficult times, when he might well have been destroyed by his own shortcomings had it not been for her. A woman who knew her much later, in the 1870's, described her thus: "Intelligent, gentle, mild, she, having come from a literary family, nurtured her husband's talent, lived for his literary interests, and feared being an impediment in his path more than anything else. In moments of grief she concealed her sorrow, not baring her own soul even to those close to her and finding relief only in prayer—she was a very pious woman."[18]

Ekaterina Pavlovna's piety and introverted personality were foreign to Pisemsky, who used her as the prototype for the frigid Evpraksiya in the novel *Vzbalamuchennoe more* (Troubled Seas, 1863); in his autobiography (I, 6) he even went so far as to emphasize the characterization of Evpraksiya in the novel as an "iceberg" (*ledeshka*). Though she may not have been an ardent wife, she still put up with all his faults and never wavered in her loyalty. In addition to managing his household and bearing him four sons and one daughter (only two of the sons survived to maturity), she performed a service for posterity by copying most of his literary production as it came from his pen. She also inserted the French phrases with which his texts are sprinkled, because being very poor at foreign languages, Pisemsky was unable to take care of them himself.[19] Ekaterina Pavlovna's task was made the more arduous by her husband's extraordinarily illegible handwriting. In the words of one of his friends, "the late Pisemsky had a dreadful hand, nobody ever wrote worse than he and he always sneered at those who wrote well."[20] In later years he often employed his wife as a secretary in the writing of letters, for if he wrote them himself, there was a good chance that their recipients might not be able to decode them. In sum, Ekaterina Pavlovna was a fortunate choice as his wife, despite the fact that she had certain shortcomings from his point of view.

During the years 1848-1850 Pisemsky was more than a little discouraged in his literary endeavors, because of his inability to publish *Is She To Blame?* and the failure of his story "Nina" to attract notice in print. Sometime after his return to Kostroma in early 1847 he had written yet another work, *The Simpleton,* but his lack of success with his first two stories so disheartened him that he several times thought of destroying it "together with other unnecessary papers."[21] Furthermore, after leaving Moscow, Pisemsky felt culturally deprived, lost in the provincial wasteland. This feeling seems to have been so strong that one wonders why he took so long to move back to the capital. Apparently his family responsibilities were primarily responsible for the delay.

After a period of provincial hibernation, Pisemsky finally began attempting to reestablish contact with the Moscow literary world. On April 7, 1850, he wrote to Ostrovsky—evidently for the first time in quite a while, as suggested by the opening phrase of the letter, "If you remember your old friend Pisemsky just a little bit." He wished to communicate his detailed opinion of Ostrovsky's play *It's a Family Affair—We'll Settle It Ourselves,* which had recently come out in the journal *Moskvityanin* (The Muscovite), but which Pisemsky had become familiar with when Ostrovsky was writing it in late 1846 during Pisemsky's Moscow sojourn. The concluding paragraph of Pisemsky's letter provides a glimpse of his unhappy frame of mind at the time. He begged Ostrovsky to write him, saying that "your letter will bring too much joy to a man who once upon a time shared his convictions with you but who now, by the will of the fates, is condemned to the dreadful existence of a provincial civil servant; a man who unfortunately up to now has been unable to smother within himself that energy of spirit which is so useless in his present position."[22]

Responding to this appeal from his erstwhile colleague, Ostrovsky promptly set about drawing Pisemsky into the circle of the "young editorial board" (*molodaya redaktsiya*) of the journal *Moskvityanin*. During the 1840's *Moskvityanin* had been the only important literary journal published in Moscow and had enjoyed considerable prestige. More recently, under the editorship of Pisemsky's former professor Stepan Shevyrev and especially his colleague M. P. Pogodin (1800-1875), the Moscow University historian, *Moskvityanin* had become primarily an organ for the publication of documents illuminating the course of Russian history. This project, useful enough in itself, could hardly have been expected to increase the journal's circulation among the general public. At this stage a group of younger men, under the leadership of Ostrovsky and the critic Apollon Grigorev (1822-1864), undertook to resuscitate the journal, even though the censorship terror was at its height. They accomplished their purpose to a remarkable degree over the years from approximately 1850 to the journal's closing in 1856, despite the fact that Pogodin retained ultimate control.

Others who belonged to the young editorial board at one time or another were the poet Boris Almazov, Pisemsky's lifelong friend, the critic Evgeny Edelson, who later served on the staff of *Biblioteka dlya chteniya* (Library for Reading) in its last days, and the publicist Terty Filippov.[23] As most of these people lived in Moscow at the time, they formed a circle in body as well as in spirit, meeting for discussion and argument in such places as Grigorev's apartment. Geography prevented Pisemsky from actively participating in the group's meetings, and Ostrovsky became his chief contact with the circle, but he is usually considered one of their number, and he did publish the bulk of the early works that brought him renown in *Moskvityanin*.

On April 21, 1850, soon after his first letter and apparently in response to an answer of Ostrovsky's that has not been preserved, Pisemsky wrote once more to his unofficial Moscow representative, enclosing the manuscript of *The Simpleton*, which had long reposed in his desk drawer. Pisemsky evidently sent Ostrovsky only the first part of the manuscript, retaining the second because it still required reworking. He gave Ostrovsky permission to alter anything he liked in the text to bring it into conformity with the demands either of the censorship or of *Moskvityanin*'s general orientation.[24] In short,

Pisemsky was so anxious to be published again that he did not insist upon his absolute rights as an author. Ostrovsky plainly liked that portion which he had received, but Pogodin would not accept it for publication until the entire manuscript was in hand. Ostrovsky must have been sent the second part in late August or early September, for he brought the complete text of the work to Pogodin on September 4,[25] and the story was published soon thereafter in the two issues for October and the first November issue. It appeared shortly in a separate edition as well.

The plot of *The Simpleton* is based upon what might be called a marital pentagon. The characters are psychologically motivated, although the society in which the action occurs is sufficiently important to the development of events that ten years later the radical critic Dmitry Pisarev could interpret the work as an attack upon the foundations of Russian society. It is doubtful that Pisemsky had any such assault in mind, and indeed in 1850 it would hardly have been possible to steer a novelette containing sharp criticism of contemporary society past the censor and into print. Surely this was the reason that in his letter of April 21 Pisemsky informed Ostrovsky that he had entitled the work *Semeynye dramy* (Family Dramas) and underlined the ordinariness of the events described in it: "My chief thought was to expose, in the everyday and quite ordinary lives of ordinary people, the dramas which each character reacts to in his own way. I have not touched on anything in the way of the social order and have limited myself to family relationships alone."[26] Pisemsky's claim to political neutrality cannot be taken entirely at face value, since it would be a simple matter to extrapolate some of the author's attitudes in the story and apply them to society as a whole. Still, it seems clear that Pisemsky did not have strongly political objectives in writing it. The fundamental source of the conflict that leads to the story's tragedy must be sought in the heroes' personalities.

The main character, Pavel Beshmetev (the "simpleton" of the title), is a retiring person who lives mostly in a dream world: his sister Liza is the only one with whom he can establish a close tie of friendship. Liza marries a man named Masurov, while Pavel falls in love with Yuliya Kuraeva, who considers him an uninteresting boor. When Pavel tenders a formal proposal, Yuliya's parents compel her to accept it and enter into a marriage that cannot bring happiness to either her or Pavel. The fifth member of the pentagon, one who preys upon the feminine halves of both the Masurov and Beshmetev families, is Bakhtiarov, the "lion of the province," a type that attained prominence in Pisemsky's later fiction of the 1850's. When Pavel learns that his wife Yuliya is in love with Bakhtiarov, he draws the most damaging conclusions, even though in fact she has conscientiously remained faithful to him in the overt sense. Pavel's marriage is destroyed by this affair, and he sinks into apathy, drunkenness, and death as the novelette draws to a cheerless end.

Pavel Beshmetev's personality is outlined in sufficient detail to allow the reader to analyze his failure. First, Pavel is not physically attractive: he has long arms and a sunken chest, is rather "ill-constructed and even clumsy." Laziness, one of his besetting sins, is clearly reflected in his demeanor. Yet if one looks more closely at his "broad, pale and irregular face," one discovers something pleasing: a fascination with the life of the mind (I, 423). Indeed, he has a reputation in provincial society for his unusually thorough education and his ambition to become a professor, although that same society clearly does not sympathize with this ambition. Had Pavel possessed any inner drive, this social disapproval might not have stopped him. He fails to attain his objective because of his own lack of staying power. It should be added that his intellectual propensities are more talked about than shown in the novelette.

Pavel's inborn sloth leads him to withdraw from the real world into the sphere of daydreams, where anything may be attained with marvelous ease. Consequently, he feels little inclination to make friends in the real world, and even among his intellectual peers at Moscow University, "he would come [to lectures], take a seat somewhere in the back of the room, take notes and then leave. He did not make friends with a single one of his colleagues and did not even say hello to a single one of them. At home . . . he led a most monotonous life, that is, he would eat, study, and then lie down on the bed and think, or rather daydream" (I, 440). Occasionally he longs to break out of this isolation, as when late at night he walks along the Moscow streets, gazing through windows at the festive people within and thinking of their pleasant existence (I, 440). However, he lacks the social polish, the will, and the financial resources to participate in the frivolous life of Moscow society and so remains an outsider.

Yuliya Kuraeva, by way of contrast, is much involved in worldly pursuits—attending balls, eating well, sporting fine clothes, gossiping about the neighbors—and displays not the slightest wish to daydream or to educate herself. She is also very selfish, little inclined to adapt herself to others if that can be avoided. Pavel and Yuliya are thus spiritually and morally very far apart, and the social institution of marriage cannot bring them together.

Had their courtship been less perfunctory, Pavel might conceivably have realized that Yuliya would be an unsuitable wife for him. However, attracted by Yuliya's physical beauty, Pavel in the beginning worships her at a distance. She appears in his world first in Moscow, later in the provincial town where they both live. In Moscow, he watches from his apartment window as she goes out for rides; in the provinces, after he meets her at a party, he writes to his sister that Yuliya looked to him like an "ancient statue" (I, 449), a phrase that underlines the purely external nature of their relationship. The two hardly talk together until after they have become officially engaged, and even then the conversation turns upon such simple-minded topics as whether Pavel likes to play cards, his age, or what he was doing in Moscow (I, 489). It is not until some time after marriage that Pavel realizes how unsuitable as a wife is the girl of his dreams. But after all his disenchantments he continues to love the "phantom" Yuliya whom he had created in his mind, though he "despised and hated" the flesh-and-blood, everyday Yuliya (I, 565). The disjunction between the world of his fantasies and the unpleasant, intractable actuality leads to tragedy for the inexperienced, weak-willed Beshmetev.

Being a clear-headed and sensible girl by worldly standards, Yuliya readily perceives that she and Pavel are unsuited to each other, but she is forced to marry him by her imperious father, who sees the union as a means of righting his sorry financial affairs. Her consent is obtained through argument and threat, and on her wedding day she weeps so inconsolably while being dressed for the ceremony that she has to be practically carried to the carriage (I, 507). Thus, to a degree Yuliya cannot be blamed for wishing to take revenge upon the husband who inflicted such humiliation on her, although at times she is excessively callous, as when she insists upon attending a ball even though Pavel's mother is on the point of death (I, 514 ff.). Nor is Pavel to be held entirely accountable for the marriage disaster, for he loved his fiancée sincerely and, blinded by passion, did not realize the true state of her feelings. The greatest burden of guilt must be borne both by Yuliya's father, who forced the two together for mercenary reasons, and through him, by society, which permits parents to exercise such power over their children. The bad effects of the initial misstep are compounded by Yuliya's impatience with her essentially good-hearted husband and by Pavel's inexperience in the ways of the world and his readiness to leap to conclusions. In short, society creates and enforces the bond between Yuliya and Pavel, without which no conflict would have arisen, but the conflict itself is spawned by psychological traits within the heroes that are only partially conditioned by their society. The tragedy results from a conjunction of the couple's illusions about life, their personal short-comings, and social conventions.[27]

The difference in tone between "Nina" and *The Simpleton* is striking, although they share a fundamental similarity in that both heroes are roughly parted from their false conceptions of the world. However, in "Nina" the hero refuses to abandon his dreams com-pletely even when he has seen the truth, whereas Beshmetev's fan-tasies are pitilessly shattered, to be replaced by nothing. This latter approach became one of Pisemsky's literary trademarks, and it may be surmised—although there are no documents to prove it directly—that he went over to this jaundiced view of life in the period 1847-1850. Though the first version of *The Simpleton* was written about the same time as "Nina," the second half at least was considerably reworked in 1850, by which time the author's pessimistic outlook had been firmly established. "Nina" thus stands alone in the body of Pisemsky's work as the literary product of a more optimistic ap-proach to reality, which proved to be an artistic blind alley for him.

Pessimistic though Pisemsky may ordinarily have been, he cer-tainly had cause to be gratified by the reception accorded his first major published work. Suffering nothing like the oblivion visited upon "Nina," *The Simpleton* was discussed by a number of leading critics and outstanding journals. Aleksandr Druzhinin, who was to become one of Pisemsky's closer associates in the latter part of the decade, was among the first to note the appearance of the new lit-erary star. In October 1850, before *The Simpleton* had been fully published, he wrote in *Sovremennik* (The Contemporary) that it was "absorbing," in spite of the fact that it showed a great deal of borrowing.[28] Ostrovsky concluded his own enthusiastic review of the story, which he had promoted vigorously from the beginning, with a declaration that his search for blemishes in it had ended in failure.[29] Although *Moskvityanin* could have been accused of prejudice in favorably reviewing a work printed in its own pages, *Biblioteka dlya chteniya* was also favorable, welcoming the story as "one of the most remarkable works of the last year." Noting that 1850 had been a poor year for literature in general—as it was in fact—the anonymous reviewer maintained that "Pisemsky's story is one of those phe-nomena which could not help attracting general attention even in a most fruitful literary period."[30] The critical chorus was marred by occasional dissident notes, as when the reviewer for *Otechestven-nye zapiski* complained that Pisemsky's characters did not develop psychologically,[31] but on the whole Pisemsky could only have been heartened by the reaction.

Impelled by the critics' praise, Pisemsky began to devote a greater portion of his time to literary endeavor. He had to take time that should have been given to his civil service employment and his growing family in order to write as much as he did in 1850 and 1851. "I am a family man and I am engaged in very serious and difficult employment," he wrote in August 1851. "Only the night is left for my literary occupations, and circumstances must turn out very favorably so that under such conditions a man can gather his forces for work."[32] Nevertheless he managed to work on four items during this period: *Sergey Petrovich Khozarov i Mari Stupitsyna (Brak po strasti)* (Sergey Petrovich Khozarov and Mari Stupitsyna [A Marriage of Passion]—most often cited by subtitle), "The Comic Actor," the long short story "M-r Batmanov" (M. Batmanov), and his first play, *Ipokhondrik* (The Hypochondriac). None of these can be ranked among his best writings, but collectively they represent a giant step toward the significant works of his next few years.

When it came to publishing his writings, Pisemsky found himself ever more closely attached to the young editorial board of *Moskvityanin*, largely through Ostrovsky's mediation. However, at first he thought of placing *A Marriage of Passion*, the next piece readied for print after *The Simpleton*, in *Otechestvennye zapiski*, since at that time he did not feel a special loyalty to *Moskvityanin*. To this end he conducted negotiations with the journalist and literary historian A. D. Galakhov, his go-between with the magazine, who had previously handled *Is She To Blame?* during its unsuccessful attempt to clear the censorship. On December 1, 1850, Pisemsky almost went so far as to promise *A Marriage of Passion* to *Otechestvennye zapiski*.[33]

Meanwhile Ostrovsky, impressed by his friend's literary achievements, pestered Pisemsky in late 1850 to contribute to an almanac with which he was connected. Pisemsky tried to put the playwright off, saying that he had only just begun "The Comic Actor" and could not possibly publish it before the middle of February.[34] When Ostrovsky persisted, Pisemsky finally gave him portions of *The Hypochondriac*, which were published in the almanac at the end of February 1851.[35]

During this important month in Pisemsky's life he made his first expedition to Moscow, specifically to strengthen his literary and intellectual contacts. Arriving in the ancient capital on February 8, he immediately descended upon Ostrovsky in a state of ill health caused

by the vicissitudes of the journey from Kostroma.[36] It was then that
Ostrovsky took advantage of his friend's weakened state to persuade
him to sell A Marriage of Passion to Moskvityanin rather than Otechestvennye zapiski; he wrote to Pogodin sometime between February
9 and 12 that he had purchased the novelette for 1,000 rubles;[37]
Pisemsky could be a shrewd bargainer even on his sickbed. Although
Pisemsky had made no firm commitment to send the story to the
other journal, it would have been justified in resenting his action.
He displayed such a lack of scruple in financial dealings more than
once in his lifetime.

One reason for Pisemsky's going to Moscow was plainly his desire
to meet and confer with Pogodin. On February 12 he was the fea-
tured guest at a literary evening held at Pogodin's. It was an important occasion, since Pogodin arranged such festivities only about
twice a year. This particular event gave Pisemsky his first significant
chance to display his talents as a reader, by reciting fragments of
The Hypochondriac, probably the portions scheduled to appear in
Raut na 1851 god (Rout for 1851), as well as two chapters from
A Marriage of Passion.[38] As a result, he succeeded in establishing
himself successfully in the Moscow literary world in the space of
about a week. He returned to Kostroma around February 15 and
resumed his literary production.

During his week in Moscow the fledgling author had done more
than merely engender vague good will for himself. At some point
he concluded a formal agreement with Pogodin, by whose terms he
undertook to furnish Moskvityanin with a certain number of works
for which he would be paid in a stipulated way.[39] Undoubtedly
Pisemsky was aware that Pogodin's proverbial stinginess made it
essential to conclude specific contracts with him rather than rely
upon oral agreements. As it turned out, Pisemsky had good reason
to be cautious, for though he received partial payment for A Marriage of Passion at the time the contract was signed,[40] he was unable
to extract the remainder until at least June, and then only after he
had written several acrimonious letters to Pogodin and refused to
supply any further stories until he had been fully compensated for
A Marriage of Passion. Eventually the situation was straightened
out and Pisemsky sent in the other items he had legally undertaken
to provide ("The Comic Actor," The Hypochondriac, "M. Batmanov," and "Pitershchik" [The Petersburger]). While bound by this
contract, Pisemsky could publish almost nowhere but in Moskvityanin.[41] Once he had discharged his contractual obligations, he never
appeared in the journal again. The portion of his correspondence

with Pogodin that has been preserved is heavily concentrated in the years 1851-1852 and deals mostly with business matters; only scattered letters survive after 1852, when Pisemsky had ceased publishing in *Moskvityanin*. These facts seem to support the supposition that Pisemsky's connection with the rejuvenated *Moskvityanin* was primarily a matter of legal obligation, if perhaps secondarily a matter of personal loyalty to Ostrovsky, and that Pisemsky never felt very close to the younger men gathered around it as a group.

Before Pisemsky was quit of Pogodin, the editor managed to extract further profit from him by publishing the first "collected edition" of Pisemsky's works. The idea had occurred to Pogodin as early as late 1852, when he had thought of publishing a three-volume edition to incorporate those works of Pisemsky's that had appeared theretofore in *Moskvityanin*.[42] After some hesitation over the title he chose *Povesti i rasskazy A. F. Pisemskogo* (Stories and Tales of A. F. Pisemsky), which gave critics with no other nits to pick the chance to carp that one of the main items in the collection was a play, *The Hypochondriac*. The edition included unmodified versions of everything else the author had published up to that time with the exception of "Nina" and *Bogaty zhenikh* (A Rich Fiancé). The edition was poorly printed, for which the author apologized when sending a set to Maykov. The fault, he claimed, was Pogodin's, "who does everything on the basis of economic calculations."[43] Nevertheless, the 1853 edition marked Pisemsky's first important excursion from the world of journal publication into the sphere of books, and it furnished the stimulus for several reviewers to write moderately extensive articles evaluating the author's career to date. The judgment was not always favorable, especially by the older critic K. A. Polevoy, who overdid things in pronouncing Pisemsky imitative, repetitive, predictable, and deficient in his command of the Russian language.[44]

Although legally and morally wedded to *Moskvityanin* during 1851 and 1852, Pisemsky plainly longed to initiate a liaison with either *Sovremennik* or *Otechestvennye zapiski*, or both. Throughout 1851-1855 (especially during the early part of the time) *Sovremennik* was the more serious contender of the two. Nekrasov, one of its guiding spirits, had commented favorably on the excerpts from *The Hypochondriac* published in *Raut*,[45] and evidently he approached Pisemsky about this time in the hope of acquiring something for his journal. Anxious to oblige Nekrasov but also bound by his commitments to *Moskvityanin*, Pisemsky cannibalized the unfortunate *Is She To Blame?* to produce the novelette *A Rich Fiancé*. Publication was begun in *Sovremennik* in October 1851, quite possibly before the entire piece had been completed in manuscript.[46] Pisemsky felt compelled to write on and on merely for the sake of length, since he was being paid by the page. As a result, *A Rich Fiancé* emerged as one of the least successful of his early works.

This unhappy experience must have soured Nekrasov on Pisemsky to a considerable degree. In any event, his moderate enthusiasm for the story "M. Batmanov," published in September 1852, was strongly tempered by disgust at Pisemsky's "coarseness." "And then it is astonishing," he added in a personal letter to Turgenev, "how little trouble the author experiences in resolving the most difficult problems. After this story, though I don't know why, I can't think of him in any other way than as a *literary policeman*, who resolves all the problems of life and the heart with a club! But then the reason all this is so irritating is that he has a great deal of talent."[47] Nevertheless, Nekrasov's attitude toward Pisemsky remained more positive than negative, and Pisemsky published in *Sovremennik* both his works for 1853, *Razdel* (The Division) and "Leshiy" (The Wood Demon). The following year he sold to the magazine one of his best short stories, "Fanfaron" (The Braggart). Most important, Nekrasov negotiated for the purchase of his first novel, *Tysyacha dush* (*One Thousand Souls*), and for a while labored under the misapprehension that the book had been promised to him. Nekrasov was therefore understandably furious when Pisemsky suddenly sold it to *Otechestvennye zapiski*: "This gentleman," Nekrasov wrote to a friend, "after having made arrangements with us for 2,000 [rubles], considered himself justified in not even warning us that he was being offered more and sold the novel to Kraevsky [the publisher of *Otechestvennye zapiski*] for 3,000."[48] By 1855-1856 Nekrasov was thoroughly disgusted with Pisemsky, who made his last appearance in *Sovremennik*'s pages in late 1855. Pisemsky then moved to *Otechestvennye zapiski*, where he published sporadically from 1854 through 1858.

The works written during Pisemsky's provincial years may be grouped in several categories. The problem of love and marriage in contemporary society is central not only in *The Simpleton* but also in *A Marriage of Passion* and *A Rich Fiancé*, two of his longer productions of this time. The hero of *A Rich Fiancé*, Stepan Gerasimych Salnikov (known as Stepochka), eagerly tries to gain a wife, only to encounter ultimate failure. Stepochka seeks the hand of a poor orphan, Vera Pavlovna, who has been brought up by her uncle. Although she is not attracted to this well-intentioned but clumsy young man, her relatives are ready to compel her to accept him for his money and future prospects, until another relative, a wealthy prince, intervenes to insist that she be allowed to marry the man of her heart, the romantic young Shamilov. When eventually the prince dies and Shamilov as fiancé proves unfaithful to Vera Pavlovna, she agrees to marry Stepochka in order to placate her uncle. Before the marriage can take place, Vera Pavlovna comes down with consumption and dies, leaving Stepochka broken-heartedly determined never to marry at all.

The figure of Shamilov, characteristic of Pisemsky's early period, has occasionally been interpreted as a forerunner of Turgenev's Rudin from the novel of the same name, and indeed there are some parallels. Shamilov wins Vera Pavlovna's heart because of his fascinating external appearance and his boastful plans for the future. In reality, however, he is a fraud who almost believes his own deceptions. For instance, he claims to be composing an article on *Hamlet*, which really consists of nothing more than a few opening paragraphs. When he sets to work on a translation, he quickly discovers that the task is too demanding and abandons the project. Insofar as Shamilov is a man of words without deeds, he is akin to Rudin; like Rudin, he arouses the love of a pure, idealistic girl whom he plans to marry but in the end betrays. On the other hand, Rudin's personality is much more complex than Shamilov's. Though neither weathers his crisis, Rudin is at least potentially more capable of action, and in the name of a higher cause. For this reason Turgenev was justified in attaching an epilogue to *Rudin* describing his hero's death upon the revolutionary barricades. Shamilov would never have considered sacrificing his life for any cause: he is primarily concerned with his own comfort. In fact, Shamilov leaves Vera Pavlovna mainly because she will not allow him the intimacies of marriage before the wedding, nor will she marry him until he has established a place for himself. Shamilov cannot meet the requirements of even this limited test, imposed on him by a woman stronger than he.

A Marriage of Passion revolves about the collapse of a marriage that originally was strongly desired by both participants. It is the wedded state that tries the two, since at the time of their union neither was sufficiently mature to foresee the problems that would arise. Pisemsky commented in one of his letters that the "chief thought in the novel was the mocking of shallow natures making a pretense at love."[49] By this statement Pisemsky emphasized, as he had earlier for *The Simpleton*, the psychological rather than social character of the work. This was a politic move at the time. The story describes the campaign of the hero, Sergey Petrovich Khozarov, to win the hand of "a guileless creature of nineteen, rosy, fresh," named Mari Stupitsyna. After the elimination of a number of obstacles the wedding takes place, but the two principals soon turn out to be poorly prepared for life together. Khozarov is unable to overcome his habit of borrowing to cover expenses. Mari, still very much a child, thinks that her husband should spend all his time with her, fondling her and tending to her needs. When he fails to do so, she decides that she is being neglected and strikes up dalliances with other young men. The characterization of the young couple made by another person toward the end of the story is replete with Pisemskian cynicism: "[Khozarov] is a repulsive and greedy borrower of other people's money, he is a corrupt intriguer, incapable of even understanding a decent woman . . . [Mari], it seems, doesn't know how to do anything but kiss; first she spent all her time kissing her fiancé and her husband, but now she has started kissing other admirers as well" (I, 413-414).

A Marriage of Passion, like *The Simpleton,* may be regarded as a revision of "Nina," the difference being that the suitor achieves his aim of marriage and then is disillusioned with his own wife rather than someone else's. By Pisemsky's lights such a denouement was unavoidable when a fuzzy-minded young man became infatuated with a shallow girl. However, since the author had reason to fear that a pessimistic ending might attract the censor's disfavor, and since one story had already been blocked by the censorship, he added a happy conclusion to the journal publication, which was quite out of joint with the body of the story. As this ending had it, Khozarov almost miraculously acquired sufficient funds and ceased borrowing; Mari matured rapidly and approached becoming a model wife.[50] When the novelette was republished for the first time, Pisemsky eliminated this epilogue, as he was fully aware of its falseness.

Two moderately significant stories, "M. Batmanov" (1852) and "The Braggart" (1854), constitute the second category of fiction typifying Pisemsky's early period. The intensely self-centered characters depicted in these stories are variants of Lermontov's Pechorin in *A Hero of Our Time,* the strong and fascinating character who derives one of his chief pleasures in life from exerting power over others while remaining emotionally uncommitted himself. Both stories were produced under English influence, for the original title of "M. Batmanov" was "Moskvich v Garoldovom plashche" (A Muscovite in Childe Harold's Cloak), and "The Braggart" was inspired by a reading of Thackeray's *Book of Snobs,* which had appeared in Russian translation in *Sovremennik* in late 1852. "The Braggart" originally bore the subtitle "Odin iz nashikh snobsov" (One of Our Snobs) and was intended as the first of a series of "several biographical sketches" under the general title *Nashi snobsy* (Our Snobs). Pisemsky was never good at completing cycles, and the story was left to stand alone.

Batmanov is the purest example in Pisemsky's characters of Lermontov's "hero of our time." The story chronicles the adventures of a man who lays no claim to idealism (as Shamilov does for instance); he is simply a professional seducer bent on profitable conquests. His callous outlook is illustrated by a brief story he tells of himself:

"I was eighteen," he began, lighting up a cigar and seeming to lose himself in his reminiscences. "I fell in love with a certain girl, beautiful as a houri; our passion knew no bounds: just as soon as we were left alone we would start kissing; we parted; a correspondence was begun which, however, ceased after a year, thank God. One fine winter morning I hear that this girl has arrived in Moscow with her fiancé to attend to her dowry. I go to see them with, I assure you, the most innocent intentions: to congratulate her and wish her happiness and a pile of children. But unfortunately I perceive that she is very much in love with her fiancé, who is a first-class blockhead, and that they are both drowning in joy; and since I can't bear to see such things among mortals, I began trying to prove to her that she was in error and that her heart's most recent choice was stupid and dull. At first she got angry; but then I succeeded in persuading her and the engagement was broken off."

"What then?"

"I don't know; two days later I left for St. Petersburg" [III, 79-80].

"M. Batmanov," though not especially significant in the entire corpus of Pisemsky's work, is at least important because it is the first story boasting as a major character the coarsely amoral cynic who later became a Pisemskian type.

The hero of "The Braggart," Shamaev, though fully as egotistical as Batmanov, lacks his almost demonic qualities. Shamaev exploits the weaknesses of those around him for his own advantage because he has been brought up to think only of himself and to use others for the promotion of his personal welfare. The story's original title, "Matushkin synok" (A Mama's Boy), pointed up its central theme: the fate of a child pampered beyond reason by his mother. When Shamaev reaches maturity, he utilizes his mother's almost pathological attachment to him in order to lead a life of pleasure without thought for the consequences. At the end he is overtaken by the sins of his youth, reduced to penury, and left by the author to an uncertain future, for he still has not mastered his profligate impulses. When sending the manuscript to Nekrasov, Pisemsky had included two variant endings, because his story dealt in part with the civil service and he feared the censorship. One ending was presumably more optimistic than the published finale and could have been used to mollify the censor had this proved necessary.[51]

Shamaev's mother is primarily to blame for twisting his personality, and for this fault she later pays a terrible price, although her love for her son prevents her from fully realizing the consequences. When he was an infant, she had insisted on giving him whatever he wanted, even to allowing him to put his hand into the fire. She changed nursemaids and tutors constantly until she found one as willing to spoil the child as she was herself (III, 165). Shamaev grows up with the barest modicum of education, convinced that the key to existence lies in making the proper contacts in high society and living beyond one's means.

Shamaev is in fact able to exist in this fashion for an extraordinarily long time, mostly because his natural charm impresses people upon first meeting and persuades them to finance him in his profligacies. His powerful charm even affects the narrator, his uncle, a sensible individual who is under few illusions about his nephew's character. When the uncle meets Shamaev for the first time as a young adult, not having seen him since he was a child, he is swayed by his nephew's elegant appearance and begins to think that perhaps he has been unjust in previously condemning him for unfilial treatment of his mother (III, 177-178). However, this error is quickly corrected when he hears Shamaev expatiating earnestly upon the advantages of making a wealthy match. Therein lies the secret of his self-seeking charm: he is not cynical about his addiction to wealth and comfort, but sincerely believes that they alone constitute the good life for which all should strive. He can be extremely generous with money when he has it, lavishing expensive gifts upon his mother, his wife, and even his uncle, while at the same time being not at all bothered by the unethical way in which he has obtained the funds or by his neglect of his family when he is short of money. It is as though part of his conscience had been cut away.

Although Shamaev's charm exercises only a brief sway over the wise narrator, it causes serious grief to the two women in his life: his wife and mother. His mother receives nothing but ingratitude in return for her sacrifices. He spends all the money she can raise for him, but when she comes to live in the same town while he is preparing to be married, he rents a small apartment for her, conceals her presence from his future in-laws, and does not plan to invite her to his wedding (III, 186). Despite this, her love is such that a kind word from him is sufficient to repay her for any spiritual anguish. Shamaev's wife is eventually more perceptive than his mother, but by the time the scales drop from her eyes she is irrevocably wed. She tells the narrator that when she married, at only seventeen, she was so much in love as to be incapable of reason. The person most to blame for the marriage was her father, who was completely taken in by Shamaev and, after having refused her sisters a kopeck, settled upon her a dowry of 30,000 rubles, which was promptly squandered (III, 203). Although she realizes that her husband is irresponsible, she continues to love him in a weary, wary sort of way. Her father, however, becomes disgusted and finally orders her to return to the parental roof in order to avoid total ruin. The strain of having to choose between her husband and her father is so great that she gives birth prematurely and before long dies (III, 209). Shamaev is left both a widower and a pauper. For a time he has gotten along on his image, but when substance is demanded, he is exposed as morally bankrupt.

Artistically "The Braggart" is one of Pisemsky's more successful efforts of his early period. In form it is cast as a narrative monologue, delivered by the local Kokin sheriff or district police officer, Shamaev's uncle, who also relates the tale of "The Wood Demon." As a rule Pisemsky did better when he worked through a narrative monologue or dialogue and could use the intonations of natural speech. Indeed, he may be regarded as one of Nikolay Leskov's teachers in the *skaz* technique, although he was far surpassed by his pupil. In addition to being distinctly individual, Shamaev was the embodiment of a certain social type existing in contemporary Russian society, which readers apparently recognized, for the story enjoyed immediate popularity with the public. Pisemsky wrote to Nekrasov in October 1854 commenting on its success in the provinces and rejoicing over reports of approval in the capital.[52]

Beyond these two groups of stories, dealing primarily with problems of marriage or with some variant of the Lermontovian "hero of our time," two other categories of works may be discerned in Pisemsky's early period. One group, depicting the peasantry, will be discussed in the following chapter. The other category has to do with the theater, either directly or indirectly. It includes the short story "The Comic Actor" and the plays *The Hypochondriac, The*

Division, and *Veteran i novobranets* (The Veteran and The New Recruit).

"The Comic Actor" is the one early story that Pisemsky devoted to the question of the artist and society. It is partly autobiographical, for Pisemsky always regarded himself as having missed his calling on the stage, being obliged to perform strictly as an amateur, before audiences who were not always capable of appreciating him. Perhaps for this reason the story ends almost violently. Pisemsky refused to modify the conclusion in spite of Ostrovsky's advice. It appeared in its entirety in the first November issue of *Moskvityanin* for 1851.

The story describes a true artist at soul who is addicted to drink and the theater, just as Pisemsky was. Stranded in a provincial town, the hero Rymov is invited to play Podkolesin in Gogol's *The Marriage* at an amateur theatrical evening. His acting talent is so great as to attract notice, and a collection for his benefit is taken up after the performance. But in his heart Rymov despises these philistines, who are devoid of any aesthetic sense, and he contemns his host, who has insisted on presenting, along with Gogol's play, a worthless farce of his own composition. Rymov's feelings emerge at a dinner where he drinks too much and begins to berate his hosts: " 'Mikhailo Semenych [Shchepkin, the great actor] has praised me, the genius himself has praised me, do you understand that? Or can't you do anything but concoct idiotic comedies and dramas? . . . Get away from me,' he cried, shoving at people. 'Actors! Writers! I despise you all, you swineherds! . . . Get away from me!' " (III, 70). Rymov is escorted out and the affair ends in a scandal. In such scenes as this Pisemsky clearly implies that between the man of genius and the ordinary person is fixed an abyss that cannot be bridged.

The Hypochondriac was the first and best of the three plays from Pisemsky's early period. It also has some autobiographical features. If the hero of "The Comic Actor" shared with his creator an inordinate craving for the theater, contempt for bourgeois provincial society, and addiction to alcohol, Durnopechin, the chief character in the play, suffers from an acute case of the same sort of hypochondria that Pisemsky displayed and which later developed to such proportions as to become a standing joke among his friends. Durnopechin's will is paralyzed by his agitation over imaginary ailments, while unscrupulous relatives and neighbors seek to exploit his weakness for their own benefit. In particular, an old maid and her roughneck brother attempt to bully him into a marriage, from which Durnopechin is delivered through no effort of his own.

The Hypochondriac, though unnecessarily long, makes fairly entertaining reading. True, some scenes are reminiscent of Gogol, and for this imitative quality it attracted the disapproval of certain critics. For instance, Druzhinin remarked that in reading the play one is constantly interrupted by characters who have stolen in from elsewhere: Podkolesin from Gogol's *The Marriage,* Osip from his *The Inspector-General.* "Oh," exclaimed Druzhinin, "if only Mr. Pisemsky could devise a way to forget, if only for a little, everything that he has read in the Russian dialect!"[53]

Discouraged by this and similar reactions from St. Petersburg organs, such as *Otechestvennye zapiski* and the newspaper *Sankt-Peterburgskie vedomosti* (St. Petersburg News), Pisemsky lamented that perhaps much of his effort over the preceding year and a half had gone for nought.[54] But he did not lose heart to such a degree as to stop writing for the theater. In January 1853, exactly a year after publication of *The Hypochondriac,* he came out with his second play, *The Division,* in *Sovremennik.* Having taken seriously the earlier criticism, he felt that in this play he had "avoided the shortcoming of the first [comedy], namely the absence of a plot,"[55] but in fact *The Division* was neither an artistic nor a popular success and has since fallen into well-deserved oblivion. The problem of the plot, which Pisemsky thought he had solved, instead overcame him. Pisemsky mistook the inclusion of abundant detail for good plotting, to the end that the reader loses his way among intricacies of domestic squabbling that are barren of meaning. As a consequence, the story line, which concerns family strife over the division of an inheritance left by a wealthy relative, lacks dramatic force and direction. *Otechestvennye zapiski,* which found the play "rather boring," justifiably decided that it belonged "more to the sphere of jurisprudence than literature."[56]

Pisemsky's third dramatic effort, the playlet *The Veteran and the New Recruit,* published in *Otechestvennye zapiski* for September 1854, was a patriotic piece written and staged during the Crimean War. It depicts an old warrior-father's willingness to send his third son off to war even after he has learned that his two elder offspring have perished in battle. The play is of almost no importance for an understanding of Pisemsky's work.

In the scholarly literature one occasionally discovers references to Ostrovsky's influence upon Pisemsky as playwright. It is perfectly true that Ostrovsky was an intimate friend of Pisemsky's at the beginning, that he served as his major link with the Moscow literary world, and that he began publishing plays a few years before Pisemsky. However, to the extent that Pisemsky was imitative at this time, his most important model was Gogol. His relationship with Ostrovsky was one of independent equality, with neither appreciably influencing the other. In this connection it is well to recall that Ostrovsky was some three years Pisemsky's junior, so that the older man would have been little inclined to look upon the younger as a superior. From time to time Pisemsky sent Ostrovsky long letters with analyses of his friend's plays offered in a spirit of helpful criticism. He also followed Ostrovsky's successes closely and sincerely rejoiced over them. Thus, in 1850 he sent Ostrovsky a lengthy analysis of *It's a Family Affair—We'll Settle It Ourselves*, which he ended with the solemn proclamation that the play was a "merchant-class *Woe from Wit*, or to put it more accurately, a merchant-class *Dead Souls*."[57] Ostrovsky in turn offered Pisemsky advice on his work, although none of his counsel has survived in written form. Moreover, Ostrovsky tended to consider Pisemsky superior to himself, as the following incident shows. When Pisemsky's first play, *The Hypochondriac*, was brought to Moscow and read by the author, Ostrovsky felt uneasy when comparing it with his own play *The Poor Bride*, on which he was then at work. "My comedy has been held up for a few days," he wrote to Pogodin on November 2, 1851, "because I have heard Pisemsky's comedy and found it necessary to polish up (*podkrasit*) my own a little so as not to have to blush (*krasnet*) for it afterwards."[58] As a result, Pisemsky the playwright cannot justly be considered a disciple of Ostrovsky's; the two worked on an equal footing.

The reaction of contemporary critics to Pisemsky's works during the years from 1850 through 1854 was generally favorable, although not universally so. *Moskvityanin* on the whole approved of his stories and plays, despite the fact that Apollon Grigorev, the journal's chief critic and one of the finest critical minds of nineteenth-century Russia, had many reservations about him. Grigorev long maintained that Ostrovsky was the white hope of Russian literature, and he therefore resisted mightily any notion that Pisemsky could be superior to Ostrovsky. Consequently Grigorev wrote relatively little about Pisemsky in this period, although what he did write was at times astonishingly perceptive.

Biblioteka dlya chteniya ordinarily encouraged the budding author, as did *Sovremennik* so long as Druzhinin was its main critic. However, Druzhinin tended to interpret Pisemsky as he wished him to be rather than as he was in fact. Thus, Druzhinin hoped to promote the quality of "gaiety" in Russian literature generally and discerned a sizable amount of it in *A Marriage of Passion*. "This gaiety," he wrote, "pervades the entire first part of this novel which has just been begun, crops up every minute in a whole series of adept remarks and comments, and leaves the reader under the influence of constantly pleasant sensations."[59] But a scant few months after these words were written, Druzhinin became disturbed when Pisemsky seemed to diverge from the path the critic had laid out for him: "When Pisemsky abandons his gaiety and strives to create something which is either very moving or very picturesque, his powers leave him and I fail to discern the entertaining raconteur in him."[60] Druzhinin's interpretation of Pisemsky as the "entertaining raconteur" was at best one-sided. Although it cannot be denied that *A Marriage of Passion* and many other of his early short stories make enjoyable reading, they were never meant merely to furnish entertainment: they had a more serious artistic purpose.

Another of *Sovremennik*'s critics, Nekrasov, approached Pisemsky in gingerly fashion. For a time he hoped to lead Pisemsky in the right direction according to his own lights, but then gave up the task as impossible. His personal relationship with Pisemsky in after years was not cordial. *Otechestvennye zapiski* occupied approximately the same position with regard to Pisemsky as did *Sovremennik*, recognizing his talent but expressing serious reservations about him. A typical comment was, "Last year we continued to find ourselves pleasantly mistaken upon beginning one of Pisemsky's comedies or novels, and unpleasantly disenchanted upon finishing it."[61] At least one critic, Ksenofont Polevoy of *Severnaya pchela* (Northern Bee), could not comprehend why Pisemsky should be accorded any stature whatever among contemporary Russian authors. Despite such dissident voices, most critics of the day agreed that Pisemsky's was a major contribution to Russian literary life, and by 1855 he had gained a considerable reputation among the reading public.

However, there were other "critics" of an official sort whose opinions had more immediate effects upon him did than the praise or censure of the reviewers writing for the intellectual journals. All during the period from 1848 to 1855 the censors were extremely strict, sometimes capricously so, and as he wrote, Pisemsky always bore in mind what the censorship might find objectionable. After his misfortune with *Is She To Blame?* he became more wary and experimented with various schemes designed to slip his writings past the censorship. For *A Marriage of Passion* and "The Braggart" he adopted the expedient of variant endings. The softer finale for *A Marriage of Passion* was actually published for fear of the censor but then discarded when no longer needed. A second way in which Pisemsky could circumvent censorial roadblocks was by trying the Moscow censorship as opposed to the St. Petersburg one, because the Moscow censors tended to be more liberal. Thus, when preparing his comedy *The Division* for publication, he summarized the plot at length for Nekrasov and suggested that he submit it unofficially first to the St. Petersburg censors so that it could be sent through the Moscow censorship if the former balked.[62]

Although Pisemsky's anticensorial tactics over this period were usually crowned with a species of success, he suffered defeat in connection with the staging of *The Hypochondriac*. The play was passed for publication with little fuss, but the censor Gedershteyn raised objections to its staging, which was forbidden at his behest on March 14, 1852. Gedershteyn, who apparently espoused lofty and positive standards for Russian literature, argued that the playwright had erred in concentrating his attention upon uncultured people. "Thus, in this comedy . . . there is not a single decent character. Even though the hero, Durnopechin, is a member of the gentry, he still is made into the plaything of low, coarse people because of his illness. The other characters possess no moral standing at all . . . In addition to all this, the depiction of a man's illness, the comedy's main thought, dragged out as it is for four acts, cannot be entertaining and is even unpleasant."[63] Pisemsky, nonplussed by this decision, immediately took all the steps he could while in distant Kostroma to obtain a reversal of the edict, but by May it had become obvious that no such thing could be expected. He was obliged to wait patiently until the censorship yoke was lightened before his play could be performed for the first time, in 1855. These bad experiences with the censorship were only the first of many, and for the rest of his life he could never feel free from the specter of actual or potential censorial interference.

Personal Difficulties

While Pisemsky was building his reputation among Russian literary men, changes occurred in his personal and business life. In 1850 he resigned his position as special agent—the employment that had furnished his art with so much raw material from life—and assumed the duties of an assessor for the provincial administration (*assesor Gubernskogo pravleniya*). This was a more commonplace sort of employment than his previous position, which had required him to travel to outlying areas of the province, but it left him with more free time for writing. Furthermore, in due course his family began to increase. His eldest son, Pavel, was born on March 29, 1850; little more than a year later, in May 1851, a second son, named Apollon, was brought into the world. Pavel survived to a bleak maturity, but Apollon lived only until the December following his birth.

Despite the literary successes of 1851, which caused the leading journals of Russia to seek contributions from him, the end of that year was a difficult time for Pisemsky personally. Not only did his son die, but word circulated that the governor of the province was leaving, and it was rumored that Pisemsky's post would be abolished. If this happened, he feared he might be left without resources. He suffered from frequent headaches, which hindered his writing. Another cause of concern was the seemingly unending exile from Moscow's intellectual life. As a result of this combination of circumstances, Pisemsky cast about desperately for some means of transferring himself to Moscow before he became mired forever in the Russian provinces. Having been informed by Ostrovsky that there was an opening for a school inspector in Moscow, in December 1851 Pisemsky wrote to Shevyrev to request his assistance in obtaining this post, which would enable him to return to the capital. Ostrovsky also lobbied to have the position given to his friend, but in the end nothing came of all this activity, and Pisemsky was condemned to spend another three years in Kostroma.

The winter and spring of 1852 passed slowly for Pisemsky, especially since he kept hoping that he would be able to move to Moscow. He was occupied by his literary labors as well as by the task of providing for his expanding family: the third annual addition, Nikolay, was born on October 10, 1852. Although the new son was a fresh source of domestic contentment, he was also another drain on their resources. For a while Pisemsky contemplated becoming a feuilletonist for *Moskvityanin* and sending in correspondence from the provinces, so as at least to make capital from his unhappy situation, but this good intention came to nought.

Although Pisemsky's fears about the security of his position proved unfounded for the time being, the new year of 1853 brought him little joy. Always expecting the worst in business and in life, he was frequently not disappointed. He consistently inclined to attribute his misfortunes to his "enemies," most of whom existed only in his mind. Thus, when a new governor was sent to replace the one under whom Pisemsky had served closely between 1848 and 1850, he was certain that his connection with the old regime would ensure his downfall through the intrigues of these "enemies." As he wrote to Pogodin on January 20, "Our new governor does not get along with Prince Gagarin, our former vice-governor, and my Kostroma enemies have succeeded in making it appear that I was the latter's bosom friend; I am not guilty of this either in body or soul, and I have never previously belonged and do not now belong to any party in the civil service; in spite of this I am out of favor, so that I not only can expect no promotion but I am even waiting to be kicked out of my present position at any moment."[64]

For a while it seemed that Pisemsky's apprehensions were ground-less, since nothing untoward occurred immediately. Indeed, things seemed to be going very well. He made a major excursion from Kostroma to St. Petersburg in the latter part of September and the first part of October 1853, stopping off in Moscow both ways. When in Moscow, he stayed with Ostrovsky and visited Pogodin. In St. Petersburg he made the personal acquaintance of the poet Apollon Maykov, his relative by marriage, with whom he had already corre-sponded for some time. It is also likely that on this occasion he was introduced to *Sovremennik*'s guiding spirits, Nekrasov and Ivan Panaev. Upon his return to Kostroma it appeared that his "ene-mies," far from gaining ground in his absence, had actually been routed. He was notified of his promotion to the rank of Titular Coun-cillor (Titulyarny sovetnik), and the governor suggested that he take over the editing of the unofficial section of the *Kostromskie gubern-skie vedomosti* (Kostroma Province News), since each province had a provincial newspaper with an official and unofficial section. In view of his new duties, he was to receive a salary increase.

As it seemed that he would be living in Kostroma for some time, Pisemsky made a few attempts at stimulating the cultural interests of the provincial public. To this end, early in 1853 he took advantage of several opportunities to act, for which he garnered local renown. On the 14th of January he participated in a theatrical evening given for the benefit of the poor, and a little later, during Shrovetide, he displayed his histrionic talents on the Kostroma amateur stage in the well-worn role of Podkolesin from Gogol's *The Marriage*. Even his wife Ekaterina Pavlovna performed a few songs for this occa-sion.[65]

It must have been at roughly this point that Pisemsky acquired his first real literary protégé, the playwright Aleksey Potekhin (1829-1908). Potekhin was also living in Kostroma, and the two beginning authors must have sought out each other's company as an antidote to the philistine atmosphere surrounding them. Reportedly they spent almost every evening together for about two years (probably 1852 and 1853). Potekhin sometimes read Pisemsky his works but more frequently listened to his elder adviser. When he moved to St. Petersburg at approximately the same time as Pisemsky, he felt closer to him than to any other literary figure in that great city.[66] Pisemsky and Potekhin were the two most important contributions made by Kostroma to Russian literature of the nineteenth century.

Life has a way of toying with people, lulling them with a sense of security just before dashing them against the rocks. So it was with Pisemsky. He was gaining fame as a literary man, and his civil service salary seemed sufficient to ensure a livelihood. But then the fundamental shakiness of his position was abruptly revealed at the end of 1853, when he was ordered to transfer from Kostroma to Kherson, a place to which he could not transport himself and his family because he lacked funds. The only option was resignation from the civil service and withdrawal to his ancestral estate of Ramene, in the vicinity of Chukhloma, one of the remoter areas of a remote province. Kostroma may have been a provincial city, but at least it was a city, whereas in Ramene Pisemsky would be compelled to live nearly in isolation, a prospect that he found decidedly distasteful. But there was nothing else to be done.

Situations that at first seem to be misfortunes often have compensations. In this instance, Russian literature benefited from Pisemsky's personal unhappiness, for life in enforced rural idleness gave him the opportunity to devote full time to writing, and he produced a worthwhile body of prose during the year spent in Ramene. Indeed, this period in Pisemsky's career is reminiscent, if on an inferior level, of Pushkin's famous "Boldino autumn." In the winter Pisemsky began writing the best portion of what was to become his finest novel and most outstanding work, *One Thousand Souls,* although four years would pass before it was brought to completion. In addition, he composed at least the opening of the third and last story in the cycle *Ocherki iz krestyanskogo byta* (Sketches of Peasant Life), "Plotnichya artel" (The Carpenters' Guild), as well as the short story "The Braggart." Never again would he produce so much of lasting worth in so short a period.

At the time, however, Pisemsky resented his disguised good fortune. In a way, his rage over his enforced seclusion in Ramene was a microcosm of his attitude toward all his provincial years. While

writing some of his best works, he was personally extremely unhappy. Paradoxically, and without realizing it, he longed to tear
himself from the very source of his best inspiration.

Although the winter at Ramene was unpleasant, Pisemsky cheered
up somewhat with the approach of spring. "I am in a blissful state
now," he wrote to Maykov in May 1854, "reveling in the spring,
which is marvelous here."[67] In June he described to Ostrovsky his
pastoral occupations, which consisted in playing with his children,
riding horseback, fishing, wandering about, and waiting for the
mushrooms to appear.[68] But no matter how diligently he endeavored
to deceive himself, the joys of the simple life could not satisfy him
for long, and when fall set in, he was in such low spirits that he
stopped work on *One Thousand Souls* and looked forward only to
reaching St. Petersburg and beginning a new life there.[69]

In view of Pisemsky's long-standing connections with the Moscow
literary world, one may wonder why in 1854 his glance was directed
toward St. Petersburg rather than Moscow. Aside from the obvious
explanation that St. Petersburg, being the political capital as well
as a cultural one, nurtured a more extensive and varied intellectual
and literary life and therefore possessed a natural advantage over
the ancient Russian capital, Pisemsky at that time found the St.
Petersburg literary atmosphere personally more congenial. At least
in St. Petersburg, he argued, writers "did not play the Tartuffe,"
whereas in Moscow one encountered "hypocrisy, sanctimony . . . and
irksome, senseless Slavophilism," attributes quite repulsive to him.
"To Petersburg, to Petersburg (V Piter, v Piter)!" became his
cry.[70]

At the very end of the year Pisemsky's cherished dream of ex-
tricating himself from the backwoods of Russia became a reality.
The *Kostromskie gubernskie vedomosti* recorded that during the week
of December 8-15, 1854, A. F. Pisemsky arrived in Kostroma from
the Chukhloma district and then continued on his journey to St.
Petersburg.[71] The provincial was leaving the provinces.

II

The Provincial in the Capital

Pisemsky arrived in St. Petersburg presumably around the middle of December 1854 and promptly set out to seek civil service employment. Luck was not with him, for he was able to obtain nothing better than a place in the Ministry of Appanages (Ministerstvo udelov, which managed the crown estates), with no salary attached. We do not know precisely why he accepted an unsalaried position; probably he felt obliged to be employed somewhere and hoped to be in line for a paying post in the ministry when one fell free. Certainly this employment, which he retained until 1857, made it more difficult for him to support his family through literary work. But now at least he was moving in the vortex of Russian literary and intellectual life, liberated from the isolation of Ramene.

Pisemsky's arrival in St. Petersburg further contributed to strengthening the capital's cultural supremacy over Moscow. By 1855 a large portion of the best Russian writers of the day had congregated there, leaving only a few hold-outs like Ostrovsky in Moscow. The quickening of literary activity at this time was accelerated by the vast relief felt by nearly every Russian following Czar Nicholas' death. To be sure, in czarist Russia it was almost traditional to greet the beginning of each reign with hopeful optimism, but the enthusiasm engendered by this particular change of regime was greater than usual after the painful restrictions of the censorship terror. Moreover, within a few years, on February 19, 1861, the new Czar Alexander II would enact the greatest reform in Russian history, the emancipation of the serfs. The early years of his reign were a period of preparation for the far-reaching political reforms to be introduced in the first years of the 1860's. It was a time of great expectations, which for once were not disappointed.

In the field of literature the years from 1855 to about 1858 were an era of continued good feeling, although a discerning eye might have noted the danger signals of dissension in the publication in 1855 of Nikolay Chernyshevsky's essay *The Aesthetic Relation of Art to Reality*. For the time being, however, Chernyshevsky and his radically materialistic view of art seemed little more than a foreign element in the body cultural, and the threat he posed to established ways of thinking was still far from obvious. The predominant literary critics of the day were the so-called "aesthetic" critics, primarily Aleksandr Druzhinin, Pavel Annenkov, and Vasily Botkin. Although their antagonists accused them of preaching the doctrine of "art for art's sake" and denying art's social utility, in point of fact they rarely argued in support of such an extreme view. They did maintain, in opposition to the radical critics, that a work of literature should be judged primarily on aesthetic grounds and to a much lesser degree on the basis of social utility. The radical critics reversed these priorities: as Nekrasov later put it in a noted phrase, "You do not have to be a poet, but you are obliged to be a citizen." Moreover, the aesthetic critics generally supported the existing political system, though they sometimes viewed it as needing reform in particular areas, whereas the philosophical radicals were persuaded that the system ought to be overthrown. The latter interpreted any social criticism in literature as an attack upon the very foundations of society, whereas the former saw it as a call for eliminating incidental abuses. In 1855-1858 this split between aesthetic and radical critics, which would become so sharp a few years later, was still mostly glossed over, although an early evidence of it was the polemics aroused by Pisemsky's *Sketches of Peasant Life* of 1856.

The best established writer among those active at this period was probably Ivan Turgenev, who created a stir with his novel *Rudin* in 1856, to be followed in 1858 by *A Nest of Gentlefolk*, in which he attempted subtly to demonstrate the inefficacy of prevalent Slavophile ideas; at the same time he wrote several apolitical love stories and novelettes. Pisemsky's old friend Ostrovsky continued to write excellent pieces for the theater throughout the decade. He owed much of his reputation to the tireless efforts on his behalf of Apollon Grigorev, who refused to abandon hope that Ostrovsky would some-

day say the "new word"—of what it would consist Grigorev did
not know, but he thought Russian literature was nonetheless waiting
for it. Among the rising talents were Lev Tolstoy, whose *Sevastopol
Stories* attracted much notice in 1855-1856, and Mikhail Saltykov-
Shchedrin, whose *Provincial Sketches* of 1857 first launched him
on a career of bitterly trenchant social criticism while he at the
same time held high bureaucratic posts with the government. Two
outstanding names in poetry were those of Nikolay Nekrasov, a major
exponent of social involvement in literature, and Pisemsky's kinsman
Apollon Maykov, who preferred to view society with detachment or,
when possible, retreat to classical antiquity. Despite occasional disagreements, these few years were a fruitful time for Russian literature, when literary men supported and aided one another instead
of indulging in mutual recriminations. Thereafter the situation
would change drastically for the worse.

The St. Petersburg milieu affected Pisemsky in various ways, many
of them unfavorable, while he himself had a definite impact upon
their literary world. He was a phenomenon, and it is instructive to
analyze, with the help of anecdotal memoir material, the ways in
which his contemporaries viewed his peculiar personality, primarily
in his St. Petersburg period, but in later years as well. In the eyes
of the civilized literary elite of the capital Pisemsky embodied the
essence of the Russian provincial. He had about him an elemental
coarseness thought typical of the Russian *muzhik,* or peasant, but
quite unexpected in a literary figure of standing. The critic Annenkov described him thus in an extensive essay intended to define his
characteristics as man and writer: "Everything in him was open
and simple. He produced in everybody the impression of a *wonder*
(*dikovinka*) in the midst of St. Petersburg, though not a simple
wonder that people merely glance at and then pass by, but the sort
that stops you and forces you to think about it a great deal and for
a long time . . . All his judgments belonged to him, to the nature
of his practical intellect, and displayed no connection with the doctrines and beliefs then most prevalent among educated people."[1]
Another memoirist, emphasizing Pisemsky's elemental, "earthy"
qualities, said that there was something in him which reminded the
beholder of a "young bull."[2] In other words, Pisemsky had managed
to escape the coating of civilization with which almost all his contemporaries had been veneered and to retain the native simplicity
of the uncorrupted Russian mind. Such straightforwardness could
either attract or repel, and it must be admitted that at first his uncomplicated naturalness repelled more of his associates than it at-

tracted. A surprising exception was the overcivilized Turgenev, who was fascinated by Pisemsky and to whom Pisemsky responded so warmly that a lifelong friendship sprang up between them.

Several of those who knew Pisemsky well agreed that he was endowed with an acute mind, although it had not been significantly shaped by education in the conventional sense. He had passed through Moscow University untroubled by an enduring thirst for learning. He never acquired any competence in a foreign language, so that when he later traveled abroad he was unable to observe European civilization as closely as he might have or to communicate effectively with foreigners ignorant of Russian. Like the ordinary tourist, wherever he went he took with him his private corner of Russia as insulation. This is not to say that he was ignorant of the works of foreign authors: he read them in translation and mentioned foreign writers frequently in his letters and his fiction. Nevertheless, he had little unmediated contact with European culture, which turned out to be advantageous to the extent that it left him more truly "Russian." As Annenkov phrased it in 1856, Pisemsky had a "simple Russian intellect, which is incapable even of reflecting foreign phenomena."[3] He was, as another friend commented, "without any foreign influences, full of purely Russian characteristics of an anticultural type."[4] It was precisely this peculiar "Russianness" of his writing which attracted the attention of certain contemporary foreign students of Russian literature.

In contrast, those who objected to the coarseness of Pisemsky's behavior could sometimes be intemperate in their comments. Nekrasov once wrote to Turgenev, in reference primarily to Pisemsky as writer, although the sentiment may be applied to Pisemsky the man as well, that one had to be very cautious with him: "He is a sloven and one is well advised to examine every little button on him, for otherwise under his buttoned-up coat one may find a hole in his trousers or a glob of filth."[5] Nekrasov exaggerated very little here, for among St. Petersburg circles Pisemsky was legendary for the unabashed crudity of his public behavior. Avdotya Panaeva, Panaev's wife and Nekrasov's mistress, who disliked Pisemsky intensely, indignantly reported cases where Pisemsky, in the course of giving readings in polite society in the presence of ladies, would leave the room and then return still adjusting his clothing. Furthermore, he offended his audiences by belching loudly and frequently.[6] Indeed, Pisemsky's belching became so scandalous that a contemporary satirical *sonnik* (dream-book) explained that seeing Pisemsky in a dream meant that one would "read one's own work in an aristocratic salon and belch there from a democratic horseradish.'"⁷ Such public displays did Pisemsky's reputation little good. In all probability, however, Pisemsky did not deliberately seek to offend in this manner. His belching seems to have been caused by an organic digestive disorder that afflicted him from youth and became acute in old age. Since he could not avoid belching altogether, he apparently chose to do so frankly and without apology.

Such characteristics as these led Pisemsky's contemporaries to view him as the archetype of the Russian peasant. That Pisemsky was more than willing to promote this image of himself may be perceived from a famous encounter between him and Grigorovich, a dandified type who had made his literary reputation in the late 1840's and early 1850's through sentimentalized depictions of the peasantry. One day Pisemsky backed Grigorovich into a corner of a St. Petersburg bookshop and began berating him: "You really should give up writing about the peasants (*muzhiki*). Why should you gentlemen do this sort of thing? Leave this to us; this is our area, I'm a peasant myself!'"⁸

In the opinion of the literary elite Pisemsky's peasant qualities were accentuated by his native Kostroma accent, which he made no effort to correct. Speakers of this dialect may omit the jod between two consecutive vowels or contract two consecutive vowel sounds into one, so that the word *ponimaet* comes out *ponimat*, for example. According to a contemporary observer, Pisemsky did not affect this pronunciation; he had been raised to speak in this fashion and was too indolent to modify his speech habits later on. It was also possible, this observer thought, that on occasion Pisemsky emphasized his accent in order to appear more exotic to his interlocutors.⁹ Be that as it may, Pisemsky's Kostroma accent was one of his trademarks.

Pisemsky's personal appearance, his actions, his provincial speech, and especially his descriptions of peasant life in several stories published during the 1850's have sometimes led him to be considered a Slavophile—an adherent of the view that Slavdom, because founded upon the doctrines of the Orthodox Church and the idea of mutual love rather than on Roman Catholicism and force, was set apart from the West and should follow an independent historical path.¹⁰ This is an error. It is true that in the early 1850's he was connected with the young editorial board of *Moskvityanin*, which has a reputation for having been Slavophile, but it seems that in fact there were hardly any convinced Slavophiles among them, although some of them sympathized with portions of the Slavophile teaching. Certainly Pisemsky was never a genuine Slavophile. He had no appreciable contact with the orthodox Slavophiles such as Ivan Aksakov, and never later published in any journal that could be considered remotely Slavophile, with the exception of *Zarya* in the late 1860's. Although his contact with the latter-day Slavophiles gathered about *Zarya* seems to have been responsible for the introduction of a few Slavophile elements into his novel *Men of the 1840's*, this was only a moderately significant and in any case temporary aberration. In fact, one reason for Pisemsky's decision to move to St. Petersburg rather than Moscow in 1854 was his distaste for the Slavophile coloration of some Muscovite literary circles. Many years later Pisemsky worked himself into a rage over the Pan-Slavs' exploitation of the Russian Ethnographical Exhibition of 1867 in Moscow for their own political purpose of uniting all the Slavs of Europe under the aegis of the Russian Empire. He wrote to Turgenev at the time that it was "difficult to imagine anything more stupid, senseless, and childish (*igrushechnee*)" than the Exhibition, and referred scathingly to the "bouquet . . . of empty noise and falsehood" which was an invariable attribute of the Pan-Slav slogans mouthed so vigorously on that occasion.[11] Finally, in 1880 toward the end of his life, Pisemsky wrote a letter to his French translator on the subject of Slavophilism, although the movement he discussed was as much Pan-Slavism as Slavophilism. Here he argued that the Slavophiles were mostly wealthy aristocrats who neither knew the people nor were known by them. Slavophilism, he stated, had been conceived in imitation of the Pan-German movement to unite the German lands, but whereas the Germans at least possessed a common culture, the same could not be said for all the different Slavic countries. He added that the Slavophile (meaning the Pan-Slav) dream of uniting the Slavic tribes remained for the time being nothing more than "religious and linguistic sentimentalizing." The "brother Slavs" occupied the unenviable position of poor relations in regard to Russia.[12] Such statements demonstrate clearly that Pisemsky did not sympathize with either Slavophile or Pan-Slav aims and ideals. The peasantry of which he wrote was a purely "Russian" peasantry, not a "Slavic" one.

Pisemsky's anti-Slavophile sentiments could not be equated with lack of patriotism, nor should the critical and cynical tone of much of his fiction be taken as an indication that he was in any sense a revolutionary. He was fundamentally committed, though sometimes not enthusiastically, to the system as it then existed. When foreign powers attacked Russia, he could support even such a rigid regime as that of Nicholas I. Thus, during the Crimean War in 1854 he wrote in a personal letter, not intended for publication: "I don't understand what we have done to these shameless people [the Allies]. I cannot imagine a more moderate foreign policy than the one which the Emperor has always pursued."[13] Pisemsky contributed to the war effort through his published writing, especially the patriotic playlet *The Veteran and the New Recruit*, which was promptly staged in 1854. In 1856 he printed a moving description of a captain who had participated in the defense of Sebastopol. There is not a hint of sarcasm in his under-stated discussion of the magnificent "characters who had been forged in the terrible school of almost inhuman self-sacrifice" or in his account of the toasts to the czar, the commanding admiral, and the men of Sebastopol.[14]

In his later years Pisemsky was less uncritically patriotic than he had been in his youth, but still he welcomed the Russo-Turkish War of 1877-1878 as an antidote to the smug, self-seeking bourgeois atmo-sphere of the day. The conflict provided an opportunity for the re-vival of heroism, and one memoirist has reported that Pisemsky expressed hope that during the struggle "the knight might awaken at least for a time" in Russian society.[15] After the war's victorious conclusion Pisemsky used to visit the health baths in Moscow partly for the purpose of talking with soldiers returned from the campaign, whom he termed "heroes."[16] Once again, when Russia was beset by external enemies, Pisemsky was more than ready to proclaim alle-giance to his homeland.

Pisemsky was also prepared to defend Russia's monarchical system against any genuinely revolutionary transformations. Al-though he found much to complain of in contemporary Russian life, revolution as an alternative was completely unacceptable to him. Indeed, he thought that the Crimean War had been fomented by frustrated revolutionaries of 1848, who, he wrote, "simply cannot forgive Russia either for its calm during that period of explosion of shallow little passions or for the terror they felt in the face of the northern giant while planning their vile, piratical plots."[17] During the mid-1860's Pisemsky even attempted to picture himself as a convinced supporter of the regime, although he was never com-pletely successful in persuading the authorities of the truth of his claim. When the regime became more oppressive, Pisemsky com-plained bitterly, but he still conceded grudgingly that the ultimate blame lay with the revolutionaries. Once in 1864, upset over the fact that the censorship had forbidden the publication of one of his plays, Pisemsky exclaimed: "Things have gotten so vile that they are much worse than before. And it's all because of this idiotic revolution, which has provoked a reaction and made it possible for all of Russian vileness to raise its head once more.''[18] The revolutionary movement effectively blocked many of the liberal reforms that Pisemsky would have liked to see instituted by offering the government an excuse to undertake repressive measures against both reformers and revolutionaries alike.

Pisemsky expressed horror that the radicals should go so far as to seek to assassinate the czar. Such an attempt was first made in April of 1866 in St. Petersburg by a young man named Karakozov, who fired at the emperor as he passed on the street. According to an account that gained wide credence at the time, Karakozov's aim was deflected at the critical moment by a native of Kostroma named Komissarov. When later a special celebration was arranged in Komissarov's honor, Pisemsky hastened to send him a congratulatory message referring to "our mild and magnanimous monarch" and the "bestially insolent assassination attempt.''[19] In short, Pisemsky's sympathies were entirely on the side of the existing regime in times of crisis, although his loyalty flagged occasionally in calmer periods.

The simplicity and directness of Pisemsky's personality attracted some as an expression of the Russian spirit untainted by foreign influences, but he also exhibited certain less pleasant aspects of the "national character." The most important of these was his tendency toward excess in sexual matters, in eating, and especially in drinking. Indulgence helped to undermine his health, which would have been poor enough even had he led a more regular life. His association with a group of St. Petersburg literary men, gathered around Druzhinin, who "drank more readily than they wrote" and engaged in stubborn carousing,[20] reinforced his inborn inclination toward debauchery. His wife exerted a restraining influence upon him, and occasionally he felt compelled to use subterfuge to conceal his drinking from her. One of his associates in the mid-1850's, who claimed that Pisemsky brought him to the verge of alcoholism, reported that Pisemsky was afraid to drink in front of Ekaterina Pavlovna. Whenever he wished to down a glass of vodka in his wife's presence, he would say to her: "Please leave the room, my dear, I want to use an indecent word." When she complied, he swallowed the vodka.[21] An amusing anecdote is told of Pisemsky's drinking in connection with his attendance at open houses held by the poet Lev Mey in the latter part of the 1850's and the early 1860's. Though Mey provided poor wine for his guests, both he and Pisemsky could still consume it in quantity. One evening while dining at Mey's,

Pisemsky became so engrossed in conversation that, without noticing, he poured vinegar into his wine glass and emptied it in two or three swallows without so much as blinking. When a startled friend pointed out that he had been imbibing vinegar, Pisemsky replied bemusedly: "You might have a point . . . I guess it is a bit like it . . . But it doesn't matter, because Mey's wine is always rotten stuff anyway."[22]

Pisemsky's fondness for alcohol was not invariably this humorous, especially for his wife. One of his friends, E. Ya. Kolbasin, described in a letter an occasion when Pisemsky came to visit him in a state of utter intoxication, "babbling such nonsense that it was pitiful to look at him." Kolbasin took him home to the care of his long-suffering wife.[23] But in order to get him there, he had to ignore Pisemsky's suggestion that they "drop in to visit the girls," another weakness of Pisemsky's that Ekaterina Pavlovna was forced to overlook. Pisemsky was probably never systematically unfaithful to her with any one woman, but he evidently patronized prostitutes regularly. The most appalling account of Pisemsky's debauches known to us was recorded at a considerable remove in time and space, so that it has undoubtedly been embellished and may even be apocryphal. Once, probably in the 1850's, Pisemsky received a considerable sum of money owed him by a journal. He then went home and, after supplying his wife with a portion of the money for household needs, announced that he was off to have a good time. He disappeared for five days and nights. On the sixth day he was found in a snow-covered field near Moscow, clad only in a pair of boots, with peasants running after him demanding that he be arrested. He was never able to explain how he had come to be in such a situation.[24]

Pisemsky's passion for drink in the 1850's caused the members of his circle to bestow upon him the nickname "Ermil," after the late eighteenth-century poet Ermil Kostrov (c. 1750-1796). Toward the end of his life Kostrov became such an alcoholic that he was forced to depend on friends for a corner in which to sleep.[25] By the mid-nineteenth century Kostrov's name was synonymous in the intellectual folklore with the concept of the author-drunkard. Many anecdotes about his drunkenness were in circulation, and in 1853 the playwright Nestor Kukolnik even published a play about him. This explains the fact that in the correspondence of Pisemsky's associates in the years between roughly 1855 and 1858 he was frequently referred to simply as "Ermil."

Pisemsky overate as well as overdrank. Since his digestive system was not especially sturdy, his gargantuan appetite aggravated an already unsatisfactory condition. Annenkov once wrote to Turgenev that Pisemsky was ill as a result of overeating. The delicate Turgenev might overeat on a piece of *blanc de volaille,* he observed, whereas Pisemsky had to feast on a bull before he collapsed, but the end result was the same.[26]

Not all of Pisemsky's illnesses were the result of debauchery. Some were the fruit of his imagination. He was eternally fearful of cholera and other diseases. He consulted doctors constantly, but usually disregarded their advice or else refused to accept their opinion that his illnesses were products of his mental state. Although later his hypochondria approached the point of mania, the fact that he wrote *The Hypochondriac* in 1852 shows that even in his earlier years it was well developed. The unsympathetic Botkin met Pisemsky at Ostrovsky's once in 1856 and reported that he looked very ill; it turned out that he had been reading medical books and discovering that he had all manner of pernicious diseases. Botkin suspected, probably correctly, that many of his troubles stemmed from too much alcohol.[27] Pisemsky also had the hypochondriac's habit of searching for diseases in other people as well as himself. When Ivan Panaev was sick, Pisemsky would regale him with horror stories on his visits and pose such inapposite questions as, "Are you sure you don't have cancer?"[28]

The *mnitelnost* (tendency to see disasters where they are not) that lay at the root of Pisemsky's hypochondria exhibited itself in other areas as well, to such an extent as to make him a walking collection of phobias. To take a trivial example, he is reported to have been in terror of dogs: a very modest canine standing in his path was sufficient to cause him to break into a sweat and refuse to continue his journey.[29] In 1855, when he ventured onto the sea to give a reading on the Grand Duke Konstantin Nikolaevich's frigate, Pisemsky started in fear upon hearing a salute fired—he thought a bombardment had begun. On the way back to shore in a small boat he was agitated lest the craft run into underwater rocks, shoals, and even mines.[30] Several photographs of Pisemsky show a man with prominently protruding eyes, the result of fright over all the photographic apparatus before which he was placed for a sitting. Pisemsky confessed in a letter that when facing the camera, he experienced, "if not fear, at least considerable perturbation."[31]

On other occasions Pisemsky invented more serious disasters. He once told Annenkov that often, upon returning home, he "stood at the threshold of [his] door with sinking heart: what if the house had been burglarized, what if somebody had died, what if there had been a fire—anything could happen." Annenkov was persuaded that Pisemsky had made these remarks completely seriously.[32] Another memoirist recalls that once when Pisemsky's son Pavel was unexpectedly delayed, his father leaped to the conclusion that Pavel had most certainly perished in a train wreck. He was preparing to claim the corpse when Pavel's appearance, alive and well, put an end to his gruesome fantasies.[33] The excessive alarmism illustrated by these anecdotes was apparently a constant trait of his personality.

Furthermore, Pisemsky suffered from a number of intellectual inconsistencies. Though one should be careful not to exaggerate the significance of such contradictions, a few deserve mention. One striking inconsistency involved his attitude toward the material side of existence. Perhaps the most persistent theme in the whole of Pisemsky's fiction is contempt for those whose sole aim in life is material security and "comfort," those prepared to make any sacrifice to avoid the disaster of bankruptcy. Yet Pisemsky himself was not the least mercenary writer of his day. He bargained shrewdly whenever selling his literary works, and toward the end of his career he demanded considerably more than his writings were worth and made sure that he received every ruble due him. Indeed, it is more than possible that the anguish Pisemsky suffered whenever one of his works was forbidden by the censorship arose from the loss of remuneration rather than from fervent attachment to the abstract ideal of intellectual freedom, although perhaps the latter played a minor role in his considerations. At any rate, in private life Pisemsky was in no way superior morally to his comfort-minded fictional personages.

Again, this writer who despised any sort of social deceit or favor-seeking in his literary creatures was nevertheless ready to pull whatever strings were accessible to him, sometimes in devious ways, in order to benefit himself. When certain of his plays experienced censorship difficulties in the 1860's and 1870's, Pisemsky dispatched letters to the Minister of the Interior or anyone else in authority who might be induced to overrule a decision unfavorable to him. In these letters he more than once stretched the truth in presenting himself as being in total sympathy with the existing regime. Pisemsky was also willing to request personal favors for himself and his family through influential acquaintances.

A letter of Pisemsky's in September 1864 to the publisher A. A. Kraevsky furnishes a striking example of his petty intriguing.[34] In the letter Pisemsky informed Kraevsky that he had contracted to compile a regular news column for the *Moskovskie politseyskie vedo-*

mosti (Moscow Police News). The column had previously been done very poorly, he asserted. He was certain he could do a better job, but at the same time he was afraid that the "swine" who ran the paper would be too dense to recognize the improvement. Pisemsky therefore asked Kraevsky to remark in one of his feuilletons—presumably for the St. Petersburg paper *Golos* (Voice)—that "in the *Moskovskie politseyskie vedomosti* there finally has appeared a chronicle which it's possible to read, a chronicle written without a lot of useless words, but rather clearly, briefly, and intelligibly." When he showed this comment to his superiors, Pisemsky argued, his position, which paid him 100 rubles in silver, would be assured. It is not known whether Pisemsky actually began writing the column or, if he did, whether Kraevsky complied with his request.

The indisputable gulf between Pisemsky's preaching and practice is shown in yet another, even more startlingly inconsistent action. It has been described by the actress Aleksandra Shubert, a relatively close friend of his during the 1870's and one whom there is no reason to suspect of bias against him. She reported that "once Pisemsky came to visit us and, seeing that my husband was wearing a medal, completely seriously crossed himself and pressed his lips to the medal."[35] If Shubert was correct in assuming that Pisemsky did this "completely seriously"—about which it is difficult to be certain—then Pisemsky cannot be listed as one who was undeviatingly contemptuous of social distinctions and the bureaucratic mind.

Pisemsky's religious views were a component part of his intellectual and spiritual profile. For most of his adult life his attitude toward religion seems to have been the common one of indifference coupled with disrespect for those official representatives of the Orthodox Church, the clergy. This posture is reflected in his fiction. In *Men of the 1840's,* for example, he created the repulsive Father Silivester, who makes the suppression of the schismatics his mission in life (V, 529 ff). A disreputable priest in "Kapitan Rukhnev" (Captain Rukhnev, 1878), in order to avoid unpleasantness with the authorities over an illegitimate child he has fathered, lets it be known that the infant expired soon after birth and, to further his deception, buries a small coffin containing a dead cat (VII, 428-430). However, in the last few years of his life Pisemsky turned to religion as a source of strength while undergoing a series of severe personal trials. In a dispirited letter of 1876 to Turgenev, describing his psychological state in dark colors, Pisemsky added, "Thank God that the religious feeling developing more and more within me affords a certain peace and support for my suffering soul.''[36] In later years Pisemsky's letters to close friends frequently ended with the formula ''May God keep you'' or some variant thereof. His letters to his son Pavel, when the latter was studying abroad in 1875, almost invariably conclude with a form of the sentence ''I embrace and bless you,'' often preceded by a ''May God keep you.'' It is true that these were more or less conventional formulas in Russian correspondence of the time, but the emotional context in which Pisemsky employed them is such that they cannot be dismissed as devoid of specific content. In Pisemsky's final novel, *Masony* (The Masons), he had originally intended to concentrate upon Masonry as a religious movement, an idea that probably would not have occurred to him seriously in his youth. Thus, in his declining years Pisemsky's earlier indifference yielded to a growing sense of religion's importance in his life.

As a person's living quarters mirror his personality to a large extent, one would expect Pisemsky's particular traits of character to be reflected in his surroundings. The memoirist and writer P. D. Boborykin has left us a description of one apartment in which Pisemsky lived, on the Sadovaya in St. Petersburg. A sizable, light dwelling on the second floor, it was decorated with lithographs of such writers as Pierre Béranger and George Sand (why precisely these two is something of a mystery). In a corner of his study hung a fur topcoat, under which reposed a chamber pot. ''He kept the fur coat there,'' Boborykin explains, ''because he was afraid that it might be stolen from the entryway, and the 'vial of wrath' . . . because he was too lazy to leave his study to take care of his natural needs.''[37] Such details are indicative not of Pisemsky's laziness, since anyone who wrote as much as he can hardly be considered lazy, but of his slovenliness, coarseness, and lack of respect for the niceties of life.

Although Pisemsky enjoyed questionable renown in contemporary society because of his vices, he was noted for certain positive achievements in addition to his writing. One of these was his skill as a reader and, secondarily, as an actor. All who heard him declaim his own writings concurred that in this area he was endowed with great ability, and he did not hesitate to exploit this strength to win public acclaim for his literary works. His friend and protégé Ivan Gorbunov characterized a reading of ''The Carpenters' Guild,'' presumably given in 1855, as, ''not a reading, but acting on a high level of competence; each character emerged as if alive, with his own tone, his own gestures, his own individuality.''[38] Druzhinin pronounced Pisemsky "an actor at heart" and expressed no little approval of his ability as a reader.[39] Almost all other commentators on this subject agreed that Pisemsky was one of the outstanding readers of his day, at least within Russia. It should be noted, however, that when Turgenev attended three of Charles Dickens' readings, he was forced to downgrade Pisemsky: "In the face of this genius," he wrote, "all our readers—Pisemsky, Ostrovsky—are transformed into something less than a fly."[40]

Pisemsky's interest in dramatic reading was intimately linked with his love for acting, which had first expressed itself in his dedication to amateur theatricals while a boy, at the university, and later in the civil service in Kostroma. Upon moving to St. Petersburg, he continued to participate in amateur theatricals, playing in several benefit performances, especially around 1860. Most observers considered him quite successful, and Pisemsky himself was so convinced of his histrionic prowess that he occasionally argued about the stage with professional actors. Still, he never approached greatness as an actor, even in the Russian context. An observation of Annenkov's helps to explain both Pisemsky's success as actor and reader on the lower levels and his ultimate failure in the upper artistic reaches. According to Annenkov, in portraying a person, Pisemsky always selected his most prominent trait and built the entire characterization around it, sloughing off all subtleties and shadings.[41] In other words, he sought a unity in each character and, if he did not find it, created it forcibly. In this lay both his strength and his weakness as an actor, and it was probably this narrowness of conception that led Turgenev to rank him so far below Dickens as a reader.

Literary and Social Critic

After settling down to his nonpaying employment in St. Petersburg, Pisemsky maintained his literary associations with the city's journals, *Sovremennik* and *Otechestvennye zapiski*, while continuing his boycott of *Moskvityanin*, in which he had published nothing since the end of 1852. He had become, however, temporarily, a St. Petersburg writer exclusively. In 1855 he published two fictional works: "Is She To Blame?" in the February issue of *Sovremennik* and "The Carpenters' Guild" in the September issue of *Otechestvennye zapiski*. This "Is She To Blame?" incidentally, is not the same work over which Pisemsky worried in the late 1840's and early 1850's but which was forbidden by the censorship.

On the subject of "Is She To Blame?" relatively little need be

said about plot structure alone. In this respect the story falls wholly
into the tradition of Pisemsky's early "family dramas," dealing
with the conflict between the requirements of family and society
and the impulses of the individual heart. The plot was prepared
according to Pisemsky's standard recipe, calling for girl, brother,
loving bystander, unloved husband, and heartless seducer, plus a few
other characters, combined without much variety. The heroine, Lidiya
Vankovskaya, agrees under duress to marry a repulsive individual
named Ivan Kuzmich Maraseev, who happens to be one of her family's major creditors. This unhappy union sets the stage for the
predictable drama. Lidiya's heart is subsequently conquered by a
man named Kurdyumov, the "provincial lion," to whom she gives
herself. The story ends inconclusively and gloomily.

If the plot is not very original in Pisemsky's repertoire, "Is She
To Blame?" at least holds interest as an exercise in the appraisal
of appearances. The question in the story's title plainly refers to
Lidiya, who is driven by well-nigh irresistible external and internal
forces to contract an unsuitable marriage and then to betray her
husband. The reader must therefore answer the query in the
negative, although not without important qualifications.[42]

The narrator, who plays the role of the faithful bystander and
promptly falls in love with Lidiya on first meeting her, says of her
that, even though she was not a great beauty, "there was in her
something unusually kind and good which attracted you to her
involuntarily at first glance" (III, 218). Although the narrator
may be considered a prejudiced observer, Lidiya's brother Leonid,
one of the most admirable persons in Pisemsky's fictional world,
who had a clearer and more intimate view, loves her deeply and says
of her that "she is not very pretty, but she has a marvelous character" (III, 228). In short, Lidiya's beauty is primarily a beauty of
the spirit rather than the flesh, a type of beauty that even a cynic
of Pisemsky's stamp ordinarily would not suspect of masking deception.

Nevertheless, when the narrator returns to Moscow some five years
after Lidiya's marriage, his suspicions are aroused, for though
Lidiya is obviously happy to see him again, she is also disturbed and
seems to be concealing something from him (III, 250). After a
time the narrator decides that she is having a secret affair with
Kurdyumov, an affair which she conceals not only from the world
at large and from the narrator, but even in some peculiar way from
herself. Thus, when the narrator, holding up before her gaze what
he considers the "truth" and pointing out that Kurdyumov had

displayed interest in her only after her marriage, Lidiya recoils in horror. "Sometimes it's terrible to talk to you," she says. "You are capable of extinguishing a woman's faith both in herself and in others" (III, 262). She concocts a plausible explanation of her supposedly innocuous attraction to Kurdyumov, claiming that after her marriage neither her mother nor her brother would have much to do with her (this seems illogical); the narrator, who might have supported her, was gone; and her husband was cruel to her when drunk. She obtained sympathy from Kurdyumov alone. At the same time she insists that she is "not in love [with Kurdyumov], but I like him (ne vlyublena, a lyublyu ego)" (III, 273). By such means Lidiya is able to shunt the narrator off the track and temporarily rescue her own illusions. Though at one point he ragingly scorns her in his mind as a "deceitful intriguer" and resolves to "tear the mask from her" (III, 272)—an attack she could not have withstood—he accepts her version, gives her the benefit of every doubt in his own mind, and vigorously defends her reputation in a conversation with outsiders who had imputed evil to her.

Then, all at once, Lidiya's world disintegrates. Leonid challenges Kurdyumov to a duel to save his sister's honor, is wounded, and dies of his injuries. Kurdyumov is jailed for his part in the duel. Ivan Kuzmich, after having left her, returns to his wife, but with his health so undermined by drink that he soon dies. After these successive trials, Lidiya abandons her attempt to explain away her actions to herself, just as the narrator has come to believe her protestations of innocence: when the narrator proposes to her, she refuses him in a letter confessing her affair with Kurdyumov. She berates herself for having deceived the narrator and concludes that she is unworthy to be his wife (III, 287). At the story's conclusion the narrator adds one final sentence pointing out that Lidiya has declared herself unequivocally to blame and asking whether she is correct in this. The best reply is that by her own high standards she is at fault; but by more ordinary measurements—or even by her own standards tempered by mercy—she is not genuinely to blame for a situation imposed upon her by external circumstances. When all is said and done, the most interesting element in the story is not its commonplace plot but the description of Lidiya's gradual realization of the true state of her feelings toward Kurdyumov, leading up to her confession.

In early 1855 Pisemsky's creative energies were concentrated on his first novel, *One Thousand Souls*, begun a year before during his sojourn at Ramene. The novel's hero, Kalinovich, resembles his creator in that he starts out in the provinces as a civil servant with literary ambitions and later moves to the capital. In 1854 Pisemsky could write knowledgeably about Kalinovich's life in the provinces because he was familiar with the milieu, but a description of Kalinovich's further adventures had to await the author's acquaintance with the capital. At the end of March 1855 he informed Ostrovsky that he was giving readings of both *One Thousand Souls* and "The Carpenters' Guild" before "various mighty ones of this world" in St. Petersburg.[43] His friend Ivan Gorbunov, who later became a minor literary figure, recalled that when he first arrived in St. Petersburg in April 1855, he went right away to see Pisemsky, whom he found working on *One Thousand Souls*. Gorbunov sat for whole days with Pisemsky as the latter wrote, so that part of the novel was composed in his presence, and he even received a few chapters from an early draft.[44] By late July Pisemsky had started the third part. He hoped to finish the work by the end of the year, but in this he was disappointed, for the novel did not appear in print until 1858. Too many other things interfered.

For instance, the abundance of activities and friendships available in St. Petersburg was distracting, especially for a man bent on taking full advantage of his new location; the cultivation of friends and the frequenting of literary salons took up much time. It was at this period that Pisemsky met the rising young author Lev Tolstoy and attended readings of some of his works. After hearing one of Tolstoy's Sebastopol stories, Pisemsky reported that during it his "hair had stood on end . . . The thing is written in such a pitilessly honest fashion that it is difficult to read it."[45] Of course, Pisemsky could not content himself with listening passively to others' readings: he was eager to present his own work to the public, and more especially to those who might be able to assist him in piercing the censorship barrier. His most significant reading of 1855, occurring in June, was a recitation of the then unpublished "The Carpenters' Guild" on the Grand Duke Konstantin Nikolaevich's flagship.[46]

In the middle and late summer Pisemsky was busy attending to the staging of his first play of importance, *The Hypochondriac*, which it had become possible to present after Nicholas I's death and the subsequent general liberalization of intellectual life. The play was premiered in St. Petersburg on September 21, 1855, and later staged in Moscow. Though hardly the theatrical event of the year, the première aroused comment. Nekrasov, for instance, devoted several pages in the October issue of *Sovremennik* to a discussion of

the play, commenting that the characters were magnificently drawn
and true to life. At the same time, Nekrasov thought, the work suffered from a lack of any guiding thought: "Before you there passes
a series of scenes from life which in reality you would survey without either sympathy or indignation." In other words the play was,
if anything, too close to life, devoid of inner meaning, just as life
often seems to be. Nekrasov ended with the hope that in the future
Pisemsky would discover the correct literary path, namely, the tradition of Gogolian humor with a purpose.[47]

It was also in the pivotal year of 1855 that Pisemsky made his
first and only serious attempt at a lengthy piece of literary criticism.
Although he occasionally disbursed literary counsel in personal letters to authors,[48] in general he rarely displayed any interest in
writing criticism for publication. However, he made an exception
for the posthumous publication of the second part of Gogol's *Dead
Souls*, when he printed a discussion of it, dated July 1855, in the
October issue of *Otechestvennye zapiski*. This break with custom
may be partially explained by the fact that Gogol is the one author
who may without reservation be considered a mentor of the early
Pisemsky, whose letters contain numerous references to the master's
works and opinions. Gogol's death on February 21, 1852, had been
a sore blow to Pisemsky in the provinces. "He died of agonies while
surveying [Russian] reality from afar," Pisemsky wrote darkly to
Pogodin at the time, "but will a very long life be granted to us
who are forced by poverty and family responsibilities to live in this
well of banality and to be completely dependent upon it [?]"[49]
At about the same time Pisemsky confessed to Ostrovsky that he
had wept quietly upon reading Pogodin's note in *Moskvityanin* on
Gogol's death and asked Ostrovsky to send him a portrait of the
great writer.[50] In view of his strong attachment to Gogol, it is not
surprising that Pisemsky should have commented publicly upon
the appearance of Gogol's work in 1855.

The article, entitled "Sochineniya N. V. Gogolya, naydennye posle
ego smerti: *Pokhozhdeniya Chichikova, ili Mertvye dushi*. Tom
vtoroy (5 glav)" (N. V. Gogol's Works, Found After His Death:
Chichikov's Adventures, or Dead Souls, Volume Two [5 chapters]),
adhered to the unfortunate pattern of many nineteenth-century
Russian critical pieces, which consisted mainly of tediously long
quotations from the work under review. It begins with a brief discussion of the literary epoch in which Gogol first appeared and
whose primary shortcoming, in Pisemsky's opinion, was its straining
for effect, its "striving . . . to create something greater than its

powers would permit'' (VII, 437). Even Gogol suffered from this in the beginning, but later he was able to overcome it and introduce a genuinely original humor. Gogol's humor, in contrast to that of his predecessors, did not spring from a feeling of ''personal insult'' but rather was directed against ''mankind's moral shortcomings and diseases of the soul'' (VII, 438). He had likewise surmounted the ''literariness'' of his predecessors, which had made them seem unnatural and forced. Although the second part of *Dead Souls* exhibited many of Gogol's strengths, at the same time it had numerous weaknesses. Several of these stemmed from the author's wish to cultivate a lyricism with which he was not naturally endowed; Pisemsky regretted that somebody had not told Gogol: ''You are by nature a great humorist and not a lyricist, and all your lyricism is engulfed by your humor, just as a brook is engulfed by a long, wide, and swift river'' (VII, 456). This remark is a good illustration of Pisemsky's inclination to analyze a literary figure exclusively in terms of his most important trait. Such an approach yields conclusions that, though possibly diverting, are ultimately misleading, because they leave out of account too many factors. In conclusion, Pisemsky issued a call to his fellow writers to heed the lesson of Gogol, who had erred in attempting to describe things of which he had no experience and about which he could not therefore be truthful. ''Keeping the great master's mistakes in mind,'' Pisemsky wrote, everyone ''should move along his chosen way without forcing himself to do something beyond his powers. Everyone, while remaining demanding of himself aesthetically, should in proportion to his talents tell the *truth* to the public'' (VII, 458).

Nekrasov commented on Pisemsky's venture in criticism in the course of his miscellaneous remarks published in the November 1855 issue of *Sovremennik*. Though Nekrasov's overall opinion of the article was adverse, he admitted that it contained a few observations of value. ''The author's view of Gogol is shallow and one-sided in general,'' Nekrasov wrote. ''He measures Gogol by a rather ordinary standard and sometimes arrives at strange conclusions.'' Indeed, Pisemsky dispensed advice with such assurance that he gave the impression that he could have improved upon Gogol in certain areas. Nevertheless, Nekrasov concluded, it was gratifying to find an article of even this stature amidst the current trivia.[51]

Nekrasov's attention to both the staging of *The Hypochondriac* and the Gogol article raises the question of whether he was attempting to win Pisemsky over to the incipient radical camp during this critical year of his life. The phrase ''incipient radical camp'' is appropriate here because in 1855 *Sovremennik* was two or three years away from becoming a consistently radical organ: many foreign elements, such as the aesthetic critic Vasily Botkin, still clung to it. Apparently Nekrasov did hope at this time to convert Pisemsky to his view of literature, even though he recognized Pisemsky's shortcomings and in 1854 had referred to him as a "sloven." It was probably this hope that moved Nekrasov to devote so many printed words to Pisemsky's activities in 1855. Pisemsky's next major work to attract Nekrasov's notice was "The Carpenters' Guild," included in his chief collection of peasant tales.

Ocherki iz krestyanskogo byta (Sketches of Peasant Life), one of Pisemsky's most universally acclaimed books, was published in 1856. It brought together three previously published and more or less unrelated short stories dealing with the peasantry: "The Petersburger" (1852), "The Wood Demon" (1853), and "The Carpenters' Guild" (1855). This collection, along with the play *Gorkaya sudbina* (*A Bitter Fate*) and the two short stories "Staraya barynya" (The Old Proprietress, 1857) and "Batka" (The Father, 1862), constitute almost the entirety of Pisemsky's writing about the peasantry. Yet because of such works, Pisemsky has earned the false reputation of being primarily a chronicler of peasant life.

The *Sketches of Peasant Life,* classifiable as "long short stories," are certainly among Pisemsky's more successful efforts. The first two are recounted by one of the characters, who has participated in the action described, so that they verge on being dramatic monologues; the third, though basically narrated by the author, contains a great deal of dialogue in which peasants participate. In each story the plot, while interesting, is subordinated to the creation of a certain atmosphere.

The hero of "The Petersburger," named Klementy, is a sturdy peasant transplanted from his native village to St. Petersburg, where he works as a painter. The term for such uprooted peasants was *pitershchik,* the Russian title of the story. While striving to fend off loneliness in the capital, Klementy strikes up an acquaintance with one Palageya Ivanovna and her aunt, on whom he wastes all his substance. Once his money is exhausted, he is rejected by his paramour and returns to his native village. When three years later the narrator meets him again in St. Petersburg, he has managed to recoup his losses and overcome the temptations of women and drink. The narrator expresses his satisfaction at the solid character of the Russian peasant, which has enabled him to reestablish himself after so many misfortunes.

Like Anany Yakovlev, the hero of Pisemsky's classic play *A Bitter Fate,* Klementy belongs to that special category of peasant who found life in the capital preferable to village existence. But it is precisely because he has been removed from his native environment that Klementy is exposed to so many disastrous temptations. He has several reasons for leaving the village: an economic one (there are no factories in the vicinity and the soil is too poor for profitable tillage), a marital one (he does not get along with his wife), and a frivolous one (the stay-at-homes envy those who return from St. Petersburg with wonderful stories about their adventures). Once in the city, he enriches himself through his entrepreneurial prowess rather than by the application of any particular professional skill. As a wealthy provincial, he then provides a tempting target for the unscrupulous, who are quick to gather around him.

The two major actors in the drama are nevertheless relatively innocent. Each is influenced for the worse by an older relative: Klementy by his uncle, who introduces him to Palageya Ivanovna, and she by her aunt, who forces her to lead Klementy on when she really does not wish to. In this way the older generation exerts a corrupting influence upon the young. Deception and pretense play a crucial role in the development of the relationship between the two young people. The old woman who serves as Klementy's go-between remarks to him that Palageya Ivanovna "is a fine girl and not the sort that you maybe suppose" (I, 601). Upon completing the story, the reader is still not certain what manner of woman she is, since she has been seen through the eyes of a lover who is thus incapable of regarding her dispassionately. Their entire relationship is imbued with pretense. For instance, Klementy's love for Palageya Ivanovna is first strongly aroused when they go together to the theater. Klementy has always loved the theater, preferring unrealistic plays with "foreign princes in bright clothing." Palageya attracts Klementy also because she sings beautifully, but this is merely a performance, not at all revelatory of her true self—the self that she conceals, under pressure from her aunt, until the day she throws Klementy's presents in his face and tells him to leave her.

It is likewise Klementy's desire to put up an impressive front that drives him to disastrous involvement with Palageya and her aunt even when his reason tells him he is acting foolishly. He is shocked to discover that they live in a slum residence but still allows the aunt to needle him. When she, for selfish motives, accuses him of being either poor or stingy, he embarks upon the road to financial ruin by providing her and Palageya with a sumptuous apartment and expensive presents. His false pride prevents him from acting rationally: "We've got a hundred in the pocket but act as if we've got thousands," he says (I, 603). Despite what he can see in his more lucid moments, Klementy blunders ahead until he is abandoned by those who have exploited him and has to be removed virtually under guard from the corrupting city and returned to the healing village.

After a year of moral convalescence in the village Klementy returns to St. Petersburg and regains his former affluence. When the narrator runs into him, he is "wearing a coat of wolf-fur and something like jack-boots, with a gold ring on his finger" (I, 610). Thus it would appear that Klementy, though not a peasant *kulak* who exploits the labor of others, is interested solely in his personal comfort. Strangely enough, Pisemsky not only fails to condemn this crassly materialistic ideal, he even seems heartily to approve of it, although in a man of higher social station he would have damned it in no uncertain terms. In Pisemsky's gallery of heroes Klementy stands out as almost the only instance of a man whose ambition to wear soft raiment and "gold rings" the author looks upon with approbation.

The second story in *Sketches of Peasant Life* is "The Wood Demon," subtitled "The Story of a District Police Officer." It chronicles the misfortunes visited upon the peasantry when a lackey who has served his master in the city is sent to supervise his country properties, a responsibility for which he is not qualified. The district police officer, who is the narrator and the story's positive hero as well, immediately recognizes the lackey, Egor Parmenov, as a rogue, and he supervises the supervisor closely. For quite a while, however, he remains ignorant of one of Parmenov's chief hobbies: utilizing his position to obtain sexual favors from the peasant women under his authority. In particular, he seduces a girl from a neighboring village and confines her as a prisoner in the manor house. When finally he must release her, he instructs her to claim that she had been abducted by a "wood demon." When the police officer finds out about the situation, he has Parmenov replaced as supervisor by one of the local peasants and exposes his amorous escapades in the presence of his wife, who until then has been ignorant of them but thereafter makes his life supremely miserable.

The motif of the story is the city's corrupting influence on the nearly unblemished morality of the countryside. The district officer clearly understands the opposition between city and country. He remarks that the *burmistry* (estate managers for an absentee landlord appointed from among the local peasantry) are on the whole greatly superior to *upraviteli* (estate managers sent out from the city). This is so not only because the peasant manager knows the local situation infinitely better and is usually more in sympathy with his fellow peasants, but also because he has not been corrupted through "living a free life" in the city, that "spoiler of men" (I, 614-615). The police officer worries lest the virulent moral infection represented by Egor Parmenov in turn corrupt the peasantry (I, 644).

The peasants among whom Parmenov makes his appearance dwell in an isolated area, and their moral standards are related to this isolation. They are so wonderfully well-behaved and obedient, according to the police officer, that if one scattered gold on the street and told them not to touch it, nobody would dare approach (I, 620). In his first ten years of service he hardly had need even to visit the area. The purity of the collective character is reflected in miniature in the purity of the peasant girl Marfa, whom Parmenov seduces. She was a hard worker and, even though she possessed a loving nature, according to her mother's testimony, never had anything serious to do with men until the age of twenty (I, 628).

Parmenov, that spreader of urban infection, destroys this potentiality for good. Even his physical appearance makes an immediately unfavorable impression: his face is greasy, his eyes are small and shifty, he is dressed foppishly, with a vest, gold watchchain, and in particular, a "gold ring on his dirty hand" (I, 615-616). He clearly has adopted civilization's vices without any of its virtues. Parmenov's activities jibe completely with his appearance: he is a lackey in soul as well as by calling. He would deceive his master grossly were it not for the police officer's supervision. In order to seduce Marfa, he utilizes the charm of his pseudo-urbanity in the eyes of a simple peasant girl, deceitful promises, alcohol, and finally forcible restraint. Before releasing her, he terrifies her into pretending that she has lost the power of speech and was abducted by a wood demon, in hopes of playing upon the superstitious credulity of the peasants so as to conceal his misdeeds. Even if they do not believe the hoax, Parmenov is confident that the peasants' mumbling passivity will prevent them from informing on him.

When Parmenov is eventually brought to account, not only for his abduction of Marfa but for his affairs with several other women as well, the police officer taxes him with his misdeeds in the presence of the entire peasant commune, and that body is happy to endorse their master's removal of Parmenov from his position (I, 648-649).

Although Parmenov and his wife continue to reside in the vicinity, they are separated from the local community as if in a quarantine, and he is dubbed "the wood demon" for his exploits. Parmenov's victim Marfa, despite her bitter and tearful repentance, also undergoes punishment. She bears his child, which she insists upon raising, but thereafter no honest peasant will marry her. She withdraws into herself, becomes very pious, and communicates with nobody (I, 651). Thus, by means of the ruthless amputation of its infected members as well as the infecting agent, the peasant community is restored to its former moral equilibrium.

The plot of "The Wood Demon" is sufficiently detailed to maintain interest at a relatively high level. Its principal shortcoming is that although the chief narrator and Marfa's mother, the two who do most of the talking, emerge as interesting and well-rounded characters, little is learned about the inner world of the two most important persons in the drama, Parmenov and especially Marfa. Had Pisemsky made them more vivid, the story would have been more satisfactory.

The final tale in *Sketches of Peasant Life,* "The Carpenters' Guild," is told in the first person. The narrator in this instance appears to be a nearly autobiographical figure. He is addressed by one of the characters in the story as Pisemsky, and *The Simpleton* is mentioned in the text. The plot involves a peasant exploiter, Puzich, who contracts to do work utilizing the labor of other peasants to whom he has lent money and who can redeem their debts only by laboring for him at scandalously low rates of pay. The narrator arranges to have Puzich and his "guild" put up a threshing barn on his estate. As work progresses, the narrator talks to the peasants about their life. For instance Sergeich describes peasant marriage customs in detail. Another peasant, Petr, relates to the narrator a harrowing tale of family hardships. The story concludes with a murder. After drinking at length in the tavern, Puzich attacks a bystander. When Petr, along with others, steps in to halt the fight, Puzich falls upon him in a drunken fury. His patience finally exhausted, Petr raises Puzich into the air and dashes him to the ground with such force as to kill him instantly. Petr is arrested and the story ends inconclusively.

From the point of view of economy of means, "The Carpenters' Guild" is the least successful of the three stories in the collection. The main narrative line, involving Puzich and Petr, is heavily obscured by a mass of digressions, which usually take the form of conversations between the narrator and various peasants. These asides at first distract the reader and then begin to weary him. The story is plagued by what might be termed an "ethnographical prolixity" into which Pisemsky tended to fall in the middle 1850's.

At the same time this very feature makes "The Carpenters' Guild" the most valuable story of the three in the sense that from it the untutored reader may learn much about the life and psychology of the Great Russian peasant. The gallery of peasant types pictured sympathetically by the narrator is extensive, even though he himself remains a "master" (barin) and can never be fully admitted to the peasant's confidence. For instance, when the narrator is negotiating with Puzich over the construction of the threshing barn, the village elder Semyon, who is the narrator's right hand man and maintains liaison between the common muzhik and the landowners, repeatedly warns his master that he is offering too much, and he listens to Puzich "with that badly concealed inattentiveness and disdain with which a good peasant usually hears out the knavish chatter of one of his fellows" (II, 9). The three peasants working for Puzich in the guild are positive, admirable characters. Petr, for example, inspires respect even in Puzich. He can be extremely straightforward, as when he tells the narrator to his face that if he had been as intelligent as his father, he would never have given Puzich such a sum as 100 rubles for the barn (II, 21). Again, Petr makes no concessions to the master in recounting the tale of an illness that had been visited upon him through witchcraft, describing the ways in which he had tried to discover who was hexing him and the steps he had taken to free himself of the enchantment. When the narrator in his superior wisdom ventures to take the notion of witchcraft lightly, Petr practically insults him, saying that the masters are often too bright for their own good (II, 36-37). The narrator's good-humored willingness to abandon the field of contest to his opponent makes it seem that Pisemsky was ready to concede to Petr a superior sort of irrational wisdom denied to the educated. In another place Pisemsky inserts a vignette of the master's coachman David, a peasant addicted to contriving farfetched lies about his master, such as that he was "a count, a general, that he had a thousand serfs" (II, 42). Pisemsky always displayed indulgence toward a prevaricator who plied his trade for the sheer pleasure of it, and he looks upon David with even more detachment than usual. As was the case with Klementy and his ideal of "comfort," Pisemsky regarded superstition of the sort displayed by Petr and the lack of truthfulness exhibited by David as mere foibles when found among peasants, although he condemned them roundly in representatives of higher social classes.

Puzich, however, is treated with no such indulgence. He makes a bad first impression upon the narrator with his foppish dress and pretenses to religiosity, praying at length when he first enters the room, and further acquaintance merely strengthens the feeling of repulsion. Puzich's most prominent trait is greed: it becomes evident to the narrator at the conclusion of their financial negotiations that he was one of those "who cannot even talk about money calmly and without nervous excitement" (II, 12).

"The Carpenters' Guild" differs from the other two stories in the *Sketches* in that comparatively ordinary peasants are described more or less in their native habitat. In contrast, the peasant hero of "The Petersburger" is an unusual person placed in an extraordinary environment. Furthermore, the corrupting element among the guild peasants is not an outsider, like Egor Parmenov in "The Wood Demon," but a native exploiter. Whereas the peasant community can restore its equilibrium simply by ejecting Parmenov, Puzich can only be eliminated by means of physical destruction, like a cancer.

The appearance of the *Sketches of Peasant Life,* especially the third story, stimulated much public and private discussion. In particular, Nekrasov and Vasily Botkin reacted strongly to "The Carpenters' Guild," entering into an extended correspondence about it. Their discussion began when Botkin in Moscow and Nekrasov in St. Petersburg at nearly the same time (mid-September 1855, just after the story's initial publication) started to write each other long letters on the story and, secondarily, on the contrast between Pisemsky and Turgenev. Theirs was among the first of a long series of considerations of this contrast by various critics. It seems that Turgenev, after hearing the author read "The Carpenters' Guild," had appointed himself a propagandist for the work, and his remarks had led both Nekrasov and Botkin to expect extraordinary things of it. When the story appeared in print, however, both felt that it had failed to measure up to their expectations and attributed Turgenev's enthusiasm to Pisemsky's declamatory skills.

In a letter of September 14 to Nekrasov, Botkin took an especially negative attitude, holding that the story's form was unsuccessful, seemingly "concocted" by the author, and that Puzich was a "falsely conceived and badly executed character." The story as a whole lacked "moral significance" and was therefore worthless as literature. The most favorable thing Botkin could say was that it contained a "fairly skillful imitation of peasant speech," truly a left-handed compliment.[52] On September 23 Botkin reiterated these basic sentiments, in condensed form, in a letter to Turgenev.[53]

On September 16—probably before reading Botkin's letter of the 14th—Nekrasov wrote a lengthy missive to him expounding his slightly more positive view of "The Carpenters' Guild." Nekrasov felt that its strength lay in its depiction of the *muzhiks* but that the story's good facets were submerged in a sea of "chatter" at both the beginning and end, which made it "boring." And if it bored even him, a professional literary man, he asked, what would it do to the ordinary reader?[54]

Influenced by the personal friendship between Turgenev and Pisemsky, Botkin and Nekrasov were tempted to draw literary comparisons between them that were unflattering to Pisemsky. In a letter of September 19 Botkin agreed with Nekrasov that a writer should love truth first and foremost, as did Pisemsky, but he claimed that "Pisemsky is bad from another angle: he has no concocted theories, but then neither does he have that higher contemplation or view of things possessed only by poetic intellects. In his works reality is reflected drily, without any perspectives, without that transparency which alone makes it possible to delve deeply into works of art. To this day Turgenev has not been completely successful with a single one of his characters, but nearly all of them possess an airy perspective and in nearly all of them one senses a higher view of the phenomena of this world."[55] Nekrasov was unwilling to go so far in downgrading Pisemsky by comparison with Turgenev: he rightly felt that Pisemsky was better at reproducing the intonations of folk speech. But he did agree that Turgenev far surpassed Pisemsky in "intellect" and in subsidiary areas such as taste and tact.[56] Pisemsky, incidentally, had his own ideas on the relative merits of the *Sketches* and Turgenev's writing. In late 1856, after reading the latest collection of Turgenev's stories, Pisemsky compared his own stories most unfavorably: "I leafed through them [the *Sketches*] and was ready to spit in my own face, because everything seemed so dry and prosaic."[57]

Later in 1855 Nekrasov stated his opinion publicly in one of his catch-all reviews, where he maintained that Pisemsky's best story to date had been "The Petersburger." Then, damning him with faint praise, he declared that "after the masterful sketches by Dal, Turgenev, and Grigorovich, Pisemsky's sketches are of course the best in Russian literature."[58] One may surmise that Pisemsky did not relish being ranked below Dal and Grigorovich as a chronicler of the peasantry.

The publication of *Sketches of Peasant Life* also furnished the stimulus for one of the more important debates in print between the aesthetic and radical camps in Russian criticism during the latter half of the 1850's. It was the aesthetic critic Druzhinin who first seized upon the *Sketches* as an excuse to write a moderately extensive article dealing primarily with the question of "pure" versus didactic art. Writing in *Biblioteka dlya chteniya* for January 1857, Druzhinin interpreted Pisemsky's work as representative of the new brand of literature, which had dealt a heavy blow to the "old didactic theories of the old criticism," that is, to the criticism of the later Belinsky. By his faithfulness to life and his impartial evaluations of people and events Pisemsky supplied a valuable counterweight to the tendentious school in literature. Moreover, Druzhinin professed to detect in "The Carpenters' Guild" "an original sort of quiet poetry, not subtle and not like that of [the poet] Fet, but still extremely attractive in its practicality and healthy development."[59] Druzhinin was justified to a point in emphasizing the story's "poetic" qualities, but since these qualities did not resemble the ordinarily accepted "poetic" values, others were certain to disagree. Chernyshevsky was among them.

Picking up the gauntlet of his ideological opponent, the radical Chernyshevsky published his own comments on the *Sketches* in the April 1857 issue of *Sovremennik*. This "review" consisted not so much of a discussion of Pisemsky's work as an attack on Druzhinin's theories. Druzhinin erred, he said, in assigning Pisemsky a place in the history of Russian literary development of the 1850's by misinterpreting his approach. The critic imagined that "the essential trait of Pisemsky's stories of folk life is the conciliatory and joyful impression they produce."[60] Declaring that this was plainly nonsense, Chernyshevsky cited page after page in which the *Sketches* painted a grim picture of Russian reality, such as the descriptions of the avaricious and tyrannical Puzich. It could even be maintained, Chernyshevsky argued, that nobody had ever sketched the life of the peasantry in darker colors than had Pisemsky. Pisemsky, Chernyshevsky held in effect, far from wreaking a transformation in the Gogolian tradition of "critical realism" (as it later came to be called), had rather added his own original contribution to it, and his work was not a corruption but a development of the Gogolian heritage. Thus, Chernyshevsky and Druzhinin, reading the same text, interpreted it in utterly different ways. Each read his predilections into a piece written without predilections.

In conclusion Chernyshevsky made an observation that helps explain the violent change destined to occur in Pisemsky's political fortunes at the beginning of the next decade. In his article on Gogol, Pisemsky had written that the master was devoid of lyricism. Chernyshevsky could not agree, but he did think the comment might be employed to good advantage in the interpretation of Pisemsky's own work. Despite Druzhinin's opinion to the contrary, there was no lyricism in Pisemsky's literary approach. Instead, one of his chief characteristics was his "calm, so-called epic tone." Some critics had interpreted this tone as a sign of moral indifference, but in Chernyshevsky's opinion Pisemsky was not in the least morally neutral. He sympathized with his good characters and detested the bad ones, but without blatancy. His tendency was toward subtlety, and hence ambiguity.

This "subtlety" of which Chernyshevsky spoke is, I believe, responsible for many one-sided interpretations of Pisemsky's work that have survived to the present. Except in a few instances, mostly dating from his later period, Pisemsky was too much aware of the complexity of human life to create a character who was completely good or utterly bad from the moral point of view. His descriptions are neutral artistically, if not always morally, and during the height of his career he did not force his views upon the reader, who was therefore left with a sizable task of interpretation. Even a close consideration of his work does not yield clear-cut results, and a loose analysis may cut in any one of several directions. It was because of such variant interpretations that in the 1850's and early 1860's Pisemsky could be claimed as an ally by both the radical and conservative camps.

Among the Literary Groupings

As the 1850's wore on, Pisemsky moved further from the incipient radical grouping around *Sovremennik* and closer to Druzhinin and his allies. After 1855 Nekrasov apparently ceased trying to win Pisemsky over. Although he had made lengthy and occasionally positive comments on Pisemsky's work in his correspondence and published writings before 1856, thereafter he usually ignored him. Evidently he came to agree with the sentiments voiced in a letter of Grigorovich's to him: "Upon first making his [Pisemsky's] acquaintance I realized what sort he was . . . He is nothing but filth and grease, and there is not in his entire make-up a single facet corresponding to our convictions; in a word, he is foreign to us. You feel this just as soon as you see him. And trust my intuition: he will not last very long in literature and among literary men."[61] Ironically enough, before long Grigorovich himself had abandoned the progressive cause. Nevertheless, as a perceptive observer, he had discerned from the start that the basically apolitical and nonideological Pisemsky could never conclude a full alliance with the radical groupings in Russian intellectual life.

Instead, Pisemsky found himself being gradually drawn into the ranks of Nekrasov's opponents as the ideological configurations in Russian literary life shifted during the years 1856 and 1857. Thus, the conservative organ *Moskvityanin*, Pisemsky's first real literary haven, ceased publication in 1857 with the appearance of the final issues for 1856. Apollon Grigorev had made desperate attempts to avert its demise, and with good reason, for after 1857 he never again controlled a major journal. When in 1856 it became clear that *Moskvityanin* would not survive, a few men, led by Botkin and usually thought of as belonging to the "aesthetic camp" in Russian literature, attempted to subvert *Sovremennik* for their own purposes. The crucial position to seize was that of chief critic, held at the time by Chernyshevsky. The aesthetic camp's replacement candidate was Grigorev, who refused to join the *Sovremennik* staff except on condition that Chernyshevsky be altogether ejected. It was clear that Grigorev, a critic who assigned to art a central place in human affairs, could not work harmoniously with the author of *The Aesthetic Relation of Art to Reality,* who held that art was in every way inferior to life. Botkin tried unsuccessfully to bring pressure to bear on Nekrasov, the editor of *Sovremennik,* in Grigorev's behalf, writing to him in April 1856 that "Grigorev is incomparably more talented than Chernyshevsky, but the latter is incomparably more sensible" and that "Grigorev is incomparably nearer to us in everything than Chernyshevsky is."[62] Botkin probably misinterpreted Nekrasov's frame of mind at the time, for it is likely that Nekrasov never seriously considered replacing Chernyshevsky with Grigorev.

Nevertheless, for a time Nekrasov delayed a decision and strove to remain on good terms with both camps. In the spring of 1856 he concluded an agreement with Lev Tolstoy, Turgenev, Ostrovsky, and Grigorovich by whose terms these authors agreed to publish exclusively in *Sovremennik.* For all practical purposes this covenant remained a dead letter. In August 1856 Nekrasov went abroad, to

return only in June 1857. While he was gone, Nekrasov turned
Sovremennik over to Chernyshevsky, who promptly brought in his
protégé Nikolay Dobrolyubov and, by his uncompromisingly radical
stance, estranged the four writers who Nekrasov thought were
safely in his pocket.[63] When Nekrasov was afterwards forced to
choose between his literary friends and the firmly entrenched
Chernyshevsky, he cast his lot with the radical camp. He eventually
broke completely with Turgenev and parted company with Botkin
as well.

Any attempt at defining Pisemsky's relationship with the more
conservative camp—primarily Grigorev, Ostrovsky, Botkin, Turgenev, and Druzhinin—must take particular account of developments over the years 1855-1857. Of these five men, Pisemsky was
closest to Ostrovsky and Turgenev during this period. He sent
frequent and cordial letters to his old friend Ostrovsky, but the
latter's geographical remoteness in Moscow and his relative disin-
terest in ideological matters led him to remain pretty much aloof
from the intellectual battles in St. Petersburg. For some time he was
nearer the *Sovremennik* camp than any other, although he made
strange company for such as Chernyshevsky and Dobrolyubov.

In the 1850's Turgenev was one of Pisemsky's most dedicated
supporters. Besides vigorously promoting "The Carpenters' Guild"
among his friends, in 1857 Turgenev wrote of Pisemsky's "The
Old Proprietress" that he was "astounded by the firmness and true-
ness of its outlines," adding that Pisemsky was a "professor of
literary drawing" (*professor literaturnogo risunka*).[64] In Turgenev's letters of 1856 to friends in Russia, he more than once
inquired worriedly about Pisemsky's "spleen." Turgenev's corre-
spondents kept him informed of Pisemsky's real or imagined illnesses as well as his drinking bouts. For his part, Pisemsky fully
reciprocated Turgenev's affection, especially at this period. One of
Turgenev's friends reported that once when Pisemsky was in his
cups, he had made a strong statement about his feelings for
Turgenev: "[Pisemsky] was complaining about you, saying that
he loved you passionately, as if you were his lover, and is always
jealous of you. This is true; he loves you very much, and there
aren't very many people who can boast of his love."[65] Even when not
intoxicated, Pisemsky could write embarrassingly intimate letters to
Turgenev, of the sort one might expect from a lover. An example is
a letter of 1857 in which he berated Turgenev for his lengthy
absences: "It is obvious that you don't love us even a hundredth
as much as we love you; during your absence I have been deprived

of the greater half of my moral existence in life, which is not over-rich in joys as it is.''[66] With the passage of time Turgenev's attachment to Pisemsky weakened, while Pisemsky's remained strong, but Turgenev never ceased to aid his colleague when he felt he could, and in the 1870's mutual adversity drew them closer together once again.[67]

Pisemsky's other immediate associates were not so well disposed toward him as were Ostrovsky and Turgenev. Apollon Grigorev never looked upon Pisemsky either as man or writer with much approval, for all that he was one of his most brilliant interpreters. A cordial personal relationship never existed between them. Vasily Botkin at first violently opposed Pisemsky and professed bewilderment over the friendship between him and Turgenev. He once wrote to Turgenev that, though he disagreed with the thesis of Chernyshevsky's *The Aesthetic Relation of Art to Reality* that art should serve as a mere surrogate for reality, he did think it could be profitably applied to the literature produced by ''Pisemsky and tutti quanti.''[68] As late as the end of 1856 Botkin was still contemptuous of Pisemsky's achievements: ''How little significance Pisemsky has in spite of his mastery of color and line!'' he exclaimed to Turgenev.[69] Before long, however, Botkin moved to St. Petersburg, where he got to know Pisemsky better and discovered he was not so detestable after all. By January 1857 Botkin was noting that Pisemsky had drawn ''much closer to all of us,'' and after hearing a reading of ''The Old Proprietress,'' he was more willing to acknowledge the author's virtues. Although he could not bring himself to repudiate his former views entirely, he criticized Pisemsky much more sympathetically.[70] In short, if Botkin never became one of Pisemsky's proponents, at least he softened his opposition to the literary current that Pisemsky represented.

Druzhinin's published opinions of Pisemsky's works in the early 1850's, though fundamentally favorable, exhibited a certain reserve, especially when Pisemsky appeared not to be stimulating ''carefree laughter'' of the sort that Druzhinin wanted contemporary literature to cultivate. On the personal level it took Druzhinin some time to acquire a liking for Pisemsky, even after the two began to be thrown together in St. Petersburg. In February 1856 he noted in his diary that he had met Ostrovsky the preceding summer and that the playwright had impressed him far more than Pisemsky because he was not afflicted with ''filthiness, moldiness, or imbecility''—presumably traits of Pisemsky.[71] However, by the beginning of the following year Druzhinin's opinion of Pisemsky had improved to the

point where he offered him an important position on the editorial
board of *Biblioteka dlya chteniya*. Since Druzhinin's health was
poor, Pisemsky became one of the journal's mainstays for the following few years.

Expedition to Astrakhan

An unusual event in Pisemsky's life at this time stemmed in part
from his 1855 reading for Grand Duke Konstantin. Probably at
some time during the summer of that year the Grand Duke conceived
the notion of sending prominent writers on "literary expeditions"
to lesser known parts of the empire so that they might report upon
their impressions for the information of the public and the government.[72] On August 11, 1855, he requested a high-ranking bureaucrat
to select individuals from "among our young and talented writers
(for example, Pisemsky, Potekhin *et al.*)" to participate in an
expedition of this type. They were to visit such localities as Astrakhan, Orenburg, the Volga region, and in general those areas of the
country that derived their sustenance from the water; to investigate
inhabitants who gained their living by fishing and seafaring; and to
publish their findings in *Morskoy sbornik* (Marine Almanac, the
official organ of the Ministry of the Navy). The Grand Duke mentioned Pisemsky's name presumably because of his personal contact
with him, and this reference was sufficient to ensure his being
offered a place with the project. Others willing to take part were
eventually located: Aleksey Potekhin, Aleksandr Ostrovsky, and
Sergey Maksimov. Pavel Annenkov was offered a position but refused
it; Apollon Maykov's bureaucratic superior would not permit him
to make the trip.

Pisemsky should have had little difficulty in accepting the invitation from the point of view of employment, since his civil service
position was unsalaried. On the personal level, however, it is difficult
to explain why he agreed to undertake the expedition, since he was
never an enthusiastic traveler and usually fell ill whenever he went
far from home. In all probability he reasoned that the original invitation came from too highly placed a personage for it to be lightly
refused. Furthermore, he may have calculated that if his colleague
Ivan Goncharov—that lover of the easy life—had been able to survive a circumnavigation of the globe from 1852 to 1855, he could
surely manage an excursion to Astrakhan. Pisemsky had met Goncharov shortly after the latter's return in 1855 and detected a
certain kinship between them. "I understand all his [Goncharov's]
convictions, even the capricious ones, and what is more I sympathize

with them," he wrote at the time.[73] Goncharov had begun publishing segments of his travel impressions soon after his return, some of which appeared in *Morskoy sbornik*. The entire collection, printed separately under the title *Fregat "Pallada"* (The Frigate 'Pallas'), today remains one of the major contributions in the relatively minor category of nineteenth-century Russian travel literature. Goncharov's trip obviously influenced the Grand Duke's thinking, too, for he vetoed a highly placed functionary's suggestion that the writers sent on the expedition compose their reports in accordance with a rigid formula. Konstantin Nikolaevich ruled instead that the travelers should be issued only very general instructions and otherwise be left free to write as they pleased in the hope that they would produce something on the order of "Goncharov's excellent articles."[74] In fact, the authors chosen for the expeditions were allowed considerable latitude in writing up their impressions.

Before long a group of suitable literary men was chosen for the project, its organizers making a conscious effort to send individuals, if possible, to areas in which they had grown up, so that they would not be completely unfamiliar with local conditions. By the first part of 1856 almost all the investigators were at their posts, including Pisemsky, who based himself in Astrakhan. We do not know exactly when he departed from the capital, but it was presumably sometime in late January or early February 1856; his first letter from Astrakhan was written to his wife on February 19. To say that he was acutely unhappy at being so far from home would be putting it mildly. In a letter written to Turgenev on the 20th, he conjured up in fond detail the comfortable occupations of his St. Petersburg friends. At the very time when Annenkov, Druzhinin, Goncharov, and others were dining elegantly and entertaining lady friends, he wrote, "poor Pisemsky, without his family, hungry, not even thinking about women, trembling from the cold in his repulsive overcoat, is traveling about Russia and dreaming solely about his return to Piter and his good friends, with whom he will dine, drink a bit, quarrel a little and even, perhaps, play a prank or two, and whom at the same time he embraces from afar."[75] The unenthusiastic traveler's first letter to his wife was more optimistic, although even there he did not conceal his dissatisfaction with Astrakhan. His initial impression of the city was decidedly unfavorable, as is evident from his remark that Astrakhan was "twice as large as Kostroma and 15 times as dirty and pointless." He had tried seeking diversion at the theater, but the performance and the audience were so dreadful that he had walked out after the second act. In spite of its filth, the city had a few positive points: the food was tasty and cheap, and those in authority were cooperative. He was especially grateful for the hospitality of one Yakov Yakovlevich Feygin, who did everything in his power to make Pisemsky comfortable.[76]

Overcoming the exhaustion caused by his journey, Pisemsky began writing soon after his arrival. Though he was not usually interested in things foreign, the mixture of languages and peoples found in this corner of the empire exerted a fascination upon him: the Kalmucks, Armenians, Tartars, Persians, Russians, Germans, and Cossacks all rubbing shoulders with one another made it seem as if he were in another world altogether. Nonetheless he was frequently lonely and bored, and waited anxiously for every letter from friends and relatives in the capitals.[77]

Although he spent most of his time in Astrakhan, Pisemsky made several trips of varying duration to the hinterland. For instance, he traveled by water to Biryuchya kosa, a small island located in the extensive Volga delta, returning to Astrakhan on March 24. The weather was unusually cold, and he must have suffered from his customary panic at the thought of sea travel, but he survived and even made fairly acute observations, including one linking the pelican to humankind in a fashion unflattering to both: "I found the cormorants most interesting . . . They say that the cormorants serve the pelicans . . . The pelican isn't able to fish for himself, so the cormorant does it for him, chasing the fish up to him and sometimes even putting them into his mouth, in which case he inserts his own head into the pelican's maw. Nobody knows what the pelicans give the cormorants as a reward for their services! It appears they don't give them anything! A very true image of human society!"[78]

Encouraged by his successful shorter excursion, Pisemsky later made a much more extensive boat trip to the port of Baku, traversing half the length of the Caspian Sea. The journey probably took up the greater part of April and a portion of May; at any rate he had returned to Astrakhan by about the middle of May, with his health further undermined. He had covered a large part of the Caspian Sea, visiting the Tyulen Islands and the Tyuk-Karagan peninsula in addition to Baku. After resting in Astrakhan in May, he made a trip inland to the steppe region. By June and July he was "going out of his mind from boredom and anguish,"[79] and this psychological state strongly colored his view of the indigenous population of the area. He solemnly declared to Druzhinin that "the Russian *muzhik* has more talent and sense in his little finger than a whole villageful of these people," and he was quite certain that nothing would ever come of the Tartars and Kalmucks.[80] Pisemsky nevertheless kept such adverse opinions mostly to himself and did not emphasize them in the published accounts of his travels.

It would be incorrect to infer from this account that Pisemsky's stay in Astrakhan lacked rewards. His visit was made quite pleasant by the unfailing hospitality of the Russians who were acting as his hosts. Moreover, during his trip to the Tyuk-Karagan peninsula he met the Ukrainian national poet, Taras Shevchenko, then living in exile in that remote region. The one extant letter from Pisemsky to Shevchenko makes clear that Pisemsky sympathized with the poet, esteemed his talent, and even contributed in a small way to his release by interceding with influential people on his behalf.[81] The Tyuk-Karagan peninsula was an odd place for one of Russia's leading prose-writers to make the acquaintance of the first poet of the Ukraine.

Pisemsky's health deteriorated steadily during his sojourn on the shores of the Caspian, and by early July he was so ill that he hardly had strength to write letters. He did not tell his wife about his sufferings because she was nearing the last third of another pregnancy and he feared that worry over his condition might cause complications for her. A combination of poor Astrakhan weather and what the writer considered poor Astrakhan doctors ensured the continued worsening of his health. It is not known what he did from July through September, but by late September he had cut short his visit to the southeast and was back in Moscow, staying with his traditional host, Ostrovsky. When he arrived in Moscow, he looked so terrible that his friends did not want to send him on to his family for fear of frightening his wife.[82] On October 2 he finally wrote to her about his illness, as by then she had been safely delivered of a baby daughter, named Evdokiya, who did not survive infancy. Pisemsky reported that the Moscow doctors had diagnosed his illness as primarily a result of his mental state: he complained of "nervous exhaustion."[83] After another couple of weeks he was sufficiently recovered to continue his journey, and by October 18 he was back in the capital, finished with travel for the time being. Even then he was not entirely well, he reported to Turgenev in a querulous missive of late November. He had been sick for ten months, he wrote, and had almost lost hope of ever recovering: "My spiritual sufferings have reached the point where every day I have fits of hysterics and roar like a little child."[84] Pisemsky may have been exaggerating the seriousness of his condition, but it apparently took him quite some time to recover completely from the hardships of his journey.

Esconced once again in St. Petersburg, Pisemsky set about re-vising his travel sketches for publication. However, the editor of *Morskoy sbornik,* where the reports were to appear, evidently did not feel obliged to accept all the material offered him by the literary explorers and bruised some authorial egos by refusing a sizable por-tion of it. Pisemsky was among the writers thus offended, for only four of his seven travel sketches appeared in the magazine.[85] The other three sketches—"Astrakhanskie armyane" (Astrakhan Ar-menians), "Tatary" and "Kalmyki"—were published in the pages of *Biblioteka dlya chteniya* only after Pisemsky had joined its edi-torial staff, the first two in 1858, the third in 1860.

Pisemsky's travel notes cannot be considered a significant contri-bution to Russian travel literature, although here and there they contain entertaining observations as well as worthwhile information on life in the southeastern part of the empire. The fact that Pisem-sky was never an especially sympathetic or keen observer of matters foreign to him accounts for many of the sketches' inadequacies. His inborn laziness gave rise to another striking shortcoming: his ten-dency to quote at immense length from travelers and scholars who had written about the areas of his interest. Although in some of the sketches he quotes hardly at all or limits himself to a modest two or three pages of quotation, in "Kalmyki"—a piece that was prob-ably submitted to *Morskoy sbornik* and rejected by the editor—his addiction to quotation runs riot. In the 1911 edition of Pisemsky's works this report is approximately thirty-two pages long (VII, 499-531): one citation takes up two pages, another occupies ten pages, and a third runs for three pages. The total number of pages given over to straight quotation is roughly fifteen, or almost half. And even where Pisemsky refrains from direct citation, his articles are replete with historical information of the sort to be found in any library.

Pisemsky occasionally offers personal observations. He does not entirely conceal, for instance, his unfavorable first impression of the area. When he entered the lower Volga region, he wrote, he was depressed by the contrast between the actual reality of the place and the picture he had formed in his mind while sitting in St. Petersburg. The country seemed so poverty-stricken and depopu-lated that it was strange to reflect that once upon a time the mighty Golden Horde had held sway there. Time had swallowed up all traces of them, and life could be restored to the area only through extensive settlement (VII, 461-462).

In his sketches Pisemsky devoted considerable attention to religious customs and institutions, wedding and marriage traditions, and food. In a description of an Astrakhan marketplace, for example, he speaks in detail of the various fruits and vegetables offered for sale (VII, 486); later on he quotes from a local poem a section enumerating various dishes, the makeup of which he carefully delineates in footnotes for the uninformed reader (VII, 494-495). On another occasion he devotes the better part of a page to a description of the unenviable Kalmuck diet (VII, 524).

As for courting and marriage customs, Pisemsky questioned an elderly Tartar at length on the subject and recorded some curious information on the way in which Tartar engagements and weddings are handled (VII, 480-483). He notes that among the Kalmucks a suitor not to the taste of his beloved's family may resolve upon an abduction. If he and his friends are successful in absconding with the girl, as they usually are, then nobody has the right to take her from him and the marriage may be solemnized (VII, 522-523). On another occasion Pisemsky draws upon a description of old Armenian marriage customs by the mid-eighteenth century traveler Samuel Gottlieb Gmelin in order to give his readers a notion of the rites (VII, 490-491).

The question of marriage is inevitably entangled with religious customs. Accordingly Pisemsky included in his sketches a detailed description of an Armenian Orthodox church that he visited while investigating local religious practices. His fluent use of ecclesiastical terminology while comparing aspects of the Armenian church to the Russian liturgy (VII, 489-490) makes clear that Pisemsky was familiar with the religious observances of Russian Orthodoxy. In reporting on non-Christian rituals, such as the rites of the Kalmuck Buddhists, Pisemsky goes to more trouble. In this case he furnishes a number of details about their feast-days, giving the original names for them, and describes the priests and some of their functions and equipment (VII, 520-521). His discussion is rather superficial, of the sort that might be composed by a tourist who merely reports what he was told at the time of his visit.

The remnants of a sect of fire-worshippers attracted Pisemsky's attention even more powerfully than the Buddhists, when he visited their monastery near Baku. It was inhabited by two ancient Hindus, all that were left of the former monastery population. Pisemsky's party found the two monks more than willing to demonstrate their rituals for their guests; indeed, they were even considerate enough to refrain from performing in their usual state of nudity in view of the fact that ladies were included among the visitors (VII, 539-

542). Actually this monastery seems to have been more of a tourist attraction than anything else, hardly worth the attention Pisemsky gave it.

This reportage of Pisemsky's had little to do with the sea and those who gained their sustenance from it, which was, after all, the subject that these writers had been dispatched to investigate in the remote corners of the empire. It should therefore be added that Pisemsky included an account of his sea voyage to Biryuchya kosa and also of his longer trip by water to Baku. But almost the only concession he made to the demand that he depict the ways by which the local population earned its livelihood from the sea is the discussion of sealhunting in the vicinity of the Tyuk-Karagan peninsula. The sealhunters appear rather unheroic in this passage, since their moronic prey offer not the slightest resistance when approached on the shore. They meekly allow themselves to be slaughtered, "turning tearful eyes upon their murderer." The hunters expose themselves to a modicum of peril only during the winter, when they hunt for newborn and therefore even more defenseless seals on the ice. Here the danger arises not from the seals but from the ice on which the hunter is standing, which may become detached and be carried out to open water, where he may perish (VII, 546-547). In all likelihood it was the irrelevance to maritime affairs of any of the sketches save "Biryuchya kosa," "Baku," and "Tyuk-Karagansky poluostrov i Tyuleni ostrova" (The Tyuk-Karagan Peninsula and the Tyulen Islands) which led the editor of *Morskoy sbornik* to accept only these, plus "Astrakhan," for publication. Pisemsky's travel sketches are perhaps best characterized as tourist impressions written by a moderately capable author lacking special knowledge of the area visited, who occasionally recalled that he had been enjoined to investigate matters related to the sea. It appears that neither the government sponsoring the experiment nor the writers selected were happy about their "literary expedition" as it worked out in practice. There was no Goncharov among the domestic travelers.

Literary and Journalistic Activities

Pisemsky's extended journey and its attendant discomforts temporarily curtailed his purely literary activity, so that the years 1856 and 1857 saw his name appear infrequently in print under a story. He had halted work on *One Thousand Souls*, he informed Kraevsky in June 1856, and would hardly be in a position to take it up again until his trip was completed.[86] Even such a brief piece as "The Old

Proprietress,'' which he had promised to *Biblioteka dlya chteniya,* failed to progress while he was plumbing the depths of the empire. In all probability he resumed work on it only after his return to St. Petersburg, although he completed it in a short time, and it appeared in the February 1857 issue of *Biblioteka dlya chteniya.*

"The Old Proprietress" was one of the outstanding works of the first decade of Pisemsky's creative activity. It is equipped with introductory and concluding sections of the sort that Pisemsky sometimes used (if not always successfully) as a framework for the central narrative to strengthen the reader's feeling of immersion in a particular milieu, in this case the world of the common people. The main events unfold as a series of recollections on the part of several minor participants. According to them, the old proprietress (*barynya*) of the title, Pasmurova, had raised her orphaned granddaughter from childhood and was firmly convinced that no person below the level of a prince or count was worthy of marrying her. The girl, Olga Nikolaevna, was of another mind and eloped with an impoverished neighboring landowner after her grandmother had categorically rejected his suit. The old lady refused to countenance the marriage, conspired to pry the couple apart, and eventually was the indirect cause of Olga Nikolaevna's death. In the old lady's eyes, death was preferable to an unsuitable marriage.

"The Old Proprietress" is most interesting for its psychological analyses of the main characters and, especially, for its experimentation with points of view. Although the experiment is not terribly sophisticated by modern standards, it is successful as far as it goes and marks Pisemsky's best effort at characterizing his heroes through the instrumentality of multiple narrators.

The recording narrator in this case plays a relatively inactive role in eliciting information from his interlocutors, who are usually ready enough to talk without prompting. When he stops at an inn, he meets three witnesses of these events now long past: the proprietress' blind, aged servant Yakov Ivanov, his wife Alena Ignatevna, and the outspoken innkeeper, a woman usually called Grachikha. When they commence their tale, it soon becomes apparent that Yakov Ivanov is the apologist for his mistress' tyrannical ways; Alena Ignatevna, torn between affection for Olga Nikolaevna and loyalty to her former mistress and her husband, occupies a middle position; and Grachikha presents the case for the prosecution, as she heartily disapproved of the old lady's character.

Upon first meeting Yakov Ivanov, the recording narrator is impressed by his well-kept beard, the intelligent expression on his face, and his old-fashioned but impeccably maintained dress (III, 290). Now nearing one hundred years of age, the old man exists entirely in the past and is a living representative of both its virtues and its vices. He genuinely laments the passing of the older breed of land-owners, who lived in a fashion he—if not we—could think of as "simple": they had plenty of everything and organized lavish enter-tainments for huge numbers of their neighbors. Nowadays, he grum-bles, the landowners have lost most of their money and sit at home reading books (III, 293). This old-fashioned generosity and hospi-tality in the grand manner had its underside, though, as in the severity with which the rich dealt with those who crossed them. One servant, for instance, had been released in disgrace because he accidentally lost one of his mistress' dogs (III, 294-295). Old Pas-murova would also buy up estates for much less than they were actually worth (III, 295). Yakov Ivanov agrees on the surface with the narrator's protestations that Pasmurova's purchases of land at substandard prices were tantamount to robbery, but it is evident that in his eyes the rules of morality binding on ordinary mortals did not hold for the nobility. Indeed, he himself had participated in an underhanded plot to induce Olga Nikolaevna to leave her hus-band and return to her grandmother: the husband was gotten drunk and then caught by the authorities *in flagrante* with a girl (III, 310). Although he may not have been proud of his part in the affair, Yakov Ivanov accepted unquestioningly the proposition that since the husband was unsuitable for Olga Nikolaevna, the couple should be separated by any means necessary.

Alena Ignatevna, on the other hand, is primarily Olga Niko-laevna's advocate: she takes up the narrative from her husband whenever the girl's reactions have to be described. Alena Ignatevna recalls that the granddaughter was a girl of unusual beauty, all "rosy" and finely dressed. "She would come out of her rooms in the morning like the sun," the old woman reminisces fondly (III, 299). When the conversation turns to the way in which Olga Niko-laevna continued to correspond with her lover even after her grand-mother's refusal to receive him in the house, Yakov Ivanov lays the blame on Olga Nikolaevna's maidservant, a "nasty little girl," who by her willingness to carry messages between the two encouraged her mistress to defy her grandmother's authority (III, 304). It is obvious that the maidservant could hardly have been to blame for the state of Olga Nikolaevna's heart, and the narrator can tell by looking at Alena Ignatevna that she sympathizes fully with Olga Nikolaevna's actions but does not wish to contradict her husband openly in the matter (III, 304-305).

The plain-spoken Grachikha, however, minces no words in speaking of the old lady. She clearly implies that Pasmurova was responsible for her son's (Olga Nikolaevna's father's) death because she refused to help him when he became entangled in financial difficulties (III, 298). She describes Olga Nikolaevna's abduction with relish, since this was one instance in which the old lady had been sorely bested. And it is she who recounts a fantastic tale, reflecting her own attitudes, of the miraculous happenings at Pasmurova's funeral: "her tongue stuck out two *arshins,* she turned over three times in the coffin . . . they almost couldn't bury her like they ought, as if it was some witch they were putting into the ground, everybody was terrified" (III, 315). Grachikha punctuates the conversation by entering and leaving the room at unexpected times, in particular when Yakov's defenses of Pasmurova become more than she can bear.

By considering the accounts of these three people with their varying viewpoints, the narrator as well as the reader gain an idea of the true character of the central figures. In particular, a vivid image emerges of the old lady, who thought nothing of indulging in robbery, bribery, and tyranny in order to work her will, whose crimes were made bearable only by the magnificent scale upon which they were committed. The effectiveness of the narrative device in the story, coupled with the skillful psychological delineation of both the narrators and the actors, as well as the restraint shown in the introductory and concluding sections, makes "The Old Proprietress" perhaps Pisemsky's best short story.

The story drew much attention from readers. Lev Tolstoy, who got to know Pisemsky well in the last months of 1856 and oscillated, in typical Tolstoyan fashion, between affection and detestation for him, commented after hearing the work in manuscript that it was a "charming thing, [which] seems to me to be the best of all he has written."[87] Botkin, who was by now less intransigent in his opposition to Pisemsky, wrote to Turgenev that the piece displayed "much talent in outline and coloration, the impoverishment of his view of life, a lack of poetry—in a word, all his former strong points and weak points."[88] Turgenev continued to praise Pisemsky's work despite Botkin, describing "The Old Proprietress" as a "charming thing" after he had read it in *Biblioteka dlya chteniya.*[89] Even the radical camp found much to admire. Chernyshevsky was prompted to give one of the most favorable notices he ever accorded a work of Pisemsky's, writing in the March 1857 issue of *Sovremennik,* " 'The Old Proprietress' is among the best works of a talented author, and from the point of view of artistic polish this story is unquestionably superior to anything else that Pisemsky has published up to now."[90] One could cavil at certain details, stated Chernyshevsky, but the overall picture was positive.

By the time of his return from Astrakhan in late 1856 Pisemsky was firmly committed to the conservative grouping in St. Petersburg literary circles, especially through his dealings with Druzhinin, who was spearheading the assault on the radical viewpoint. Pisemsky's personal associates at this point were predominantly men of conservative or liberal political and literary persuasion; he had little to do with representatives of radical thought. Within the domain of literature, the critical sentiments displayed in his Gogol article certainly placed him among the "right-wing Gogolians" (to coin a phrase) as opposed to the "left-wing Gogolians" like Chernyshevsky.[91] A letter of his to Maykov from the provinces, dated March 12, 1854, contained an unusually explicit formulation of his approach to aesthetic questions: "When will there arrive those blessed times when artistic criticism will see art as something that contains its own purpose within itself, when will it, in the process of analyzing Goncharov's *A Common Story,* forget even to mention its orientation but say instead that the novel is fine and artistic, that *The Inspector-General* is not at all a denunciation of bribe-takers in the civil service, but rather a comedy which people will laugh over for all time."[92] To be sure, Pisemsky made this statement to his friend and relative, a stalwart of the "artistic" camp, and it indisputably represents the extreme of his allegiance to the "art for art's sake" school of thought. But the very fact that he ever interpreted *The Inspector-General* as a comedy without social significance, of worth only as entertainment or pure literature, shows how widely his theoretical views differed from those of the radicals. The radicals might have agreed that the play was not merely a denunciation of bribe-taking, but they also would have fiercely rejected Pisemsky's interpretation of it as an entertainment piece, however lofty. Had they been compelled to choose between these two interpretations, they would have selected the first; whereas, offered the same choice, a member of the aesthetic camp would have taken the second. Pisemsky's choice placed him squarely in the aesthetic camp. The question of the interpretation of Gogol is of course not so simple, but if the issue had to be reduced to rock-bottom terms, it might well have been stated as Pisemsky defined it in his letter to Maykov.

Pisemsky's letters yield further indications of his attitude toward the radical critics. In November 1856 he wrote to his friend Almazov about Count Kushelev-Bezborodko, "a terribly nice fellow" who was thinking of financing a journal. At first the Count had been surrounded by the "Horde of Literary Locusts," by which Pisemsky evidently meant the radicals, but "then he made the acquaintance of Goncharov, Maykov, and Druzhinin, who want to direct him onto a truer path."[93] In 1859 Kushelev-Bezborodko did establish *Russkoe slovo* (Russian Word), which after being controlled by the aesthetic critics for a brief initial period, was taken over by the radicals and transformed into Dmitry Pisarev's forum. Kushelev-Bezborodko thus did not hold to what Pisemsky considered the "truer path."

Despite what must have been uneasiness on Druzhinin's part over Pisemsky's alcoholism, the rapprochement between him and the Druzhinin group continued through 1857, and around the first of October 1857 Druzhinin offered him a permanent place on the editorial board of *Biblioteka dlya chteniya*. Druzhinin had been made editor of the journal about a year before, and he plainly intended to turn it into an organ for those who shared his views. Why he should have chosen Pisemsky, who had never exhibited any particular executive abilities, as his chief aide is unclear, but it may have been that, of all Druzhinin's important literary associates living in St. Petersburg, Pisemsky was the least incapable.

Pisemsky should have been pleased to accept Druzhinin's offer, since from the time of his arrival in the capital he had not managed to find a permanent, salaried position of a literary nature. He had made one incongruous attempt, in view of his constant battles with the censorship, to obtain a place as a censor. In this connection he had written to A. V. Nikitenko, a moderate liberal influential in government circles, requesting his aid in gaining one of several censorial positions that he had heard were available. "The Ministry is well advised," he argued, "to make censors of literary men, thus, so to speak, placing the censorship evaluation of them upon themselves."[94] If Pisemsky had hoped to liberalize the censorship by burrowing from within, he proved a poor subversive, for he had no luck in his efforts to be appointed censor either in 1855 or on one or two subsequent occasions. On the other hand, several prominent authors, including Goncharov, Maykov, and Fedor Tyutchev, did serve as censors in the mid-nineteenth century, and the question of how they reconciled their literary consciences with the necessity of shackling their fellow writers is an interesting one, which to my knowledge has yet received no satisfactory elucidation. One point worth emphasizing about the czarist censorship, irksome and capricious as it often was, is that a literary man in the capitals in the 1850's dealt with only one or two censors at a time and could argue with the man responsible for passing on his work. His writing was ordinarily not censored by an invisible, omnipotent bureaucrat. Pisemsky's *bête noire* during the mid-1850's was a censor named Andrey Freygang, who censored many of his works and who is referred to several times in Pisemsky's correspondence.

Pisemsky's inability to find a salaried civil service position meant that he had to support himself by writing, and his other employment merely deprived him of valuable time that he could otherwise have devoted to literary endeavor. In fact, on March 23, 1857, he requested to be released from his position with the Department of Appanages, and he officially retired from his employment on April 20. Therefore, when the invitation to join the staff of *Biblioteka dlya chteniya* was extended, Pisemsky was more than ready to accept, for he sympathized ideologically with Druzhinin and his group, and he had no other employment to restrain him. When writing to Ostrovsky to inform him of the move, Pisemsky remarked that *Sovremennik* had withdrawn an earlier invitation to become a contributor; but the whole matter had worked out beautifully because now he could deal with the "honest Pechatkin," the publisher of *Biblioteka dlya chteniya,* instead of that "sharper (*zhulik*) Nekrasov." In the same letter Pisemsky summoned all the former members of the recently dispersed *Moskvityanin* staff, the "young editorial board," to regroup around *Biblioteka dlya chteniya.* As Pisemsky saw it, the newly reconstituted circle could accomplish two things: it could mount effective opposition to the men gathered around the new Moscow journal *Russky vestnik (Russian Herald,* begun by Mikhail Katkov in 1856), which at that point was publishing the caustic satires of Saltykov-Shchedrin; and it could remind the public of "those aesthetic requirements without which Literature cannot claim to be Literature."[95] Pisemsky's own inclinations, reinforced by Druzhinin's theories, were reflected in this second purpose, which was generally directed against the radical critics.

In spite of Pisemsky's hopes for the reincarnation of *Moskvityanin* in *Biblioteka dlya chteniya,* few of the former "young editorial board" gravitated to his journal. Among those who did was Evgeny

Edelson, who in the 1860's became *Biblioteka dlya chteniya*'s chief critic, remaining loyal to it even after Pisemsky's desertion. The primary reason for this poor response was the impossibility of reconstituting the group as it had been in the old days. Several of its members no longer lived in Moscow; and even if they had, *Biblioteka dlya chteniya* was published in St. Petersburg, so that geography would have made it difficult to sustain any feeling of solidarity. Furthermore, Apollon Grigorev was displeased to hear of Pisemsky's project in late 1857. He objected to Pisemsky's plans because, for one thing, he still hoped to revive *Moskvityanin* directly and disliked the thought of competition, and for another, because "Pisemsky was for [him] not nearly so important as Ostrovsky." Grigorev insisted on regarding Ostrovsky as the central figure in contemporary literature and referred contemptuously to Pisemsky as a "hack writer."[96] In this case Grigorev was as stubborn and unlucky as ever, for *Moskvityanin* remained defunct.

Pisemsky took up his new duties almost immediately. In an announcement of coming attractions for the year 1858, subscribers to *Biblioteka dlya chteniya* were informed that he had joined the staff and would assist in supervising certain sections of the journal, primarily those dealing with literature, criticism, and miscellaneous information.[97] Initially Pisemsky occupied a subordinate position in editing these sections, for Druzhinin had the final word on the acceptance of articles and contributions. Thus, in December 1857 Pisemsky had to apologize to Edelson because Druzhinin had refused to publish without changes an article of his that Pisemsky had previously accepted. "I have no unconditional right to demand the publication of articles I select," Pisemsky wrote. "I have evidently been hired only as an advisor."[98] But as time went on, Pisemsky gained an ever stronger voice in the management of the journal's affairs. With a steady income and responsibility of his own, he settled down and overcame his alcoholism to a great extent. When Druzhinin departed from St. Petersburg for a period in the middle of 1858, he left *Biblioteka dlya chteniya* in Pisemsky's keeping. Although Druzhinin may have had misgivings about the wisdom of this action, later he was pleased with the way things had been handled in his absence. "Talent is such a sacred thing," he wrote to Turgenev *à propos* of Pisemsky, "that a person who has it, it seems, can do anything in the world and it will come out better than when it is done by an untalented person."[99] When Druzhinin's health later worsened, Pisemsky took over as chief editor of *Biblioteka dlya chteniya*.

As a leading member of the journal's staff, Pisemsky no longer had to worry about an outlet for his writing. Thus, he could print his travel sketches that *Morskoy sbornik* had presumably rejected. More important, he could finally realize his long-standing dream of publishing his very first work of any significance, which had been written in 1844-1846 under the title *Is She To Blame?* Financial problems had caused his thoughts to revert to this early piece even before he was invited to join *Biblioteka dlya chteniya*. He reported to Ostrovsky in March 1857 that he had disinterred it, examined it as objectively as he could, and decided that further reworking was merited. The friends to whom he had read it also approved, so that he looked forward to placing it in *Biblioteka dlya chteniya* and in return receiving a comfortable sum.[100] He recast the story considerably, eliminating what he called its "bawdiness" and patching up the gaping wounds left when he had cannibalized it for stories published earlier in the 1850's.[101] Since he had already used the original title for a published work, he rechristened his novelette *Boyarshchina* before presenting it to his readers in the January and February 1858 issues of *Biblioteka dlya chteniya*.

The plot of *Boyarshchina* is the standard one of Pisemsky's early short stories and novelettes, being constructed around an unhappily married young woman, Anna Pavlovna; a young man, Elchaninov, who loves her passionately and shelters her when she is driven out by her tyrannical husband; a thoroughly rotten, lascivious count who employs all his wiles to seduce the poor woman; and a friend of Elchaninov's who loves Anna Pavlovna secretly and remains loyally by her side until her death after Elchaninov has deserted her. The story offered nothing novel to those who had been following Pisemsky's writing career, and the piece was almost entirely ignored by the critics, even though it was one of his longer works to date. Annenkov praised the "amazing firmness" with which the novelette was developed but found its motivating idea "coarse."[102] Yet the critics' silence on the subject of *Boyarshchina* proved misleading, for the transitional period of Pisemsky's career was approaching its end, and he was about to attain the zenith of his literary reputation.

III

Upon the Heights

The era of Pisemsky's maximum influence and reputation began with the completion and publication of his first full-length novel, *One Thousand Souls*. Printed in six monthly installments from January to June 1858 in *Otechestvennye zapiski,* for which it had long been earmarked, it was also issued in the same year in a separate edition published in St. Petersburg by D. E. Kozhanchikov. As a long-awaited work by a prominent author, it created a noticeable stir in the literary world.[1]

One Thousand Souls was composed in four parts. The first two depict the hero, Kalinovich, as a young man, suffocating in the provincial atmosphere of a Russian backwater.[2] Possessed of enormous aspirations, he is none too scrupulous as to the means by which he promotes these aspirations. In Part Three Kalinovich detaches himself from his provincial environment and moves to St. Petersburg, where his hopes of becoming an outstanding author are shattered by discovery that the publication of his first novel has gone virtually unnoticed. He enters upon a bureaucratic career as a means of material support and an alternative route to social prestige. In order to further his worldly plans, he compels himself to marry a young woman who, lacking in physical attractions, nevertheless has a sizable income and important connections. In the space of a single paragraph, Kalinovich then rises with blinding rapidity from a special agent (*chinovnik osobykh porucheniy*) to acting vice-governor in the same province that he had left several years before.

The fact that Pisemsky omits the details of Kalinovich's meteoric ascent and simply presents him in his new position as a *fait accompli* is a major shortcoming in the novel. The fourth and last part describes Kalinovich carrying out his duties as vice-governor and, finally, as governor. In these positions he is a paragon of righteousness, who complies rigidly with the requirements of the law and even goes so far as to jail his former patron, Prince Ivan Ramensky. Although Prince Ivan was essentially guilty, he had assisted Kalinovich in attaining his present position, and he also possessed powerful friends. Ignoring these considerations, Kalinovich continues on course almost as though he wished to be destroyed through his own intransigence. In the end his world falls apart, again very abruptly, when his wife leaves him and his enemies succeed in ousting him from his gubernatorial post. Once power has been taken from him, he is left to drag out a useless existence.

The first two parts of *One Thousand Souls,* written at least in first draft before Pisemsky left the provinces, represent one of the high points of his achievement as a novelist. They faithfully delineate the mores of provincial society as well as the psychology of the hero and those around him. The third part is intended primarily as a transitional stage to the fourth part, in which Pisemsky abruptly shifts to a novel of social criticism. Despite this transition, the last part, showing Kalinovich the high bureaucrat warring against official dishonesty, is badly integrated into the work as a whole, and it appears that for quite some time the author intended to end the book with the third part roughly as it now stands. Thus, on July 26, 1855, he wrote to Ostrovsky that he was into the third part and hoped to finish entirely by the end of the year.[3] It is almost certain that in his mind the completion of the third part was the equivalent of finishing the entire novel, especially since *Otechestvennye zapiski* announced in September 1855 that *One Thousand Souls* would appear in its pages in the coming year. As late as April 16, 1857, Pisemsky wrote to Turgenev that he had stopped work on the novel at the beginning of the third part,[4] and it seems likely that even at this date he had not yet clearly formulated the notion of a fourth part. Yet at some point Pisemsky resolved to add an additional segment, which given the unity of the first three parts, became something like an epilogue. It is precisely this last, "social" part that attracts the most favorable attention from Soviet critics, who interpret it as an exposé of the old society.

There is no simple way to analyze Kalinovich's character. Although he was evidently intended as a positive hero, Pisemsky's awareness of life's complexity led him to endow Kalinovich with a number of negative traits. Kalinovich is fundamentally driven by an intense ambition to achieve something noteworthy in this world and to make a name for himself. He exhibits an arrogance derived from a conviction of his own moral and intellectual superiority over the common herd and his deep resentment against a society which, he feels, has humiliated him. He attributes his bitterness against society to a twisted childhood and youth, when being early left an orphan, he was compelled to live in the home of a ''benefactor'' and act as little better than a servant to the children of the family. This situation galled the egotistical Kalinovich intensely. After he entered Moscow University, his benefactor died, and he was forced to live in poverty, supporting himself by giving lessons. When all these obstacles had been overcome, he discovered that the only way to make a career was through kowtowing to those in authority, which he could not bring himself to do. Consequently, when the reader first makes his acquaintance, Kalinovich has just taken up the relatively unimportant post of school inspector in a provincial town, while nursing his resentment against fate and more especially against the system that has relegated him to this position. It is thus plain that both psychological and social factors will contribute to the hero's drama in the novel, and neither strand may justifiably be separated from the other.

Although Kalinovich considers himself in many ways superior to the ordinary bureaucrat, he is also motivated by a desire shared, in Pisemsky's view, by the everyday individual: the drive for material wealth and its concomitant comforts. Indeed, Kalinovich displays this drive at an even more intensive level than the ordinary person, so that in this respect he may have been intended as an emblemic figure, a ''hero of his time'' in a highly sarcastic sense. While engaged in writing *One Thousand Souls,* Pisemsky commented to Apollon Maykov on precisely this subject: ''The chief and distinctive direction [of our age] is a *practical* one: one wishes to make a career, settle down as comfortably as possible, guarantee the future for oneself and one's progeny—these are the idols worshipped by the heroes of our time—all this is even very fine, if you wish: the desire to make a career produces useful diligence, the Comfort of all is composed of the comfort of individuals and so on, but the thing is that a man traveling this path, without looking or turning around, is forced to smother within himself the noblest and most justifiable demands of the heart and then, when his purpose is achieved, he almost always sees that what he has been reaching for was only trifles, he sees that in all his past life he has been a scoundrel, and the devil only knows why!''[5] This passage expounds what was originally to have been the novel's central thought. In earlier times, Pisemsky felt, people had been somehow more idealistic, less concerned about material success. In an entertaining passage contrasting the ''provincial misses'' of a previous era with contemporary ones, Pisemsky remarked: ''Before a young girl would have been willing to elope with some impoverished but noble Waldemar; but now there are no more elopements. Instead [today we note] dozens of cases where a seventeen-year-old girl has employed all her coquettish tricks to catch a rich old man'' (II, 219-220). Again, at one point in his novel Pisemsky inserts a cynical dithyramb on the importance to contemporary man of comfort, for which ''people take bribes and even commit crimes'' (II, 332). In Kalinovich's desire for material prosperity, which he equates in one sense with happiness, he was thus a concentrate of the failings of contemporary society.

In the novel Kalinovich is caught between representatives of two very different outlooks on life. One ideal is represented by the Godnev family, especially Nastya Godneva. Nastya embodies the best of the old traditions: she is not consumed by ambition nor unduly concerned about material riches; she is pure in soul and gives herself to Kalinovich without reservation. Her naive goodness of heart makes her at times appear slightly ridiculous in a society with pretensions to sophistication. But in their love affair Kalinovich for a time enjoys an inkling of the true happiness of personal fulfillment.

The ambition within him will not be quelled, however, especially after he meets a character who stands at the opposite pole from the Godnevs. Prince Ivan Ramensky is a typically evil Pisemskian type, the cynic who lives solely for his own pleasure and is almost devoid of redeeming qualities. There are numerous hints at the consequences of his sinister traits of character in the past, such as stories about his ''relationship with a certain very important and significant person, his former benefactor, who loved him as his own son but then suddenly sent him away and even forbade his name to be mentioned in his presence'' (II, 309). The prince was a whited sepulcher, who could conceal his genuine nature from his associates for a time but from whom people withdrew in loathing when they discovered the truth about him. He plays the role of Kalinovich's evil genius, arguing the case for the self-seeking approach to life. Once Kalinovich has been bedazzled by the luxury in which the prince lives, the latter holds forth to him the alluring prospect of an assured future through a marriage to Polina, a wealthy but unattractive woman who also happens to be the prince's mistress. In the course of his campaign the prince sneers at Kalinovich's idealistic notion that love is a prerequisite for marriage, plays upon his ambition, and gives him the selfish advice that money is all, and one must possess it in order to have any hope for advancement in the world. The prince himself will not undertake to arrange the marriage for nothing: Kalinovich must pay him 50,000 rubles if the union is successfully arranged.

The account of Kalinovich's indecision between the advocates of good and evil (Nastya and the prince) occupies the major portion of the second and third parts of the novel. Gradually but inexorably the prince gains the upper hand. At the end of Part Two Kalinovich decides to go to St. Petersburg for the furtherance of his literary ambitions. Since he has become sexually intimate with Nastya and her moral standards do not allow her to maintain such a relationship lightly, Kalinovich feels he must comfort her before leaving by swearing on her mother's grave that he will marry her and by tendering a formal proposal to her father. He does this despite the fact that he has no intention of ruining his career prospects by such an unsuitable marriage, though he has not yet sunk to the point of resolving to marry Polina. Upon arrival in the capital he breaks contact with Nastya, but later, overcome by illness, he writes to beg her to continue to love him although he will never marry her. For her part, Nastya not only forgives him but abandons her dying father to go to Kalinovich in St. Petersburg, bringing him all the money she has and moving in with him without benefit of marriage. Meanwhile the prince continues his work of subversion and in the course of time persuades Kalinovich to betray Nastya again, despite her many sacrifices for him, and to accept Polina. After lengthy hesitation Kalinovich finally chooses the prince and worldly success, giving up the personal happiness he has found with Nastya.

Wealth, Kalinovich soon discovers, cannot make him entirely happy. The thought of marrying Polina, whom he finds personally repulsive, although she herself begins to form an affection for him after agreeing to the marriage, revolts him to such an extent that he falls ill before the wedding, and the bride must be kept from the sickroom lest the sight of her destroy his determination to see the marriage through. At the actual wedding ceremony Kalinovich is "as thin as a corpse," and the description of the wedding night emphasizes the fact that wealth and personal happiness are not always linked: "In an expensive dressing-gown, in slippers studded with gold and with a face pale as death, the bridegroom passed over the silken carpet into his wife's bedroom—and then all was still" (II, 526). So deep is Kalinovich's misery on this night that at three o'clock in the morning he mysteriously appears at a fire and dashes into the burning building in order to rescue a woman. Even the prospect of death holds no terrors for the bridegroom.

Pisemsky attempts to justify Kalinovich's betrayal of Nastya in several ways, of which perhaps the most curious is his excruciating spiritual anguish. A man of sensitive soul much given to the analysis of his own spiritual condition, as befits a would-be litterateur, Kalinovich is not one of those who can betray their friends without remorse. Although in the long run Kalinovich always chooses the expedient alternative, he suffers genuine pain in doing so. Thus, his mental torment while he is betraying Nastya for the first time is intense. Later, while in the process of deciding to marry Polina, he exclaims melodramatically to the prince: "If she [Nastya] only knew of my sufferings she would forgive me. Do you realize what is going on in my soul? It's pure hell! Have mercy on me!" (II, 516). This doctrine of "justification through suffering" is made most explicit in Part Three. After abandoning Nastya for the second time, Kalinovich catches sight of Belavin, a righteous young man who, since he knows of Kalinovich's treason, despises him heartily. This is one person, Kalinovich thinks to himself, who has the right to call him a scoundrel: " 'But my Lord, I am not really a scoundrel! If only he knew of all my sufferings!' Kalinovich thought painfully, and his first intention was to go up to Belavin, no matter what, to lay bare his heart before him and to ask, demand of him not to despise him because he did not deserve it" (II, 533). Objectively, of course, the baseness of Kalinovich's actions is not diminished by his spiritual anguish, but Pisemsky seemed to feel that a tortured blackguard was morally a notch above a completely heartless one.

In the fourth part of the novel Kalinovich finally attains his coveted fame and power, but by then the happiness he had expected to achieve through them has been transmuted into a cheerless joy over the opportunity to wreak personal revenge upon society through a strict enforcement of the law. Kalinovich's zeal for social justice is thoroughly mixed with vindictiveness. As he says to one of his subordinates responsible for feeding the prisoners: "Woe to you if the cabbage is sour or the beef rotten! I will come myself and cram it all down your throat" (II, 571). As vice-governor Kalinovich is not content with disciplining his subordinates alone; he even goes against the governor, who is plainly trying to misapply the law, and manages to obtain his removal from his post. Kalinovich is then appointed governor in his stead. He thereupon delivers to his assembled underlings a speech setting forth the policies to which he intends to adhere in his new post. Each civil servant should be guided by "the law, his own common sense, and, finally, utter readiness to do good." But it is clear, Kalinovich continues, that frequent abuses of power exist, that civil servants sometimes take bribes and demand payment in illegal fashion. If such things occur in his province, harsh corrective measures will be taken: " 'we shall of course take it as our sacred duty to eliminate and destroy all this at the very root,' he concluded more in a malicious than sincere tone" (II, 629-631). The "malice" which Pisemsky placed in Kalinovich's voice at this juncture indicates that his motives for upholding the right are not unmixed. He intends to avenge real or fancied injustice by enforcing justice.

Whatever Kalinovich's inner motivations are, the fact remains that he does much to benefit the province in his charge, both as vice-governor and as governor. Through Kalinovich, Pisemsky seems to argue that it is impossible to do good in a fundamentally corrupt society except by evil means. As the editors of the journal *Russkaya beseda* (Russian Discourse) noted disapprovingly at the time, he preached the "strange doctrine" that one "may become dishonest in order to be honest."[6] Pisemsky might have agreed that this contention appeared "strange" at first glance, but he would probably have replied that it reflected a deeper level of reality than that to which his critics were accustomed. "Though I am wealthy," Kalinovich tells Nastya toward the end of the novel, "I lead an almost ascetic life. When I was a civil servant I worked day and night, hired spies with my own funds, and became a stool-pigeon and a detective myself in order to expose some unimportant abuse" (II, 623). Besides the argument that good can be accomplished only by evil means, Pisemsky gives another reason not to condemn Kalinovich for his villainy. A society that is no better than he—and in most cases even worse—has no right to pass judgment on him. For example, a man who for ten years betrayed others in order to ensure good dinners for himself and his guests for the rest of their lives cannot justifiably condemn Kalinovich. No, the author concludes, "if we must blame something, then let us blame the age, since that's a good abstract concept!" (II, 507-508).

In the novel's fourth part, which depicts Kalinovich as the "ideal civil servant," Pisemsky formulates still another social prob-

lem: is it possible for a single reformer, however wealthy and powerful, to prevail for long against the mores of a corrupt society? The
answer clearly is no. Kalinovich's subordinates, who have seen reformers before, realize that if they put up no resistance, the inertia
of society will eventually break him. Let yourselves be shorn like
sheep, says one character, and before long the shearer's hands will
blister (II, 633). In fact, this is what occurs. Once Kalinovich of-
fends people who are too highly placed, his hands are swiftly removed from the levers of power. Thereafter he can only sulk,
conscious both of his failure and of the fact that he could not really
have hoped for anything but failure. This last attitude was made
explicit in a passage, deleted from the novel's final text, where
Kalinovich comments sadly on the state that he has served: "In
order to repair the machine it is pointless to take out one little bolt
at a time from the old thing; rather you have to tear the whole
thing down at one go and put in entirely new parts. For the time
being one cannot foresee even a glimmer of anything decent: the
same sort of vileness that has been, is now and will continue to be."[7]
Soviet scholars attempt to interpret this passage as meaning that
Kalinovich's struggle against society had brought him to practically
revolutionary conclusions.[8] It seems much more likely, however, that
Kalinovich is advocating not a revolutionary transformation but
rather a moral regeneration of the existing system. One replaces
all the parts in the machine with new ones, but the machine itself is
the same as before. The difference is that now it functions properly.
At the same time, as a political realist, Kalinovich was aware of the
extreme unlikelihood of any such transformation's occurring in
Russian society. From this derives his pessimism.

Several reviewers were unreservedly enthusiastic over *One Thousand Souls*. An editor of *Otechestvennye zapiski*, S. S. Dudyshkin,
used the novel as the basis for a discussion of didacticism in art, as
Druzhinin had treated *Sketches of Peasant Life* a short time before.
Although Dudyshkin found *One Thousand Souls* socially useful, he
also credited it with achieving this utility without sacrificing artistic
quality. Consequently, Pisemsky could be favorably contrasted to
the *oblichiteli* (exposers or muckrakers) active at the time, writers
who produced novels and stories solely for the purpose of "exposing"
bribe-taking and other abuses of the existing system. Pisemsky's
novel included exposure but was not confined to it. Dudyshkin com-
plimented Pisemsky for not hesitating to grapple with the important
problems of the day while at the same time having the sense to
approach them from the point of view of the living people involved.[9]

Evgeny Edelson, though perhaps slightly prejudiced, voiced unqualified praise for the book, calling it "one of the best adornments
of our belles lettres for the past year."[10] Druzhinin was more reserved, making several criticisms of detail but approving Pisemsky's
animosity toward the "literature of exposure." "As a practical man
who has experienced the manysidedness of human nature in real
life," wrote Druzhinin, Pisemsky was not tempted to simplify reality in the manner of the muckrakers.[11]

Not all the critical reactions to *One Thousand Souls* were as favorable as these. Even Pisemsky's ally Annenkov—possibly following
up a comment in Druzhinin's review that Pisemsky was the "most
practical and *businesslike* (*delovoy*) of all our recent Russian
writers"[12] —composed a long article, "O delovom romane v nashey
literature" (On the Novel of Affairs in Our Literature),[13] in which
he mostly criticized Kalinovich. This character, Annenkov argued,
was so predominant that "all the other characters in the novel exist
by his mercy," possessing no independent standing. Yet Kalinovich
was essentially a negative character, one of whose chief motivations
seemed to be a "conviction of the necessity for persecution," so that
he could not be believed when he claimed that almost all the actions
leading to his appointment as governor had been pure and holy.
Despite this, Annenkov considered *One Thousand Souls* a substantial contribution to Russian letters.

Annenkov's was not the only negative reaction from the more
conservative camp in Russian criticism. Mikhail de-Pule, writing
in the Slavophile *Russkaya beseda*, found Kalinovich to represent
nothing more than another abortive attempt at picturing an ideal
bureaucrat.[14] Nikolay Akhsharumov, a minor novelist and critic,
published an extensive and very adverse review.[15] Fedor Dostoevsky,
who had read the first two parts of *One Thousand Souls* while living
in Siberian exile, wrote to his brother expressing astonishment at
his enthusiasm over it. The book "is only a mediocrity, even though
golden, but still only a mediocrity," Dostoevsky exclaimed. "It is
nothing but old themes put together in a new way. A magnificent
pastiche drawn from others."[16] The differing viewpoints of the
Dostoevsky brothers serve as an excellent illustration of the split in
the nonradical camp over the evaluation of the novel.

For their part, the radical critics generally wrote little about
the book. Nekrasov maintained complete silence on the subject.
Chernyshevsky, who by then had ceased to produce much literary
criticism, limited himself to fleeting remarks. Dobrolyubov, one of
the few radical critics active at this time, for some reason felt an

aversion to Pisemsky and never accorded him more than passing mention. He merely touched on *One Thousand Souls* in the course of an attack on Akhsharumov's review, in which he vigorously disputed the latter's contention that the novel's defects were attributable to the "malicious influence of the realistic school." While maintaining that the "critical realist" tradition was valid, Dobrolyubov denied that Pisemsky was in fact working within this current. He did agree, however, with certain of Akhsharumov's "very accurate remarks concerning the artistic falsity of Kalinovich's character."[17]

Another contributor to the burgeoning radical movement, Saltykov-Shchedrin, was ambivalent in his attitude toward Pisemsky's novel. For instance, he wrote to Annenkov that he liked the work very much but felt that Pisemsky had erred in allowing a school inspector to ascend to the seat of gubernatorial authority. Summarizing the situation with typical crudity, Saltykov argued: "when does it ever happen that staff school inspectors marry princesses [Kalinovich for a time dreams of marrying Prince Ivan's beautiful daughter]? In our society careers are advanced more simply: through staunch devotion, the licking of hands and other parts of the body, etc. The author is mistaken in extracting his hero from too low a class, from which nobody ever rose to the top."[18] Less than a week later, however, Saltykov's view of Pisemsky had shifted markedly: "No matter how Pisemsky grinds away at those dolts of his, he still cannot breathe the breath of life into them."[19]

It is plain that contemporary evaluation of this novel, which has endured as one of Pisemsky's best works and falls just short of being a classic, was not at all unanimous. The bulk of the dissatisfaction focused on Kalinovich as the novel's dominant person. Some critics scolded Pisemsky for attempting to create a social novel instead of a consistently psychological one. The more radical critics, on the other hand, were entirely in favor of social novels but reproached this one for not being true to contemporary Russian life. For all this controversy, *One Thousand Souls* firmly established Pisemsky as an important writer and was his first major work to attract the notice of a foreign critic.[20]

A Bitter Fate

The period of Pisemsky's greatest renown lasted for only a few years, roughly from 1858 to 1862. This period witnessed several major shifts in the course of Russian history. The chief historic event was the emancipation of the serfs in 1861, a reform welcomed in the beginning by both the liberal and the radical elements in Russian society. Before the decree had actually been issued, anticipation of its appearance and uncertainty as to the form it would take sufficed to impose a considerable degree of political harmony upon the country. But when it developed that the act of February 19 did not grant the land free and in perpetuity to the peasantry but instead burdened them with redemption payments to the landowners extending far into the future, dissatisfaction mounted among the peasants and the more radical segments of the intelligentsia. In the following months the peasants engaged in frequent "disturbances," some of which had to be suppressed by force. The revolutionary intellectuals hoped to exploit the rural and urban unrest for their own purposes. There soon emerged a clear split between the reforming liberals, who accepted the emancipation as far as it went and hoped to improve it by further modifications, and the radicals, who were loud in their demands for fundamental alterations in Russian society. The radicals, or "nihilists" as they came to be called after the popularization of the term in Turgenev's novel *Fathers and Sons,* set forth their demands as far as they could in the legal press; when this became impossible, they utilized the illegal press.

Peasant unrest was accompanied by other disturbing events, such as the extensive St. Petersburg fires of the spring of 1862, whose origin has never been satisfactorily determined but which were generally attributed to the radicals. These occurrences moved the government to resort to sharply repressive measures. The two leading radical journals, *Sovremennik* and *Russkoe slovo,* were temporarily closed down, and several radical leaders, including Chernyshevsky and Dmitry Pisarev, were arrested. These official measures succeeded in damping revolutionary agitation for a time. Then the outbreak of the Polish rebellion in early 1863 rallied public opinion to the government's side to such an extent that the oppressive restrictions could be eased.

The period 1858-1862 was eventful from the literary point of view as well. The crucial year of 1859 witnessed the breakdown of the uneasy truce between the older, established liberals and the new radical generation. In subsequent years—especially after 1861—writers and intellectuals were forced to choose sides even against their wishes. The departure of Turgenev, Tolstoy, and Grigorovich from the *Sovremennik* group after Chernyshevsky had seized effective control of the journal was a major contribution to this liberal-radical split. The radicals sneered at "pseudo-liberal" writers who contented themselves with exposing abuses within the system while assuming that the system itself was sound. Pisemsky was accused by some of adhering to this view in *One Thousand Souls,* and indeed the fourth part of the novel probably should be classified as a contribution to the "literature of exposure." When occasionally there appeared an artistically valuable work which, though written by a nonradical writer, implicitly criticized the state of affairs in Russia, the radical writers often interpreted it to suit their own purposes. The chief instance of this was Dobrolyubov's treatment of the most important novel of the period, *Oblomov,* whose author, Goncharov, far from being a radical, occupied an official post as censor at the time of its publication in 1859. Dobrolyubov read the book as a massive attack on the foundations of Russian society, which the author surely never intended, and this reading has ever since colored the novel's interpretation by critics. Dobrolyubov also interpreted the liberal Turgenev's saga of the Bulgarian revolutionary Insarov in *On the Eve* (1859) as a call for a Russian man of revolutionary action.

The exploitation by radicals of novels written by liberals could not continue indefinitely, especially after the radicals became so prominent in real life as to appear themselves in fiction. Thus, the publication in 1862 of Turgenev's *Fathers and Sons,* in which he attempted to sketch as objectively as possible the ultimate failure of a fundamentally admirable young radical, evoked differing reactions from the radical critics. Dmitry Pisarev was sufficiently clear-sighted to recognize that Bazarov's failure could only have been expected, given the society in which he had to live, but the reconstituted *Sovremennik* group, under Chernyshevsky and his singularly insensitive disciple, the critic Maksim Antonovich, pronounced the book a slander on the younger generation. After this point there was little hope of reconciliation between the liberals and the radicals. Even before 1862 the radical journals—*Sovremennik,* Pisarev's *Russkoe slovo,* and the satirical journal *Iskra* (The Spark)—had begun to cultivate their own groups of creative writers. These writers at first concentrated on describing the appalling conditions existing in the Russian countryside, implying that a social system which allowed such misery, or even spawned it, had forfeited all claim to legitimacy. It happened that most of the literary talent, however, except for Nekrasov and Saltykov-Shchedrin, was to be found among the liberals.

Pisemsky's career was an unusually faithful microcosm of the nonradical writers' situation during these years. His best known novel, play, and short story—all displaying a negative attitude toward contemporary reality—were interpreted by some radicals as indicating that their author was at least potentially one of them. But Pisemsky was at heart committed to the existing system; however much he may have disliked aspects of it, he detested the revolutionaries even more. When this fact became unmistakably clear at the beginning of 1862, he was violently rejected by those whose expectations he had disappointed. Thereafter he experienced no little difficulty in publishing his works, in large measure because of the radical rancor he had incurred.

Early in this period, during 1858, Pisemsky was exceptionally busy, absorbed primarily with his numerous business affairs. His correspondence mostly concerns articles and stories intended for *Biblioteka dlya chteniya*, which he was managing singlehandedly in Druzhinin's absence, and negotiations for the sale of rights to a separate edition of *One Thousand Souls*. So far as Pisemsky's personal life was concerned, 1859 was little more eventful than 1858, although he was elected to the Obshchestvo lyubiteley rossiyskoy slovesnosti (Society of Lovers of Russian Literature) under Ostrovsky's sponsorship.[21] All in all he seems to have settled down reasonably well to the task of running *Biblioteka dlya chteniya*, to have controlled his drinking better, and to have conducted his family life in satisfactory fashion.

The year 1859 saw the publication of Pisemsky's most brilliant drama, *A Bitter Fate*, which has since created for itself a secure niche among the masterpieces of the Russian stage. There is little information about the play's creation, for the number of Pisemsky's letters preserved from this period is small. It is first mentioned in a letter from Goncharov to Annenkov of May 20, 1859, in which Goncharov describes a reading of one act from the play given by Pisemsky. Goncharov thought what he had heard to be very good indeed, extremely "lively and true to life."[22] After Pisemsky's death his widow and son composed a brief memoir on the play's composition. According to this document, Pisemsky wrote the first three acts while living in the country near St. Petersburg. One evening while taking a stroll, he happened to meet the comic actor Aleksandr Martynov and invited him to hear what had already been written. Martynov became so excited over the play that he pleaded to be given the lead role in it, a request which astonished Pisemsky, who was thinking of a dramatic actor for the part. Moreover, Martynov contributed significantly to the play's creation by suggesting the ending that the author eventually adopted.[23]

Evidently *A Bitter Fate* was composed for the most part in the spring and very early summer of 1859: in a letter of July 21, 1859, Pisemsky informed Turgenev that he had written three and a half of the four acts but that he had become so weary of it that he had set it aside for about a month and a half.[24] This would mean that when Goncharov heard it around May 20, it must have been nearing completion. In any case, before long Pisemsky overcame his temporary antipathy, for he mentioned that he was finishing the play in two separate letters written on August 7, 1859,[25] and when the text finally appeared, it bore the date August 19.

Pisemsky's conflicts with the censorship over this play were even more acrimonious than usual. He had already had difficulty in getting the fourth part of *One Thousand Souls* through the censorship, dealing as it did with the upper reaches of the bureaucracy: only the friendly intervention of Goncharov in his capacity as censor had enabled that part to pass, and Goncharov himself was later reprimanded by his superiors for his laxity in this case. Pisemsky realized full well that the censorship would probably raise strong objections to this new drama rooted in the social conditions of Russian serfdom, to be published at a time when sentiment for abolition was running high. As Pisemsky wrote to Ostrovsky, the play "faces a great deal of difficulty with the censorship, and God only knows when it will go through."[26]

But then, astonishingly, *A Bitter Fate* was passed for publication with comparative rapidity, though not without occasioning turmoil within official ranks. The play was submitted to the censorship on October 9 and entrusted to the historian S. N. Palauzov, who approved it without any objection the following day. Thus at first it seemed that *A Bitter Fate* had vaulted the censorship with extraordinary celerity. The manuscript was returned to Pisemsky in its approved form, but then on October 19 he was required to resubmit it for the inspection of the Minister of Education, because of rumors, as Annenkov wrote to Turgenev, that "it belches unbearable shame and detraction upon the landowning class."[27] A. V. Nikitenko, who was privy to the minister's deliberations upon such matters, noted in his diary under October 23 that it had been thought inadvisable to publish the drama just at the point when the peasant problem was so acute. However, since the play was very good, it should be allowed to appear later, when tempers had cooled somewhat. Three days later, on October 26, Nikitenko recorded that the minister had summoned Pisemsky to his office, lauded the play, and promised to permit its publication after a lapse of time.[28] The minister's re-

luctance to clear the play immediately is comprehensible if Nikitenko's diary entry for October 23 is correct, where he summarized
the plot as follows: "A drama from the life of the peasants. In it
a landowner seduces the wife of a peasant, and the latter, in a fit
of rage, murders the first." If in the version originally submitted
to the censorship Pisemsky did in fact resolve the situation through
violence inflicted by a peasant on his master, then the government's
reluctance to permit the publication of such a potentially inflamma-
tory piece was understandable. Certainly a violent conclusion to the
play would have been more in keeping with the character of the
play's hero, Anany Yakovlev, than the ending as it now stands.
Moreover, at another time Pisemsky evidently considered having
Anany become the leader of a bandit gang and return to murder
his chief ill-wisher, Kalistrat the *burmistr* (serf entrusted by his
master with the supervision of his fellow serfs). Upon further reflection, however, Pisemsky probably realized that any sort of violent
conclusion would hinder the play's approval by the authorities.
Faced with this possibility, he apparently decided to yield the
point, picked up Martynov's suggestion, and at the play's conclusion
replaced sudden death by peaceful submission on Anany's part. *A
Bitter Fate* was thereafter submitted for censoring a second time
and entrusted to Goncharov, who on November 12 found it suitable
for publication with a few minor changes.[29] The required changes
seem to have been promptly effected, for the play appeared in
print in the November issue of *Biblioteka dlya chteniya.*

The plot of the tragedy is easily recounted, although the play
itself is not simple.[30] Indeed, from the psychological point of view
it is among the more complex of Pisemsky's works. The hero, a serf
named Anany Yakovlev, has been living and working in St. Petersburg for some time, leaving his wife Lizaveta to her own devices in
the provinces. In her husband's absence Lizaveta has become enmeshed in an affair with the landowner, Cheglov. Their romance,
far from being another instance of a heartless landowner's taking
his pleasure with a female serf, is a matter of deep attachment on
both sides, the fruit of which is an illegitimate child. As the play
opens, Anany has just returned from St. Petersburg. When he
learns of these developments, his sense of honor is mortally offended,
and Cheglov too suffers moral agony over the situation. Anany's
initial restraint finally cracks: he murders his wife's child by casting it to the floor and makes his escape. Eventually he gives himself up, however, and in the play's finale humbly asks forgiveness

of all those whom he may have offended before being led off to punishment.[31]

A Bitter Fate is of interest from the structural point of view. At the very beginning the reader is provided with a quantity of essential background information on Anany's stay in St. Petersburg and Lizaveta's affair through an extended conversation between peasants waiting for Anany to return with Lizaveta, who has gone out to meet him on the way. When Anany and Lizaveta arrive on the scene, the cuckolded husband is still unaware of what has transpired, and the dramatic tension is prolonged through the middle of the first act by means of a more or less irrelevant conversation about the wonders of the steam age. Finally at the end of the act Anany learns of his wife's infidelity, and the scene is set for the tragedy to follow. The second act introduces the landowner Cheglov and details his side of the case, as well as his futile attempts to arrive at an understanding with Anany. The third act depicts the fateful struggle between the lawful husband and the landowner over Lizaveta and the child. When the competition is about to be resolved in the lover's favor, the dramatic climax is reached with Anany's murder of his wife's child. Finally, in the fourth act this crime is expiated through Anany's repentance and willing acceptance of punishment.

A Bitter Fate, like several of Pisemsky's other works, is a psychological drama conditioned by the social milieu in which the characters exist. But it is also somewhat different, in that an inexorable fate seems to be directing the heroes' destinies in a classical vein. At the beginning one of the characters, commenting on Anany's reputed condescension toward his fellow peasants working in St. Petersburg, remarks that perhaps the blow about to descend on him is God's punishment for his overweening pride (VIII, 147). The course of the tragedy might have been altered at several points during the play, but the heroes' characters will not permit this. For instance, Anany might have chosen to overlook his wife's fault altogether, as did most other peasants when landowners saw fit to seduce one of their women, but his pride forbids such a resolution. Cheglov might have given Lizaveta up, but he is too deeply in love and too honorable to take this way out, though it is strenuously urged by his despicable brother-in-law Zolotilov, the mouthpiece of the hypocritical "accepted morality." Lizaveta might have abandoned the child after its birth, as Cheglov once suggests to her (VIII, 161), and thus have mitigated her lot, but she insists on bearing the consequences of her shame. Nor can she accept a separation from Cheglov, and it is her insistence upon leaving her husband that precipitates the murder of her guiltless child. Last of all, during the formal investigation of the crime, Anany's punishment would have been eased had anyone been willing to witness to the dead child's illegitimacy, for this would have been considered an important extenuating circumstance. The civil servant conducting the investigation has strong suspicions as to the true state of affairs, but even Anany will not tender a true confession, because he considers his own sin infinitely greater than his wife's and demands proportionate punishment (VIII, 194). Thus, every feasible avenue to a softening of the tragedy is more or less consciously bypassed, as if the leading figures looked upon the situation as a drama imposed upon them by a superior force. The tragedy results from a collision between pride on the one side and love on the other.

Anany's self-esteem is much in evidence in his relationship with his wife throughout the play. In fact, it would be easy to argue that self-love is more important in his marriage than any love for his wife. It transpires that he had married her in the first place by force (VIII, 164), though it is not clear why, and his cruelty toward Lizaveta is a major factor in her decision to leave him for Cheglov. Anany's pride has some positive facets, however. During his first conversation with Lizaveta after learning of his wife's infidelity, Anany tells her that during the entire time of his stay in St. Petersburg he never looked at another woman because he was conscious of his duty as a Christian and a family man. Lizaveta at first does not want to believe him but finally has to accept his word, much against her will (VIII, 158). Then again Anany makes one important gesture toward a reconciliation when he offers, out of a sense of family honor, to cover up for his wife's sin provided that she break off her affair with Cheglov entirely (VIII, 159). For a time it seems that the two may come together again, since Anany has refrained from punishing his wife physically, but in the end his violent nature wins out and his wife feels the knout.

Anany's fury against Lizaveta reaches its highest intensity when the *burmistr* Kalistrat arrives upon his master's orders to take Lizaveta and the child away from Anany. Livid at the realization that his wife has been conspiring with his enemies, Anany threatens to imprison her in chains (VIII, 182). It is this burst of rage that leads to the child's murder, but before Anany commits the crime, he asks the peasants who have accompanied Kalistrat to intercede for him. One of them begins to argue with Lizaveta in Anany's favor, but the *burmistr* cuts the exchange short and starts to prepare her for transfer (VIII, 183). It is only at this point—when he feels he has exhausted all legitimate recourse—that Anany kills the child.

On the whole, Anany's plea for help addressed to the assembled peasants fits rather badly with his character as delineated in the first three acts, and it is possible that Pisemsky inserted this passage—as well as a speech in which he asks his wife's indulgence (VIII, 176-177)—into the third act after having decided to redo the last act, in order that Anany's change of personality in the final act might not seem totally unheralded. The transformation that Anany undergoes after his crime is nevertheless profound: the murderer simply gives himself up and is brought in unbound by one of the peasants. Anany explains, rather improbably, that he ran away after killing the child, not in order to escape punishment, but rather to seek it through being rent to pieces by wild beasts in the forest (VIII, 192). One may avoid human retribution, he says, but not divine wrath. However, as the divine anger fails to descend, Anany returns to face human justice, rejecting any thought of trying to soften the punishment. At the end he asks his fellows to pray for him as he departs for prison.

If the question of the success of the last act is debatable, most investigators would probably agree that Pisemsky failed to delineate satisfactorily the character of Cheglov. The landowner is essentially a weak person, though he does stand up against Zolotilov's arguments in refusing to abandon the woman he has grown to love. Thrashing about in desperation, he concocts nonsensical schemes for ending the conflict between him and Anany, such as his mortgaging his estate and giving Anany the entire proceeds (VIII, 168), the two fighting a duel (VIII, 169), or Lizaveta moving in with him as "the mother of [his] child," not his mistress (VIII, 169). Anany rejects all these ridiculous ideas with scorn, and indeed Cheglov is made to seem so silly that there is nothing left for him but to vanish from the stage. Thereafter we hear of him only at a remove, as in the report that he was so upset by the situation as to begin coughing blood (VIII, 173), or we see his orders being carried out by the evil *burmistr*. Thus, Cheglov is not a successful character, and the play would have been strengthened had he been handled differently. Certainly there was no necessity for him to be so vacillating. He should have been an important element in the tragedy, and Anany's strength of character might have appeared more remarkable had his rival been a man of sterner stuff. In this connection, the master-man relationship between Cheglov and Anany, though of considerable importance, is not absolutely crucial to the play. Cheglov had made only limited use of his position as a serf-owner to seduce Lizaveta in the first place; and by the time of the play's action he is very much in love with her and she with him, so that the conflict engendered by the difference in social station is minor.

Certain scholars, influenced by Pisemsky's reputation as a realist who derived his inspiration from life, have sought to discover genuine incidents with which Pisemsky could have been familiar and which might have supplied the initial impulses for his literary works. Some success in this respect was achieved for *A Bitter Fate* by Ivan Milovidov, who disinterred two criminal cases involving the peasantry of the Chukhloma area that displayed similarities to Pisemsky's play. The first of these cases, dating from 1845, concerned an extremely jealous and suspicious peasant named Mikhaylov, who had killed his wife's infant son because he was far from sure that it was his. Another incident in 1857 had to do with a landowner who had raped many of his female peasants and finally was stabbed by one of his serfs in revenge for the violation of his wife and his unmarried sister.[32] There is no direct evidence, however, that the plot of *A Bitter Fate* was derived from these incidents.

Similar parallels were drawn by A. M. Loboda between *A Bitter Fate* and Ignacy Kraszewski's "Ulana" (1843). Pisemsky almost certainly read "Ulana," because a translation from the Polish was published in *Biblioteka dlya chteniya* for October 1858.[33] Its influence on his play was thought to show up in his plot, which, reduced to its bare essentials, is a love triangle involving two men and one woman. But this situation, which forms the core of "Ulana" as well, is common throughout literature. Both Kraszewski and Pisemsky added the further complication that one of the men is the master of a peasant couple, and this master uses his position as a partial aid in forcing his will upon an initially reluctant woman, who then becomes passionately attached to him. Beyond this, however, the similarities between the two works are minor: in "Ulana" no child is involved and no murders are committed, the master is a flighty sort with no permanent interest in his victim, and the hapless heroine commits suicide when, after a prolonged absence, her beloved master returns home with a wife.

Contemporary critical reaction to *A Bitter Fate* was on the whole favorable, and in some cases enthusiastic, though the play did not lack for convinced detractors. Years later it was evaluated highly by the poet and critic Innokenty Annensky, who wrote that with

A Bitter Fate began "the history of the modern Russian drama, if one may speak of the history of Russian drama at all." Annensky was impressed by the play's avoidance of cheap melodrama as well as the author's refusal to idealize his characters and his ability to present a number of ideas without making them excessively obvious.[34] Annensky justifiably emphasized the near uniqueness of Pisemsky's dramatic masterpiece, for the peasant drama *A Bitter Fate* stands almost alone in the history of the Russian theater. Tolstoy's *Power of Darkness*, though inferior as literature,[35] is one of the few Russian plays that may be placed in the same category. Tolstoy himself was pleased by Pisemsky's achievement in 1859. He thought the work "healthy, powerful and true to life, not concocted," although at the same time he objected to the detail of Cheglov's willingness to fight a duel with one of his own serfs.[36] In this case Tolstoy's democratic convictions were weaker than Cheglov's.

The radical critics tended to dislike *A Bitter Fate*. Dobrolyubov, faithful to his distaste for Pisemsky, wrote only a couple of pages about the play, to be found in "A Ray of Light in the Realm of Darkness," his famous discussion of Ostrovsky's *The Storm*. Assuring his readers that *A Bitter Fate* had by then (1860) been mostly forgotten, Dobrolyubov claimed that the play was a run-of-the-mill example of the "literature of exposure" and argued that Anany, if taken as a type, was a "slander on the Russian character and Russian life." The complexity of Anany's character was beyond Dobrolyubov, who considered him a failure.[37] In 1863 Saltykov-Shchedrin expressed most forcibly the negative point of view.[38] He could discover almost no merit in the play, professing to be amazed by the author's "remarkable lack of development" and his inability to generalize. Pisemsky's chief shortcoming in the eyes of such radical critics was that he merely depicted characters and actions, without "rising" to an understanding of the necessity for adopting the proper attitude toward his creations. "We do not demand from [an author] ideal people, but we do demand an ideal," wrote Saltykov: this was an element Gogol had always furnished the Russian reading public but which Pisemsky refused to provide.

In 1860 *A Bitter Fate* was published in a separate edition by D. E. Kozhanchikov, the same entrepreneur who had obtained the rights to the separate edition of *One Thousand Souls*. At that time Pisemsky was refused permission to have the play staged, although it was premiered soon after the emancipation, in 1863.

At the time of its initial publication the fate of Pisemsky's play was closely intertwined with that of Ostrovsky's masterpiece, *The Storm*. The two plays approached completion at nearly the same moment, and Pisemsky originally intended to publish *The Storm* in the November 1859 issue of *Biblioteka dlya chteniya*, especially since it seemed that his own drama might be held up indefinitely by the censorship. But when *A Bitter Fate* was abruptly passed by the censor, Pisemsky as editor replaced *The Storm* with his own play, leaving Ostrovsky's work to appear in the January 1860 issue for the gratification of new subscribers. *A Bitter Fate* and *The Storm* subsequently were linked even more intimately when both were awarded an Uvarov prize for drama in 1860. It was extraordinary for two plays to be awarded this prize in the same year, and the story behind the event is an intriguing though minor episode in the literary politics of the period.

The Uvarov prizes for drama and works of historical scholarship first began to be awarded in 1857 in honor of Count S. S. Uvarov, Minister of Education under Nicholas I from 1833 to 1849.[39] *The Storm* and *A Bitter Fate* were culled from a total of eight plays submitted in 1860 to the Uvarov committee for consideration. Goncharov had contributed a favorable first report on *The Storm*, and the leading Slavophile A. S. Khomyakov offered some comments on *A Bitter Fate*, which, though not positive, at least permitted the play to remain in competition. In his short review Khomyakov wrote that Anany and Lizaveta "kill all interest in the drama by their lack of interior life" and concluded that "the entire drama contains within itself all the elements of an artistic work and at the same time forms an extremely unartistic whole." A Slavophile like Khomyakov could hardly have been expected to appreciate a peasant drama painted in such dark colors. *The Storm* was then transmitted to the literary historian A. D. Galakhov, who wrote an enthusiastic commentary on it. *A Bitter Fate*, however, fell into the hands of Nikolay Akhsharumov, who may not have been predisposed to favor Pisemsky's play after having written his negative review of *One Thousand Souls*. It is likely that the committee was unaware of this particular review, for Akhsharumov seems rather to have attracted its notice by his discussion of *Oblomov* published in early 1860.

Akhsharumov was appalled by *A Bitter Fate*. The critic complained of the author's "mannerisms" in the use of language, his penchant for unusual words and expressions. He criticized all the major characters in the play, though he felt that some of the secondary ones were good. He accused Pisemsky of having selected only that which attracted notice readily because of its extraordinary nature and of incorporating it in the drama as undigested raw material. In conclusion he stated that *A Bitter Fate* was by no means an "exemplary work" of the sort the committee was supposed to recognize. As a sop, he added that the author's talent was worthy of encouragement.

Akhsharumov's comments were much too harsh for those who had requested them. Somebody highly placed in the Uvarov committee, almost certainly P. A. Pletnev, thought Akhsharumov's report justified an unusual step: both *The Storm* and *A Bitter Fate* were entrusted to Pletnev for a comparative review. His published remarks on the two plays were devoted primarily to *A Bitter Fate*, in which he discovered numerous virtues that had escaped both Khomyakov and Akhsharumov. "The greatest merit of [Pisemsky's] work," Pletnev wrote, "lies in the amazing simplicity of the drama's development. But this is not the simplicity of lifelessness [a slap at Khomyakov] or of the absence of shattering experiences. On the contrary, with each step forward, with each change in the characters' positions, everything seems more and more dreadful and distressing from a foreboding of the inevitable consequences of that fateful thread to which all are clinging openly before you." Thus did Pletnev emphasize the play's classical quality as evinced in its employment of the ancient concept of fate.

The upshot of the controversy was that Pletnev's strong recommendation of both plays outweighed the negative opinions of Khomyakov and Akhsharumov, and it was undoubtedly because of his advocacy alone that Pisemsky was granted an Uvarov prize along with Ostrovsky.[40] In his official report summarizing the events leading up to the double award, the Academy of Sciences' Permanent Secretary, K. S. Veselovsky, was obliged to resort to sophistry in order to justify the overriding of Khomyakov's and Akhsharumov's recommendations. To prepare the ground, he included a disquisition on the difficulty of evaluating literary works objectively because of differing individual tastes. He then contended that, though the earlier adverse remarks might seem to indicate that *A Bitter Fate* was substandard literature, this would be an improper conclusion, as proven by the following ridiculous argument: "the very fact that they [Khomyakov and Akhsharumov] paid especial attention to the defects of the drama under consideration may . . . serve as proof that these defects are not so noticeable as to enable one to mention them in a few words, which could be done in pointing out the drama's obvious and indisputable merits." The original reviewers may not have agreed that their emphasis upon the play's weaknesses was a sign of its superiority, but the matter was out of their hands, and feelings were soothed through the award of a gold medal for his "remarkable analysis" to Akhsharumov, the only reviewer so honored on this occasion. In this case the authorities' decision to disregard the reviewers' recommendations has been proved correct by history. Rarely have two plays of such enduring quality as *The Storm* and *A Bitter Fate* appeared in the same year, and Pletnev was perceptive in recognizing their worth immediately.

During the remainder of his career Pisemsky wrote a number of plays, several of which he submitted to the Uvarov committee in the hope of repeating his coup of 1860. The committee had introduced exacting requirements, however, and from 1861 through 1873 awarded only one prize for drama, to Ostrovsky's *Sin and Sorrow Are Common to All* (1863), even though every year it honored works of historical research and it is difficult to believe that the level of scholarly investigation in this period was so much higher than the level of dramaturgy. For instance, the committee passed over all three of the plays comprising Aleksey Tolstoy's classic trilogy—*Death of Ivan the Terrible* (1866), *Czar Feodor Ivanovich* (1868), and *Tsar Boris* (Czar Boris, 1870)—which now stands as one of the greatest achievements of the nineteenth-century Russian theater. In 1874 the committee, evidently deciding its standards had been too high for too long, lowered them drastically to grant an award to *Razorennoe gnezdo* (A Ruined Nest), a now completely forgotten play by Dmitry Minaev. Such were the vicissitudes of one scheme for the official recognition and encouragement of excellence in literature.

General Recognition

In 1860-1861, after the publication of *One Thousand Souls* and *A Bitter Fate* had brought Pisemsky a degree of literary fame, he unfortunately was so heavily burdened with editorial work that he had little opportunity for further creation, with the result that in these two years he wrote almost nothing except the novelette "Starchesky grekh" (An Old Man's Sin). If Pisemsky had been able to devote all his energy to writing, he might well have produced something even more outstanding than that which he had contrived so far; but as things actually turned out, the opportunity was allowed to slip from his grasp.

In 1860 Pisemsky was chiefly preoccupied with the affairs of *Biblioteka dlya chteniya*. His few letters preserved from this period tend to be brief and to pertain to business matters only. He had no leisure to compose the lengthy essays that he sometimes included in epistles at earlier or later periods. During the first part of the year Pisemsky's responsibilities were not so burdensome as they might have been, for Druzhinin remained esconced as the official editor of *Biblioteka dlya chteniya*. In September, however, Pisemsky unwisely assumed further duties in connection with a newly founded and obscure journal called *Iskusstva* (The Arts). This short-lived organ appeared in six issues, beginning in September 1860 and ending in December of the same year.[41] Pisemsky soon resigned his position on it, complaining that he was being blamed by the subscribers for the rascality of the publisher.[42]

Much more important than Pisemsky's temporary link with *Iskusstva* was Druzhinin's resignation as editor of *Biblioteka dlya chteniya*. When Pisemsky first learned of this development from the publisher, V. P. Pechatkin, he wrote a worried letter to Druzhinin assuring him that he had carried on no intrigues against him and stating that he himself would gladly abandon the journal were it not for the steady income it provided, which was so necessary for him.[43] In a letter of October 1860 to Turgenev, Druzhinin explained that his duties as an editor of the newly founded newspaper *Vek* (The Age) prevented him from supervising *Biblioteka dlya chteniya* closely enough to prevent it from returning to its former "tricky path." "Once it has been published in an unclean fashion for twenty years [a reference to the period when it was under the editorship of the brilliant Osip Senkovsky, who enjoyed a reputation for intellectual dishonesty]—it is hard for it to proceed on the straight path," Druzhinin wrote. "Pisemsky will have to be very cautious and beware most of all of the well-known axiom: 'Others are doing it too.' God grant him success, because things will be difficult for him."[44] One may infer from these words that Pechatkin had been advocating certain changes which appeared to Druzhinin to herald a reversion to the unsavory days of Senkovsky, and that Druzhinin left *Biblioteka dlya chteniya* because of these policy differences. In any case, officialdom raised no objections to Pisemsky's installation as editor-in-chief of the journal, and he formally assumed this position beginning with the November 1860 issue. Although he was greatly overworked at the time, laboring every day until near collapse from exhaustion,[45] his position as sole editor of the oldest *tolsty zhurnal* (thick journal) in St. Petersburg added luster to his reputation as a writer.

Despite the tasks piled on him in the latter part of 1860, Pisemsky somehow found time to work on "An Old Man's Sin." In August

1859, while still finishing *A Bitter Fate,* Pisemsky had written to Turgenev that he was planning a new novel, a "very, very long" one.[46] Evidently he later decided to condense the work, for it emerged as a novelette. Aside from this remark of 1859, "An Old Man's Sin" is hardly mentioned in Pisemsky's correspondence for the period, and all we know about its creation is that when it appeared in its entirety in the January 1861 number of *Biblioteka dlya chteniya,* it bore the date November 23, 1860. For some reason, it aroused little comment in the press.

"An Old Man's Sin," though representing a marked throwback to the Gogolian influence that Pisemsky had largely overcome by 1860, must stand as his masterpiece in the genre of the novelette. On the whole, it would nevertheless have to be ranked below both *One Thousand Souls* and *A Bitter Fate* as a literary achievement. The plot is constructed around the old *bedny chinovnik* (impoverished civil servant) theme so beloved of the "critical realist" school of the 1840's. As the story begins, the hero, Iosaf Iosafych Ferapontov, is working as a bookkeeper—a position of some responsibility—in the *Prikaz obshchestvennogo prizreniya* (Office of Social Welfare), a government agency that furnished the public with certain minimal services. No longer a young man, Ferapontov is noted for his absolute honesty and sterling character. Yet he has almost no friends. The story's intrigue begins when Ferapontov's office is visited by a young man named Bzhestovsky, who hopes to keep the estate of his "sister," the widow Kostyreva, from being sold entirely to pay her debts. When Ferapontov and the ravishingly beautiful Kostyreva meet, she makes an immediate and total conquest of his lonely soul, so that he is moved to do everything in his power to extricate her from the financial difficulties in which she is entangled. Unable to find any other way to help, he utilizes his position to embezzle money for her and is caught before he can replace it. At his trial Ferapontov is shaken by one revelation after another: testimony that Kostyreva had been nothing more exalted than a barmaid, her confession that Bzhestovsky had been her lover and is now her husband, and above all her categorical denial that she had ever received any money from Ferapontov. The trauma of these exposures is so severe for an older man who has risked all for his first and only love that he ends by hanging himself.

Although the plot of "An Old Man's Sin" turns fundamentally upon the psychology of the characters, an implicit strain of social criticism runs through it. The author makes this criticism explicit at the story's conclusion, when it becomes apparent that the authorities will accept the word of the beautiful but unscrupulous Kosty-reva against that of the honest Ferapontov. Indeed, Pisemsky implies, society was largely responsible for Ferapontov's death. He ends his tale with a gloomy observation: "To live in a society in which Ferapontovs are criminals, Bzhestovskys are just, and the judges are like the police chief [who had taken a highly formalistic approach toward Ferapontov's case]: to live in this society, no matter what you may say, one has to have a large supply of courage!" (IV, 87).

The structure of "An Old Man's Sin" is spare, if one ignores the episode in which Ferapontov travels about visiting various wealthy local landowners in hopes of negotiating a loan for Kosty-reva's benefit. This unnecessary journey serves only to retard the plot development. Ferapontov's Chichikovian series of visits to such types as the caculating miser Rodionov, the cautious miser Gavrilov, and the redneck buffoon Odintsov did provide Pisemsky with an opportunity to picture the mores of provincial society in the fashion of which he was so fond. In this case, however, he competed with Gogol too directly, and the extent to which he fell short of his mentor's achievement becomes embarrassingly evident. Pisemsky's miserly landowners lack the force of genius with which Gogol invested his characters in *Dead Souls*. And since the string of visits in "An Old Man's Sin" adds little to our knowledge of Ferapontov's own psychology, it might best have been omitted.

Ferapontov's character and psychology are sketched in some detail. He was significantly influenced by his father, the prototype of the downtrodden civil servant, who has abandoned any self-respect in an attempt to curry favor with his superiors, but who for all his abasement has hardly enough to eat or wear. Although Ferapontov rarely mentions his father, it is plain that he regards his parent's life as an existence to be avoided at all costs. Thus, when he first gains employment as a civil servant, he "shudders" upon entering the office and noting that several of the older clerks look just like his father (IV, 29). Ferapontov's character is vastly different from that of his sniveling progenitor. As a student, Ferapontov was noted for his resolute adherence to the highest moral ideals, a characteristic that emerges most strikingly in the account of his refusal to name any leaders of a nonexistent student "conspiracy" supposedly detected by the school authorities. Whereas all the other students basely pointed incriminating fingers at one another in the hope of saving themselves, Ferapontov endured a brutal caning rather than falsely accuse his fellow students (IV, 12-15). Pisemsky attempts to show in other ways that Ferapontov's character is far above the common run. We are told that as a youth Ferapontov once experienced a passionate thirst for reading, to which he devoted all his spare time for about six months, until he tired of it (IV, 26). In adulthood, "the bookkeeper thought and meditated on more elevated and noble subjects than his subordinates" (IV, 3), and "his thought was broader than the small space in which God's world appeared to him through the office window" (IV, 4). However, as is so often the case, Pisemsky offers almost no concrete illustrations to support this assertion. The most explicit evidence appears in a passage describing Ferapontov's instinctive enjoyment of nature, his singing of sentimental songs to himself that cause him to weep, and his occasional reading of the journal *Otechestvennye zapiski* (IV, 32-33). These somewhat ordinary activities were apparently meant to raise him noticeably above the general level of the surrounding society.

In his relationships with his fellows Ferapontov frequently presents an artificially cold exterior. After indulging his more tender emotions in private, he will become "ferocious" and appear at the office with a "stony and emotionless face" (IV, 33). He fulfills his own obligations punctiliously and demands the same devotion from his colleagues and subordinates, being especially hard on the young gentry who wish to work only a little for the fun of it. As is frequently the case with persons so unrelenting toward themselves, Ferapontov exhibits a tendency toward cruelty to others. While still at school, he was nearly expelled for torturing a younger student; he could offer no explanation for his behavior except to point to a phrenological "bump of cruelty" and comment that he was probably "capable of killing himself and anybody else" (IV, 20). His suppressed bloodthirstiness is again demonstrated when, after Pushkin's death in a duel, he shoots a hole in a portrait of the poet's tormentor, the journalist Faddey Bulgarin, and apparently would have been happy to execute Bulgarin himself had he been present (IV, 25). Thus, Ferapontov figures as a strong character conjoining an occasionally excessive sentimentality with a moral rigidity sometimes shading into active cruelty.

Ferapontov is able to maintain strict standards of personal morality principally because he has so few friends. The narrator had attempted to cultivate his acquaintance when they were at school together, but without much success, and the two later drifted apart. Had Ferapontov enjoyed closer contact with others, the experience might have armed him against the catastrophe of his love for Kostyreva. Instead, as a young adult he remains "a complete child and at the same time a pure idealist" (IV, 22). As the years pass, he still is so innocent of the deeper wellsprings of human vice and avarice as to fall easy prey to the unworthy woman. "Everything that was poetic in his nature, all the dreams and hopes which had been restrained and shattered in his youth, his capacity for self-sacrifice" (IV, 45), contributed to his unhappy infatuation. For such a man his first love can be his only love.

It is not only in his relationship with Kostyreva that Ferapontov's simple, idealistic character serves him ill in the struggle for survival in a society that has long since abandoned ideals. For example, he might have spared himself much effort in seeking a loan from neighboring landowners had he realized the extent to which they were guided by purely selfish interests. More important, upon his arrest he is tricked into signing a confession by the cynical police chief, who falsely informs him that Kostyreva has already admitted the embezzlement and agreed to take the debt upon herself (IV, 79). At his trial he has difficulty in recanting that which he has already confessed. The prosecution further exploits his simplicity by interrogating Kostyreva in his presence, so that finally, enraged by her perfidy, he once again admits to everything. The narrator writes that even he was so naive as to suppose that Ferapontov might nevertheless be pardoned in view of his record. This too was an idle illusion, far removed from reality: "It's obvious that I was still very young then and did not comprehend very well the people among whom I lived and moved, and it is only now, when almost an entire decade has passed, that I can see them before me as if alive, in all their frightening and monstrous significance" (IV, 85). Ferapontov's tragedy is thus a double one: that of a psychologically maladjusted person who would experience difficulty in finding a place in even a perfect society, but whose inborn aberrant propensities are certainly reinforced by harsh contact with the actual world; and that of a man whose determination to be honorable cannot be tolerated by a corrupt society. Although the psychological motif is the more fundamental, the social one is very significant.

An activity that took up a considerable portion of Pisemsky's limited time in 1860-1861, but which he loved too much to abandon completely, was the reciting of his own works and participation in amateur theatricals. For instance, he lent his histrionic talents for the benefit of a "progressive" cause of the day, the Sunday Schools, which were very much in vogue as an instrument for enlightening the masses who could attend school only on Sunday.

Staffed mostly by students seeking ways to serve the common people, they flourished until 1862, when they were closed down by the government during a period of political repression. On November 21, 1860, Pisemsky participated in an evening of readings for their benefit given by his old acquaintance Taras Shevchenko, Fedor Dostoevsky, and the poets Vladimir Benediktov, Yakov Polonsky, and Apollon Maykov. At least one observer thought Pisemsky's recitation of the first act of *A Bitter Fate* the high point of the evening.[47] Pisemsky took part in another such evening for the support of the Sunday Schools on January 11, 1861.[48] A second worthy cause he aided through benefit readings was the Literary Fund (*Litfond*), an organization founded by Druzhinin in 1859 to furnish financial aid to needy authors. In 1861 Pisemsky participated in at least two amateur play productions—Gogol's *The Inspector-General* and *The Marriage*—in which parts were taken by leading writers, including Dostoevsky, Turgenev, Grigorovich, Maykov, and Druzhinin. In *The Inspector-General* Pisemsky played the mayor. Although he was reported to have read the role extremely well in rehearsal, he was less successful when actually on stage.[49] Nevertheless, as a result of these activities Pisemsky's reputation as actor and reader reached its height simultaneously with his fame as writer and editor.

Pisemsky's success in these various areas inevitably spawned more labor and responsibility. One of his major tasks at this point was the preparation of a collected edition of his works, published in three volumes in 1861 by F. T. Stellovsky under the title *Sochineniya A. F. Pisemskogo* (Works of A. F. Pisemsky). The Stellovsky edition was the second and last collected edition of Pisemsky's writings published during the author's lifetime—the Pogodin edition of 1853 having been the first—and it therefore contains the canonical texts of almost all his fictional works published to that point,[50] with the exception of "Nina," which the author excluded. Pisemsky reworked some texts to take account of comments made by reviewers, but he effected no drastic changes at this stage. From the material point of view the Stellovsky edition was no striking improvement over the unsatisfactory 1853 edition: the 1861 edition was printed on low-quality paper, the format was not especially attractive, and the volumes were too large to be held comfortably for reading. The writer's friend Sergey Maksimov later interpreted these facts as another manifestation of the "malign fate" that had bedeviled Pisemsky both in life and in death.[51]

The appearance of the Stellovsky edition gave the critics a reason to survey Pisemsky's career, an opportunity seized enthusiastically by Dmitry Pisarev, who had recently gained prominence as a young radical critic. In fact, after Dobrolyubov died in November 1861, Pisarev was for a short time almost the sole representative of the radical camp in literary criticism. He attempted a definition of Pisemsky's place in Russian letters in three articles published in *Russkoe slovo* during the last three months of 1861. In the first article, entitled "Stoyachaya voda" (Stagnant Water),[52] Pisarev remarked that the question of Pisemsky's literary standing had long since been settled. "All one has to do," he wrote, "is to open any story or drama, any novel of Pisemsky's, in order to be convinced by the power of unmediated feeling that the personalities depicted in them are live people, who express through themselves at full strength the peculiarities of the soil on which they were born and raised." Pisarev then used *The Simpleton* as the starting point for an extended attack on much that he deemed wrong in contemporary society, especially the "emptiness of life, which gives rise to artificiality and falsity of interests, and patriarchal routine in concepts and relationships which brings family despotism along with it." One of the story's greatest virtues, in Pisarev's eyes, was that its heroes were by no means outstanding or unusual personalities: instead, they were quite ordinary people, "suffocating in a foul atmosphere, unable to find the way out into the light." Although *The Simpleton* lent itself to this interpretation of it as an onslaught against society, one may suspect that Pisemsky was not gratified by such an analysis, though no record of his reaction to the article has been preserved.

Pisarev's enthusiasm for Pisemsky reached its apogee in the second of his three articles, "Pisemsky, Turgenev i Goncharov."[53] Pisarev here not only placed Pisemsky on an equal footing with Goncharov and Turgenev, he even ranked him above them in important respects. Dismissing Goncharov briefly with a few unfavorable comments, Pisarev commended both Turgenev and Pisemsky for their honesty, their willingness to say precisely what they thought about contemporary life: "Both of them . . . have adopted a purely negative attitude toward our reality, both have looked skeptically upon the best manifestations of our thought and upon the most beautiful representatives of those types which have emerged among us. These negative attitudes and this skepticism have been their most magnificent service to society." But there were also differences between the two, and for a "sober realist" like Pisarev, Pisemsky's cynicism was more congenial than Turgenev's poeticized and sometimes sentimental approach. In Pisarev's view the unpretentious quality of

Pisemsky's realism made it superior to Turgenev's idealistic realism: "Pisemsky grasps these phenomena [of life] more deeply than Turgenev, depicts them in thicker colors, and in the vital fullness of his creations, like the 'power of the black earth,' stands above Turgenev."

Pisarev's third article, "Zhenskie tipy v romanakh i povestyakh Pisemskogo, Turgeneva i Goncharova" (Feminine Types in the Novels and Stories of Pisemsky, Turgenev and Goncharov),[54] dealt with Pisemsky only briefly. He expressed the conviction that none of Pisemsky's women was to blame for her misdeeds: everything was the fault of either her husband or her upbringing. And this was precisely the way things actually were, Pisarev maintained.

Pisarev's series of articles at the end of 1861 is one of the most favorable commentaries on Pisemsky's art ever to have appeared. Still, the significance of Pisarev's appraisal must not be overestimated, for his view was not characteristic of the radical camp as a whole. Dobrolyubov, a much more influential critic than Pisarev until his death, failed to appreciate Pisemsky's contributions to Russian literature and certainly did not claim him as an ally in the radical transformation of Russian society. He must have realized that Pisemsky's opinion of mankind was far too jaundiced to allow him to share radical optimism on the perfectibility of human nature once social institutions had been fundamentally altered. In fact, Dobrolyubov was very nearly correct in his estimate of Pisemsky's position, and whereas he mistakenly hailed Goncharov's *Oblomov* as a blow struck at the foundations of Russian society, he refrained from making such a slip in Pisemsky's case. After his 1857 review of "The Old Proprietress," Chernyshevsky mentioned Pisemsky's work very little. Nekrasov was warily distrustful of him, while Saltykov-Shchedrin was actively hostile. This leads to the conclusion that Pisemsky's acceptance by the radical camp in 1861 was far from general. The youthful force of Pisarev's enthusiasm deluded many into thinking that Pisemsky was more closely allied to the radical camp than was actually the case.

After completing "An Old Man's Sin" in late 1860, Pisemsky once more neglected fiction for a time. His sole contribution for 1862 was the short story "The Father," which appeared in Pisarev's *Russkoe slovo* for January 1862, in the brief interval between Pisarev's endorsement of Pisemsky and the sequence of events leading to the sharp rift between Pisemsky and the literary left. It went almost unnoticed by contemporary critics. Turgenev, however, expressed the private opinion that the work had turned out "pale" in spite of certain "fine individual things worthy of his [Pisemsky's] power."[55]

Though short, "The Father" is not without significance for Pisemsky's fictional world, since it treats some of the darker sides of human nature. The plot involves a landowner who punishes a young serf couple on the complaint of the husband's father, who lives with them. The landowner accepts unquestioningly the old man's contention that the young these days have no more respect for their elders. In the end, however, the master discovers that the reason for the animosity between the couple and the older man lies in the father's attempts to seduce his daughter-in-law. In consequence, he chastises the old man severely.

Clash with the Radicals

The energies that Pisemsky withdrew from fiction writing were invested instead in the composition of feuilletons and reviews designed primarily as filler for his journal. In the course of 1860 several unsigned reviews of varying lengths appeared in *Biblioteka dlya chteniya,* which may with some confidence be attributed to Pisemsky as an editor. Then in 1861 Pisemsky made his debut as a feuilletonist under the pseudonym "statsky sovetnik Salatushka" (state councilor Salatushka), writing pieces that at first dealt with the state bureaucracy. The initial feuilleton, dated December 31, 1860, appeared in the January 1861 issue of *Biblioteka dlya chteniya.* It consisted of relatively innocuous ramblings attributed to Salatushka, who was identified as "a fairly common sort of person in St. Petersburg" (VII, 586). The entire piece is written in a spirit of mild satire directed against the bureaucratic point of view and the bureaucratic milieu as it existed in contemporary St. Petersburg. In one passage Pisemsky-Salatushka displays true insight into the wellsprings of human social organization when he emphasizes the permanence of bureaucratic institutions: "I surmise that a great many changes may occur in Russia: various nationalities may coalesce, classes may be destroyed, but we bureaucrats will endure" (VII, 594). The observation is as valid today as it was more than a century ago.

The second installment of Salatushka's "Thoughts and Feelings," published in the February issue of *Biblioteka dlya chteniya,* begins in the spirit of the first, with Salatushka describing the envy that seized him at the sight of a fellow bureaucrat who had served two years fewer than he but had already been promoted to a higher rank. Salatushka then begins discussing actually existing persons in Russian intellectual life. These include Pisemsky's former colleague Druzhinin and more especially Ivan Panaev, Nekrasov's associate on the *Sovremennik* editorial board. "Just today I was looking through Mr. Panaev's literary reminiscences," Salatushka muses. "This writer must be an extraordinarily free-thinking person. I believe he is capable of writing anything in the world about anyone who has been so incautious as to admit him to his home. One wonders whether in these memoirs he will describe the cornerstone on which was founded his extremely remarkable friendship with Mr. Nekrasov, so that now the friendship between Grech and Bulgarin has lost all its charm."[56] Pisemsky was referring here to the *ménage à trois* that existed for some years among Nekrasov, Panaev, and the latter's wife, the beautiful Avdotya Panaeva, a situation everyone knew about but nobody mentioned in print. Pisemsky was most undiplomatic in bringing up the subject, and apparently he did so gratuitously and without personal provocation, for he himself is hardly mentioned in Panaev's memoirs.

Nekrasov was understandably incensed by Pisemsky's public hint at the relationship between him and Panaeva. He included a detailed summary of the situation in a letter of April 5, 1861, to Ivan Turgenev, who was in a similar position himself and could therefore be expected to sympathize.[57] In view of the fact that a woman's reputation was involved, Nekrasov was disinclined to pursue the matter further, but he was unsure how to react should Pisemsky again publish something of this nature. "I wanted to let him know about this," Nekrasov concluded, "but it is a risky business to give this man a document that does not pertain to me alone." In short, Nekrasov was in a cold fury over Pisemsky's insinuations about his personal life, and this fury undoubtedly reinforced the delayed explosion against Pisemsky that occurred in the first months of 1862.

In the third installment of Salatushka's notes, published in the March 1861 issue of *Biblioteka dlya chteniya*, Pisemsky went beyond this kind of personal nastiness to indulge, for the first time, in a general attack on the nihilists. For this purpose he describes a young "student" who mechanically mouthed parodies of the fashionable ideas of the day, such as the theory that "we must reconstruct the brain, bones, and flesh of European man, and then he will reconstruct the cities as well" (VII, 603). This student was a clear harbinger of the antinihilist period in Pisemsky's career, which would reach its peak with the publication of the novel *Troubled Seas* in 1863. The warning flags were up as early as the spring of 1861.

Pisemsky continued to compose feuilletons throughout 1861, some of which were published anonymously. Then occurred the major journalistic crisis of his life, which began in December 1861 with his emergence under a new pseudonym, "staraya feletonnaya klyacha Nikita Bezrylov" (the old feuilleton nag Nikita Bezrylov [Nosnout]).[58] His first feuilleton under this byline, untitled, makes fun of three enterprises dear to radical hearts: the considerate treatment of children, feminine emancipation, and the practice of giving literary evenings for the benefit of worthy causes. Here Pisemsky-Bezrylov mocked the very Sunday Schools for whose support he had given readings in the recent past: "Dear children!—I exclaim—you are living at a happy time for people of your age: have you heard that at the Sunday Schools to various sloven boys and girls . . . they use *vy* [the formal mode of address] . . . What does it matter that these stupid creatures have no understanding whatever of this courtesy and are even more frightened by it than anything else, and that they learn much better from some leather-lunged landowner and from regimental junior officers than from our most modern young people; all these little contradictions mean nothing: just so the rule of great humaneness (*gumannost*) be observed" (VII, 613). In addition, Pisemsky-Bezrylov jeered at the pretensions of modern women to sexual emancipation, remarking sarcastically that Russian "humaneness" had then reached the point where soon each married woman would demand two lovers (a "loving lover" and a "loved lover") besides her husband. In the capital "the loving lover should always be her husband's superior, and the role of the loved lover should be played by a young subordinate . . . stronger in body than in spirit" (VII, 614-615). Pisemsky aroused radical anger, however, not so much by his assault on the custom of holding literary evenings as by the personal comments he included in a passage referring to Panaev's reputation as a dandy and to Nekrasov's weakness for gambling, through which the latter had considerably enriched himself. Nekrasov in particular would have been offended by this second slur upon his personal character, despite the fact that the paragraph in question also contains jibes at Pisemsky himself and the staunch conservative Viktor Askochensky: "Messrs. Pisemsky and Askochensky, while conversing most cordially with each other, will preliminarily immerse themselves in thought for about a quarter-hour and then will commence reinforcing their frail bodies with salt zander (*sudak*), during which time Mr. Pisemsky . . . will with genuine ecstasy wash down this scanty fare with pure Neva water, casting contemptuous glances at the roast beef, oysters, porter and port wine resting near him. Mr. Panaev, with the utter calm of a gentleman, will, in the presence of the entire audience, count 500,000 rubles in silver belonging to him personally, and Mr. Nekrasov, in accord with his so deeply felt love for the poor and unfortunate, will with the greatest of pleasure play at trumps with an expelled cadet, and for free'' (VII, 615).

As can be seen from these passages, though Pisemsky's satire fell short of the embittered tirades that the radicals could unreel against contemporary society, it was sufficiently harsh to sting. It must have especially saddened those who had accepted Pisarev's recent analysis of Pisemsky's ''radical'' position in Russian letters; this feuilleton would justify their thinking him a renegade from the camp to which they had imagined he belonged. In any case, Pisemsky's piece provoked violent controversy.

The first reactions to it appeared in *Severnaya pchela* for January 24, 1862, and the satirical journal *Iskra* for February 2, 1862. The *Severnaya pchela* writer expressed abhorrence at Bezrylov's ''cynical derision of everything that our contemporary society has considered necessary and decent, that has made us rejoice for humanity in the blessed cause of moral and scientific progress.'' This statement was mild compared to the remarks made by Grigory Eliseev in his regular *Iskra* column, ''Khronika progressa'' (Chronicle of Progress). Exclaiming that nobody should be so crude as to sneer at the necessary reforms the radicals were trying to introduce, Eliseev launched an *ad hominem* attack on Bezrylov: ''Does this Nikita Bezrylov belong to the number of those born of woman or did he just somehow appear accidentally in human society? Is there a human heart within him? Has there ever stirred within him a human thought, has he ever been troubled by any human emotion whatever?'' Though the writer for *Severnaya pchela* at least pretended to believe that Bezrylov and Pisemsky were not the same person and that Pisemsky had probably neglected to read the feuilleton before printing it, *Iskra* was certain that at the very least Pisemsky had knowingly passed upon it. Since he had sunk to such depths, he should now be dealt with sternly. The time had passed when a writer could gain renown solely through his ability to write poems or novels: ''Now everyone . . . knows that a talent which does not genuinely strive to serve the cause of society deserves no respect at all; but a talent using its powers for the destruction of this cause is worthy of utter contempt.'' In short, *Iskra* was attempting to force upon Pisemsky an ideological task, which he, unideological as he was, would not shoulder.

Pisemsky undertook to answer his critics in the January 1862 issue of *Biblioteka dlya chteniya,* which was late in appearing. He prefaced the article "Otvet Nikity Bezrylova svoim vragam" (Nikita Bezrylov's Reply to His Enemies) with a brief piece, "Otvet Pisemskogo" (Pisemsky's Reply), in which he noted the published insults directed against him and entrusted his case to the judgment of the public, in confidence that his good name could not be destroyed by a "flourish of the pen of some zealous attackers unknown to me" (neither of the two polemical articles against him had been signed in full). In Pisemsky-Bezrylov's retort "to his enemies" he defended his stand on the three issues of children, women, and literary evenings, concluding with an ironical promise to organize another literary evening "for the benefit of talentless feuilletonists definitively driven out of all our journals as a result of the raising of the intellectual level in literature" (VII, 618).

Pisemsky did not limit his defensive maneuvers to the publication of polemic rejoinders to his ideological opponents. Taking a more unusual step, at some point between February 2 and 7 he and his supporters drew up a formal protest against the *Iskra* article. We first hear of the protest in a letter written by Pisemsky on February 7 to Ostrovsky in Moscow, pleading for the playwright's adherence to the draft copy of the protest on the grounds that, if *Iskra* can "sling mud at me, it can sling mud at anyone who gets in its way."[59] At roughly the same time Pisemsky made a similar request of another friend of long standing, Turgenev, who was then in Paris. In a letter to him Pisemsky expressed bitterness over recent events and begged Turgenev to write on his behalf to the newspaper *Sanktpeterburgskie vedomosti,* since "the public will believe your voice sounding in my favor."[60] In the meantime Pisemsky's supporters were busily collecting signatures for the protest, which in its initial form apparently was nothing more than a rejoinder to the *Iskra* article alone. Public notice of the impending protest was given on February 10 in the weekly *Russky mir* (Russian World), which claimed that about thirty signatures had already been obtained for it, including those of "editors and contributors (*sotrudniki*) from our most popular journals: *Sovremennik, Otechestvennye zapiski, Russkoe slovo, S. Peterburgskie vedomosti, Severnaya pchela.*"

Unhappily this sally into the enemy camp, through citing *Sovremennik, Russkoe slovo,* and *Severnaya pchela,* backfired on *Russky mir,* for the editors of *Sovremennik* quickly issued a statement denying that they had adhered to the protest and, worse, declaring their support for the *Iskra* article. As a demonstration of radical solidarity, this statement, signed by Nekrasov, Panaev, Cherny-shevsky, M. A. Antonovich, and A. N. Pypin, was published in *Iskra* for February 16. This prompt and energetic communication from the editorial board of the leading radical journal did much to under-mine Pisemsky's campaign.

For various other reasons, enthusiasm over the protest subse-quently subsided, and before another month had elapsed it was plain that the text would not be published, presumably because no agree-ment could be reached on the generality of its wording. In an attempt to counteract the impression made by the *Sovremennik* statement that no members of the *Sovremennik* staff had signed the protest, the editors of *Russky mir* on March 17 published the names of several of the original signers. The list included friends of Pisem-sky who would be expected to sign (Apollon Maykov, Aleksey Po-tekhin, Pavel Annenkov, Aleksandr Druzhinin, Ivan Goncharov) in addition to such a prominent radical as Dmitry Pisarev, who ap-parently had been unable to discard instantaneously his sympathy for Pisemsky and his work. However, two names one would antici-pate finding in the group were missing: Turgenev and Ostrovsky. Turgenev was already anticipating trouble from the radical critics over the publication in February 1862 of his novel *Fathers and Sons;* in addition, he was probably influenced by the thought that Pisem-sky had earlier been guilty of personal innuendo against Nekrasov, for a domestic situation that was uncomfortably similar to Tur-genev's own. Ostrovsky, who had connections with *Sovremennik* at the time, at some point between February 8 and 11 refused to adhere to the protest, giving as his excuse the fact that Kraevsky, whom he disliked, was among the signers.[61]

Inasmuch as so many important intellectual figures had initially been willing to affix their signatures to Pisemsky's protest, why did it fail? Part of the answer is supplied by a letter from Pisemsky to Turgenev in Paris, dated February 20, 1862, stating that the thirty or more persons listed on the original sheets had reconsidered their positions, and a number had ended by repudiating their sig-natures. Such a development came as an understandable shock to Pisemsky: "This has shaken me to the depths of my soul," he wrote. "If you had been in St. Petersburg, I think this would not have happened with you around: they would have been ashamed!"[62] Probably the organizers had tried to formulate a broader protest with general implications for Russian intellectual and literary life, thus alienating those who were willing to take a public stand against a specific article but were disinclined to go further.

In the same letter of February 20 to Turgenev, Pisemsky again proved himself something of a prophet, at least with regard to his own future. He remarked that the radicals wished to destroy his authority in the literary world as well as that of Goncharov and Turgenev: "And do you know what? Though perhaps only temporarily, they will achieve this! Our public is so accustomed to believing the printed word, the more so since they [the radicals], after two words, usually make the third one: we are the progressives, the most advanced, the most extreme." Pisemsky thus clearly discerned the coming course of events, for the political animosity generated by his writings and actions at this period was certainly an important factor, though not the sole one, in his subsequent eclipse.

The uproar over Pisemsky's protest flared one last time before subsiding. In the February issue of *Biblioteka dlya chteniya* Pisemsky inserted into a feuilleton by Boborykin a phrase referring to *Iskra*'s "not entirely noble little nature." The editors of *Iskra*, Vasily Kurochkin and Nikolay Stepanov, who delighted in attacking others but resented attacks on themselves, interpreted the phrase as a personal insult and in mid-March challenged Pisemsky to a duel. Pisemsky was never very brave, and the challenge upset him considerably. He refused to give his challengers satisfaction, maintaining in a letter that since *Iskra* employed strong language in its articles, he was fully entitled to reply in kind. He also proposed that the dispute be settled in court if need be. The recipients of the letter posted the original in a St. Petersburg bookshop, but as the majority of those who knew anything about the affair apparently took Pisemsky's side, the episode was terminated without bloodshed.[63]

After the question of the duel had been settled, Pisemsky made a few bitter remarks in a feuilleton published in the March issue of his journal and then abandoned the struggle to seek immediate surcease in his first journey abroad. Trips to foreign countries provided a valuable means of escape for many nineteenth-century Russian writers who found themselves in various straits. Some, who were in political difficulties with the regime, deemed it advisable to leave Russia temporarily or permanently, in which intention they were ordinarily not hindered by the authorities. Others, who like Pisemsky had become embroiled in personal or political conflicts not serious enough to involve the state, took a trip abroad in order to allow domestic passions to cool during their absence.

Though it is not known precisely when Pisemsky departed from St. Petersburg, he presumably left no earlier than April. The single letter extant from his trip was written to A. A. Kraevsky from

Dresden on May 10. In it Pisemsky declared that all he was doing was "dragging around Europe," not especially enjoying it.[64] The rest of his journey may be characterized in the same terms, so far as can be judged. On May 19 he arrived in Paris and promptly dropped in to see Ostrovsky, who was visiting there at the time.[65] Then he continued to London, where he went to great lengths to obtain an interview with Herzen. Evidently he told Herzen that he had come to London largely for the purpose of paying him a visit, and presented the exiled revolutionary with a copy of his collected works as a "sign of his immense esteem." Pisemsky had always regarded Herzen as one of the most attractive figures of the generation of the 1840's, that "golden age" of his youth, and it is likely that he expected to find in him a sympathetic listener to his complaints against the younger radical generation, with whom Herzen had also had some misunderstandings.[66] If such was his expectation, he was grievously in error, for Herzen was quite cool toward him in the course of an uncordial conversation. As a consequence, Pisemsky temporarily turned against Herzen. For example, in his antinihilist novel of 1863, *Troubled Seas*, Pisemsky caused one of his heroes to be arrested for attempting to smuggle revolutionary proclamations from London into Russia. The implication was that Herzen incited rebellion from a safe distance, using dupes as his agents so that they might suffer if detected, while the master revolutionary sat comfortably in London. Further, in a play of 1864 Pisemsky had one of his characters admit to disillusion in Herzen's cause and attack his "buffoonery [and] juvenile intention to preach his doctrines among the masses of our savage and drunken people" (VIII, 661). Herzen was not slow to retaliate: he referred to Pisemsky's creations in *Troubled Seas* as "sorely-tried freaks," spoke of Pisemsky himself with contempt, and penned a brief parody of his novel under the title "Vzboltannaya pomoynaya yama" (The Shaken-up Rubbish Heap). Despite all this, in the long run Pisemsky found Herzen's personality too compelling to remain permanently hostile toward him and his ideas.

Pisemsky returned to St. Petersburg from abroad sometime in the late summer or early fall of 1862. Within a few more months he had completed preparations for leaving the capital, which, as he wrote to Turgenev on February 19, 1863, had become "absolutely repugnant" to him.[67] The events of early 1862 had jarred him so thoroughly that he decided he could find peace of mind only by moving to the cultural capital which he had bypassed some eight years before. A weighty contributing factor in his decision seems to have been an invitation from M. N. Katkov, the editor of *Russky vestnik*, to join his journal. Sometime in the early months of 1863, probably in March or April, Pisemsky left St. Petersburg for Moscow.[68] There he established a permanent residence, subsequently making only brief return visits to the Northern Palmyra that had rejected him. The provincial capital, Moscow, was from then on to be his home.

IV

Between Radicalism and Reaction

Upon severing his connections with *Biblioteka dlya chteniya*,[1] Pisemsky formed new ties with Mikhail Katkov's *Russky vestnik*, a journal noted for its conservatism in political affairs. Although it never boasted any critics of stature, it published a remarkably large portion of important fiction in that Golden Age of Russian literature. Its extensive roll of authors included Dostoevsky, Turgenev, Lev Tolstoy, Aleksey Tolstoy, as well as Pisemsky.

At some point not long after his arrival in Moscow, Pisemsky was given an official position as director of the literary section of *Russky vestnik*. Though Katkov was thoroughly disliked by many, his relations with Pisemsky seem at first to have been rather cordial. Evidence of this appears in a passage from a letter of June 1863 to Turgenev in which Pisemsky refers to Katkov as a "hero" who was "inspiring the country" and whose "sacred cause"—by which he meant Katkov's campaign against both Polish and Russian revolutionaries—stood in need of support.[2] In this instance Pisemsky's view may have been strongly colored by the patriotic feeling engendered by the Polish uprising of 1863, since Katkov was a leading proponent of the rebellion's prompt suppression, but the warmth of Pisemsky's words is nevertheless noteworthy. In little more than a year, however, the two had permanently parted company because of personal and policy differences.[3] When Pisemsky recalled the situation somewhat later, it seemed to him that their relationship had been uncomfortable from the start: "it was obvious that they [presumably Katkov and Pavel Leontev, the chief editors] had become accustomed to a rather slavish and servile attitude on the part of their staff members and that they wanted a proof-reader instead of a co-editor.''[4] But it appears more likely that at this later date Pisemsky was projecting his current sentiments into the past and that in fact his initial attitude toward Katkov was favorable. However that may be, we lack information on the precise conditions under which Pisemsky's employment with *Russky vestnik* was terminated.

During his months with *Russky vestnik* Pisemsky began to publish in quantity once more. His preoccupation with the affairs of *Biblioteka dlya chteniya* had prevented him from bringing out much fiction during 1861 and 1862, but in the early part of 1863 he published his novel *Troubled Seas*. It is considered a primary example of the genus of "antinihilist" novels that became prominent in the literature of the 1860's. What are now termed antinihilist elements appeared in the writing of that day whenever an author attempted to picture members of the flourishing radical movement, not with unmistakable approval, but either dispassionately or with hostile intent. In the emotionally and politically supercharged atmosphere of those years, the radicals felt that whoever was not with them was against them, and therefore deserving of total obloquy. Since their cause was just, nobody should be permitted to examine its operation critically. Despite this view, many leading Russian novelists—including Dostoevsky, Turgenev, Leskov, and Goncharov—brought out books containing radicals pictured in neutral or hostile fashion, which incurred lasting condemnation from the radical critics.[5] Certainly the critics viewed the young radicals in *Troubled Seas* as proof of Pisemsky's unreserved adherence to the conservative camp in Russian letters, the more so as it first came out in *Russky vestnik,* a journal the radicals detested.

Since *Troubled Seas* is of great importance from the point of view of literary history, it is unfortunate that little information on its composition is available. The first extant letter written after Pisemsky's return from abroad in 1862, dated October 8, is also the first one to include any mention of the novel. On November 1, 1862, he informed Katkov that under certain conditions he would be pleased to sell him this "huge novel" and that he was currently writing the third part of the six parts in which it would finally appear.[6] By the end of December he had completed five of the six parts.[7] In all likelihood the book was finished by March 1863, for it began to appear in *Russky vestnik* in that month, continuing thereafter in monthly installments through August.

What we know of the chronology of the novel's composition makes it difficult to devise a satisfactory explanation for the appearance of a polemical and journalistic tone in the second half, beginning with Part Four. It is probable that Pisemsky had begun the work by late 1861, before his disagreements with the radicals, for in his memoirs Boborykin states that in the fall of 1861 *Sovremennik* was thinking of publishing the novel, two parts of which had been completed.[8] It is certain that this consideration would have been promptly terminated after the outburst of ill-feeling against Pisemsky in February 1862, and Pisemsky's change in tone could have resulted from the same experience. Yet it is difficult to see why he should have maintained his calmer outlook through Part Three, which he was writing as late as October 1862, and taken up the polemical cudgels only in Part Four. This does not fit with what we know of his quarrel with the radicals.

While writing *Troubled Seas*, Pisemsky unquestionably regarded it as potentially a major novel. In his correspondence he termed it a "serious work" which "embraces almost all of our Mother Russia" and remarked that "this novel is the work of my entire life: and whether it comes out good or bad, I will never write anything better or more powerful."[9] He remained convinced of the novel's importance even after absorbing all the abuse heaped upon him for it. Thus, in 1869 he wrote to Turgenev that "in *One Thousand Souls* [is depicted] a bygone Russia, but in *Troubled Seas* contemporary Russia" and expressed the wish that his German translator undertake a rendering of the later novel so that the European reading audience might be given an accurate notion of "our revolutionary party, than which, I think, the world has never produced anything worse and more vile."[10]

Being persuaded of his novel's significance, Pisemsky felt that he should not rush its composition. As work progressed, he gave readings to his friends and associates, most of whom encouraged him by their praise. Despite this backing and the literary reputation he then enjoyed, his psychological state at the time was such that he feared he would find no publisher for the novel, and went so far as to negotiate for its publication as a supplement to a newspaper before receiving an offer from *Russky vestnik*.

Troubled Seas disappointed nearly everyone when it came out. It is difficult to summarize the novel's subject, for it endeavors to present too extensive a panorama of contemporary society. Annenkov, while granting credit to the author for his courage in attempting such a monumental task, pointed out that even if one assumed the theoretical possibility of adequately describing the major social and intellectual movements of the preceding twenty years, the depiction would have to be enclosed within a conceptual framework, and this Pisemsky had failed to provide.[11] However, one may make sense of *Troubled Seas* by concentrating on the chief pair in the novel, Sonya Basardina, the daughter of an army officer, and her cousin, Aleksandr Baklanov. Their extended love affair is the principal thread upon which the plot is hung. After flirting with Aleksandr in a juvenile way, Sonya comes to realize the importance that the world places upon wealth and abandons him for the sake of a wealthy but unhappy marriage. Aleksandr then diverts himself by seducing a Polish girl, who falls ill and dies. He arranges a sensible marriage with the reserved Evpraksiya, who later separates from him when he renews his liaison with the profligate Sonya, but in the end returns to him for their children's sake.

While all this is going on, the reader is introduced to a vast assortment of Pisemskian characters, most of whom contribute little to the direct development of the plot, but who recall the Pisemsky of the preceding decade. Indeed, in the person of Iona Cynic, *Troubled Seas* contains the most perfect embodiment of Pisemskian cynicism in the entire sweep of his work. This character capped the tradition evolved in such scoundrels as Count Sapega in *Boyarshchina*, who resorts to any subterfuge in order to remove Elchaninov so that he may seduce Anna Pavlovna; and Prince Ivan Ramensky in *One Thousand Souls*, who arranges a marriage between his own mistress and Kalinovich for the sake of financial gain. A completely immoral being, Iona Cynic is not averse to admitting that perhaps his own wife died because he did not take proper care of her health. He contentedly recounts tales of having compelled people to give him bribes when he occupied a position of power. He cheerfully confesses that he had used his position to obtain sexual favors from women (IV, 231-233). In short, Iona Cynic is the living image of self-centered complacency: not only does he lack the slightest compunction over past offenses, but he is certain that everyone else is fully as immoral as he. The character was so vividly drawn that even the radicals praised him. Pisemsky himself favored him, for he published certain chapters in which Iona Cynic appeared in the January 1863 issue of *Biblioteka dlya chteniya*, as a farewell gift to the journal.

Had Pisemsky confined himself to the creation of such repulsive types as Iona Cynic, few would have found fault with him, for Iona Cynic represented, however hyperbolically, the corruption, cynicism, and selfishness of many upholders of the established order. However, beginning with Part Four, Pisemsky assumed an unaccustomed role as expert commentator on the sociology of Russian life and analyst of the historical sources of contemporary intellectual unrest, stirred up primarily by the radicals. He declared that the chief cause of the current unstable situation was the reaction against the reign of Nicholas I, during which Russia had resembled an armed camp more than a peaceful state; the oppression had been so intense that even the nobility doubted the regime. Education was also to blame: "Education in all branches of the state became narrower and narrower: in the officers' schools it was made senselessly strict, in the gymnasia discipline was relaxed entirely, and in the seminaries, in order not to be backward, the students began to be taught everything but dancing. From here, there and everywhere emerged young people who did not comprehend anything at all" (IV, 345).

If Pisemsky had confined himself to terming the radicals "young people who did not understand anything at all," he might have escaped their criticism relatively lightly. But he went further and depicted the young radicals in the flesh. Among the more important secondary characters in the book are Viktor Basardin, who mouths "loud phrases" of the modish revolutionary sort, and Elena Bazeleyn, a typically "dirty-cuffed" nihilist girl who preaches doctrines of free love and avidly follows the current radical line. At the end, for no valid reason, almost the entire cast of characters journeys to London, where Aleksandr and the nihilist Sabakeev are supplied with revolutionary proclamations to be transported to Russia. Aleksandr is shrewd enough to jettison his proclamations before arrival in St. Petersburg, but Sabakeev is apprehended in possession of his by the authorities.

The radicals could not forgive Pisemsky for dealing with the radical characters in the same way that he had treated all his previous creations. Far from being ideal persons, his radicals are as corrupt and self-centered as Sonya or Aleksandr, who at times sympathize with them. Pisemsky thought that addiction to radical ideology was merely a matter of fashion: these were the same people "who up to 1855 expired of ecstasy at the Italian opera and considered this the highest point of human purpose on earth," and who now had begun "with the enthusiasm and trust of schoolboys to read *Kolokol* [Herzen's émigré radical publication *The Bell*] on the sly.'' Pisemsky's radicals, like most of his other characters, are at bottom motivated by the desire for material gain or sexual lust. For instance, the author implies that Basardin advocates the destruction of the monied classes because he wants to enrich himself. The link between political radicalism and moral turpitude is emphasized when the police, after arresting Basardin, discover in his home copies of *Kolokol*, hand-copied revolutionary poems, and pictures of naked women.

Pisemsky inveighed against the radicals in *Troubled Seas* just as vehemently as he had ever attacked the crassly corrupt representatives of the established order. Aleksandr, for instance, complains of the ''students here, who do nothing and study nothing. In our day we didn't do anything either, but at least we were aware of it and ashamed of it, but these people are proud of it . . . They want to be citizens and defend the rights of the Russian land . . . What rights? . . . Who asked them to?'' (IV, 417). Now and again Pisemsky speaks, not through a character, but in his own derisive voice: ''Who are this salt of the earth, anyway, these chosen ones come to society's table . . . Witty windbags, who think the essence of the matter is to turn a sharp phrase . . . Salesmen who are able eternally to peddle their small supply of spiritual bile . . . Mature and immature good-for-nothings of all sorts, always ready to fill their emptiness with whatever you like'' (IV, 441).

After loosing such barrages, Pisemsky realized that he would be called upon to defend himself. By including sociological ruminations on the origins of contemporary unrest, he hoped to gain the protection of history for his novel. He wished to establish the claim that he was merely describing things easily observable in historical reality, rather than slandering Russian society by describing events and persons that rarely existed in fact. This tactic was employed by several other antinihilist writers, and it helped them no more than it did Pisemsky. He constructed his defense lines explicitly in the final paragraph of *Troubled Seas*: ''We undertook our labor not at all for the education of the minds and hearts of sixteen-year-old female readers and not in order to satisfy the fervent self-love of various weak-minded young men: they would do better not even to read us; we had quite another (not to say higher) purpose and we wish for much more: may the future historian read our tale with attention and trust: we present to him a faithful, although incomplete, picture of the morals of our time, and if not all of Russia is mirrored in it, at least all her falsehood has been carefully collected herein'' (IV, 549). Far from placating Pisemsky's ideological ill-wishers, this paragraph made them even angrier at his presumption in invoking the muse of history to justify his work. Some years later, however, Pisemsky made an about face when he complained to Nikolay Leskov that "the novel is evidently becoming more and more an artistic statistic of the time and history's closest helpmate."[12] That is, novelists were simply trying to describe reality as it in fact was, thereby producing raw material for the future historian. But in 1863 Pisemsky himself had not been averse to aiding future historians.

The critics reacted violently to this novel, which even Nikitenko called a "sea of tastelessness, in the which there is no end to reptiles."[13] With one or two exceptions, no favorable review appeared. Every literary faction was dissatisfied. The Slavophile newspaper *Den* (Day) berated Pisemsky for the coarseness of his descriptions, complaining that he did not confine himself to the objective "exposure" of filth and banality but actively relished the infamous scenes he concocted.[14] Apollon Grigorev, sounding like a radical, proclaimed unequivocally that the book had exposed Pisemsky as an obscurantist of the first water. "Reactions in general are blind," he wrote, "but there is hardly anything at all so blind as the reaction which this gifted author now represents."[15]

The main area of controversy was Pisemsky's view of the younger generation. A balanced critic like A. P. Milyukov agreed that contemporary youth had indeed wasted much energy on "foreign doctrines" and ingesting "ready-made ideas," but they had at the same time abandoned card-playing, carousing, and other such harmful occupations. Milyukov considered the current state of Russian society not nearly so hopeless as did the alarmist Pisemsky.[16] The problem of the relations between generations was analyzed from a conservative standpoint in a review of *Troubled Seas* published in *Otechestvennye zapiski*. "The slightest word of exposure directed against youth," wrote the reviewer, "even if the word be conscientious and just, even if it be called forth by sympathy, though not the blind sort of sympathy which can only pat people on the head— any such word our literary milieu takes as an intentional attack. But when it itself begins describing youth, it pictures it in monotonous portraits of suffering and hard labor, so that education and the milieu—that is, the older generation—always turn out to be at fault."[17] The nub of the disagreement between the generations lay in the notion of "typicality." The younger generation was pleased to regard an Iona Cynic as in some way "typical" of supporters of the existing state of affairs, but it was unwilling to agree that nihilists like Sabakeev might be viewed analogously. When radicals even admitted the existence of such individuals, they treated them as rare "exceptions." In contrast, the older generation, having learned to be more cognizant of its own shortcomings, would accept a character like Iona Cynic, but it saw no reason to exempt its offspring from the same kind of criticism. This difference in viewpoint was central to the literary clashes of the 1860's.

In view of the fact that Pisemsky's reputation was severely damaged by *Troubled Seas* until the present day, that the young radicals must have been outraged by it, and that several nonradical critics spoke harshly of it, the outward reaction from the openly radical journals *Sovremennik* and *Russkoe slovo* was astoundingly mild. The explanation must be sought in a fortuitous set of circumstances affecting the major radical critics active at the time. Although Pisarev's colleague Varfolomey Zaytsev wrote a review in *Russkoe slovo* entitled "Vzbalamuchenny romanist" (The Troubled Novelist), Pisarev himself hardly commented on it. His biographer ascribes this silence to Pisarev's inability to cultivate a genuine antipathy toward the writer whom he had once admired and to whom he had devoted such enthusiastic pages.[18] On the other hand, Maksim Antonovich, *Sovremennik*'s head critic, though he had no particular brief for Pisemsky, was so enraged by the antinihilism of Turgenev's *Fathers and Sons* that he almost ended up defending Pisemsky. Antonovich had attacked *Fathers and Sons* with irrational virulence when it appeared a year before Pisemsky's novel. Now, in his lengthy review article "Sovremennye romany" (Contemporary Novels) treating both *Troubled Seas* and Turgenev's minor story "Ghosts," he was primarily concerned with denigrating Turgenev once again.[19]

In Antonovich's opinion, *Troubled Seas* was neither very good nor so dreadful as to be condemned out of hand. It was simply cut from the same antinihilist cloth as *Fathers and Sons,* and Pisemsky was only following in Turgenev's footsteps. Consequently, Antonovich felt, it was unjust that Turgenev should have been praised for his book while Pisemsky was hounded. "I could even say," the critic wrote in one of his ingenious misreadings, "that Pisemsky, if he was not in fact, at least tried to be impartial toward the younger generation, something which was not noticeable in Turgenev." Indeed, Turgenev's shame over his reactionism should be the greater because his was the superior intellect and the larger talent; as Pisemsky was inferior to him, his fault was so much the less. Antonovich's nearly pathological hatred for Turgenev thus impelled him to swim against the prevailing currents and make excuses for Pisemsky. In this case, as in so many others, Antonovich was wildly incorrect, for today most historians of Russian literature would agree that *Fathers and Sons* was a much more objective and dispassionate portrayal of the contemporary social scene than *Troubled Seas.* Moreover, for all the maltreatment Turgenev took at the radicals' hands, he never allowed himself to become as bitter about the radicals as did Pisemsky.

We possess no published documents with information on how Pisemsky took the generally negative reaction to his book, but like several of the antinihilist novels, it enjoyed widespread popularity with the reading public. Readers apparently thought of it as sensational, and the controversy that arose over the book did not harm its sales.

First Years in Moscow

From Pisemsky's point of view, the move to Moscow was undoubtedly a wise one, since the conflicts in St. Petersburg became if anything fiercer in the years following the Polish uprising of 1863. Although the surge of patriotism engendered by the Polish conflict enabled the government to lighten its controls and proceed with further innovations, such as the extensive court reforms of 1864, the revolutionaries remained intransigent. In 1864 Chernyshevsky was exiled to Siberia and his voice thereby effectively silenced, though at the same time the government's action made a martyr of him in the eyes of the younger generation. Pisarev remained in opposition to the government, composing his critical articles in the Peter and Paul Fortress, where he was imprisoned for sedition until 1866. Many youthful revolutionaries, not content to work through the spoken or written word alone, adopted ever more radical tactics. With the attempted assassination of the Czar by the student Karakozov in 1866, the empire received its first experience of the political terrorism with which it was to contend for over half a century. The government retaliated with measures at least as stern as those it had employed in 1862, including permanently closing down both of the major leftist journals, *Sovremennik* and *Russkoe slovo.* The radicals managed to circumvent this difficulty through such tactics as taking over the politically moderate *Otechestvennye zapiski,* which after 1868 was transformed into a prominent and consistent voice of radical opinion under the guidance of Nekrasov and Saltykov-Shchedrin.

Despite the government's attempts at repression, the general intellectual atmosphere of the 1860's remained intensely radical, and many of the moderate or liberal writers of the time were pushed into the background. In this respect Pisemsky's career in 1863-1865 was typical of the experience of the moderate camp. He first fell back upon *Russky vestnik*, which remained the only important literary journal opposed to the radical hegemony in Russian life throughout the 1860's. He was not alone in his alienation from the other significant literary journals. Nikolay Leskov suffered something resembling a formal excommunication at Pisarev's hands after the publication in 1864 of his antinihilist novel *Nekuda* (No Way Out), and many years elapsed before his genius gained proper recognition. Dostoevsky opposed radical doctrine unbendingly in his journals *Vremya* (Time) and *Epokha* (Epoch), but in 1865 *Epokha* had to be closed down for financial reasons and the writer, burdened by debts, emigrated temporarily. Turgenev also resided abroad during most of these years. After *Fathers and Sons*, he wrote quite apolitical short stories until the publication of *Smoke*, his most political novel, in 1867. But *Smoke* only aroused fresh anger among the younger generation, so that Turgenev felt he had lost all standing with them and was hesitant to state his opinions publicly. Following these developments, the intellectual battleground of the 1860's was left mostly in the possession of the radical intelligentsia.

One nonradical contemporary viewpoint of some influence was latter-day Slavophilism, along with its offshoot, Pan-Slavism. The Pan-Slavs differed from the Slavophiles in their greater orientation toward the Slavs beyond Russian borders, especially the Orthodox South Slavic nations, who they hoped would eventually unite politically under Russian direction. Pan-Slav ideas claimed a number of adherents during the 1860's, enough to enable a Slavic Congress to be convened in Moscow in 1867. The object of the congress was to impress the non-Russian Slavs with Russian achievements and to promote the idea of Pan-Slav independence and unity. The Poles, however, were excluded from this scheme because they were too infected with Roman Catholicism and also because they were already partially subjected to Russia and therefore did not need to be "freed." Pan-Slav notions eventually proved useful as an ideological justification for the Russian intervention in the Balkans leading to the Russo-Turkish War of 1877-1878 and Bulgaria's liberation from the Turkish yoke. But in the 1860's the Slavophiles and Pan-Slavs limited themselves to propagandizing their theories and publishing various journals and newspapers.

Although Pisemsky had moved to the Slavophile capital, had some Slavophile friends, and was to an extent influenced by them, he generally steered clear of politics, whether radical or Slavophile.

During his initial year of residence in Moscow, indeed, he had enough pressing problems to keep him otherwise occupied. The principal problem was the presentation of *A Bitter Fate,* which until then had never been allowed on the stage. By 1863, Pisemsky thought, the question of serfdom had surely receded far enough into the past to allow the play to be produced. Submitted to the censorship in July of 1863, it was passed without hindrance and received its premiere performance at the hands of an amateur group on July 31, the author himself taking the lead role of Anany. However, the director of Moscow theaters, L. F. Lvov, at first prevented its professional staging in Moscow.[20] As Pisemsky stood in need of the financial return he anticipated from the play's presentation, he did everything he could to have Lvov overruled.

In the course of his campaign to gain support for *A Bitter Fate* from high government officials Pisemsky emphasized his trustworthiness from a political point of view and argued that by then his play was almost solely of historical interest: "Last of all my play, as far as its themes go, has already receded into history: the abuses of serfdom and the shortcomings of secret judicial processes are capable of insulting only half-insane people!"[21] Pisemsky made great efforts, through the dispatch of long letters, to gain the sympathy of the Minister of the Interior, P. A. Valuev. He had met Valuev in March 1861 at a jubilee dinner honoring the conservative poet P. A. Vyazemsky, and on April 2, 1863, he had read some chapters of *Troubled Seas* at Valuev's home. In all probability Pisemsky selected suitably antinihilist portions of his novel for presentation before the minister, but his schemes that evening were in vain, for Valuev barely listened. Instead, he was trying to decide whether he should resign as Minister of the Interior.[22] At any rate, on August 4 Pisemsky wrote Valuev an imploring letter arguing that his play was entirely fit for staging: an audience of gentry in attendance at the premiere had applauded it enthusiastically, according to the author, which proved that there was nothing "insulting" to the nobility in it, as Lvov had maintained. At one point, taking a number of liberties with the facts, Pisemsky summarized his literary career in terms that made it sound as though he had always been an ardently pro-regime writer: "I have served literature for twenty years, nothing that I have published has ever caused a scandal; my hostile relations with the so-called extremist party and finally my most recent novel, with which I hope to give the revolutionary movement a rap from which it will never recover: all this has given me some hope of receiving the trust and condescension of the government."[23] Pisemsky complained to Valuev that his play had obviously been prohibited because the Moscow authorities placed him in the same category as those "chatterboxes [the radicals], who should be forced to keep quiet at least for a while." In short, in order to gain approval for his play, Pisemsky was going so far as to advocate the suppression of the radicals' right to free speech. In this he was being opportunistic, for ordinarily he did not approve of censorship.

Pisemsky's campaign on behalf of *A Bitter Fate* was in the end successful. Lvov's "intrigues" against it were overcome, and it was premiered in St. Petersburg on October 18 and in Moscow on November 18. Dostoevsky wrote to his brother that he had run into Pisemsky on the street in Moscow on the day of the Moscow premiere and that the latter had complained of a "cabal" organized against him by the "English Club" and the "party of the landowners." Dostoevsky was sure Pisemsky had been exaggerating.[24] Pisemsky's tendency to see conspiracies everywhere thus remained strong, though in this instance he admittedly had better grounds for suspicion than in some other cases. Despite all his agitation on its behalf, the play enjoyed only moderate success with the public and did not enter the permanent repertory of the capital theaters, although from the late 1860's it became a standard item in the provincial repertory.

Grateful to Valuev for his aid in this and other matters, Pisemsky sent the minister a copy of his *Troubled Seas* plus an additional copy for presentation to the Czar, commenting in a covering letter that "monarchs should know the shortcomings of their people as well as its virtues."[25] All in all, during the period 1863-1864, when Pisemsky was working for the conservative *Russky vestnik,* writing protestations of loyalty to the government, and actively supporting the antinihilist cause in literature, he was closer than ever to the right wing in Russian intellectual life and most distant from the radicals. In late March 1864, for example, he wrote to Apollon Maykov of rumors to the effect that the poet Polonsky was considering publishing a poem in *Sovremennik:* "This is dreadful! They have run all you poets down in God knows what fashion there, but still you have not broken utterly and forever with those gentlemen . . . [Tell Polonsky that] all decent people should publish in *Russky vestnik.*"[26] In after years, however, in certain major ways he seemed to move much further to the left.

After the publication of *Troubled Seas* Pisemsky entered the doldrums, and it was not until 1867 that he once more began appearing in print in earnest, though by then he had been so thoroughly excluded from the major journals as to be compelled to publish in insignificant organs. In 1864, though, he did project a cycle of satirical sketches, to be entitled *Russkie lguny* (Russian Liars), the aim of which was to present a "whole series of types resembling Thackeray's snobs."[27] This reference to Thackeray links *Russian Liars* to Pisemsky's short story of ten years before, "The Braggart," which had also been inspired by the English writer's snobs and was to have been part of a cycle. That projected cycle had gotten no further than the one story, but the proposed series of 1864 was more fully realized. On August 25, 1864, Pisemsky informed Kraevsky that he had completed the first series, entitled "Nevinnye vrali" (Innocent Prevaricators), and that he planned several other sketches, to treat such subjects as "sentimentalists," "Russian Byronists," "Herzenites," and "Katkovites." It is unfortunate that he failed to follow through on most of these last pieces.

Russian Liars, published in *Otechestvennye zapiski* for January, February, and April 1865, passed largely unnoticed, though a provincial reviewer in an Odessa newspaper complained that one discovered in the stories, not "a malicious falsity of tendency [as in *Troubled Seas*], but simply an astounding lack of talent." The reviewer felt that the sketches bordered on pornography.[28] A century later, it is difficult to agree with such an evaluation: slight they may be, but they are scarcely pornographic or devoid of interest.

Pisemsky advanced a claim to seriousness for these sketches in a short introduction setting forth their purpose. He requested his readers to direct their attention, not to the liars themselves, but to the subjects on which they lied, for by analyzing the things about which the people of a given epoch tell falsehoods, one can make a rough determination of the "level of intellectual, moral and even political development of the country" (IV, 550). This approach may have a certain validity, but on the whole it is preferable simply to enjoy the Pisemskian characters as depicted than to look for their deep sociological significance.

In the first sketch of the series, "Konkurent" (The Competitor), Pisemsky continues his tradition of reintroducing characters from his earlier stories into later works. In this case he recalls Anton Fedotych Stupitsyn from *A Marriage of Passion*. Upon meeting a young man, Stupitsyn for no particular reason begins lying in an absurd fashion. In retaliation, his interlocutor puts him to confusion by describing a clock he had purchased for his mother, equipped with an alarm set for eight o'clock, exactly the time his mother was accustomed to arise. As Stupitsyn seems willing to accept this, the young man adds that the alarm consisted of, not a bell, but a human voice saying "Get up! Get up!" Stupitsyn remains credulous, so his opponent presses his advantage: the alarm clock even used his mother's name: "Get up, Kleopatra Grigorevna!" By this time Stupitsyn, his head spinning, has been defeated at his own game and is incapable of retaliation (IV, 553). The other stories in *Russian Liars* are similar in tone.

After the publication of this collection Dmitry Pisarev made a passing comment upon Pisemsky that seems uncannily prophetic. In a general review article of March 1865, "Progulka po sadam rossiyskoy slovesnosti" (A Stroll Through the Gardens of Russian Literature), the radical critic remarked that after the failure of *Troubled Seas*, "the only thing left for Mr. Pisemsky was to transform himself into a gay raconteur of humorous little anecdotes, and he has in fact effected this transformation on the pages of *Otechestvennye zapiski*, where he is at present describing *Russian Liars*. These little stories might with great success have figured even in the Moscow journal *Razvlechenie* (Entertainment), and I refuse to abandon hope that sometime Mr. Pisemsky . . . will indeed go off to complete his literary career with some newspaper fully as miserable as that one."[29] Pisarev might have been maliciously gratified had he lived to witness the concluding years of Pisemsky's life, for his last works were in fact published in newspapers and journals nearly as "miserable" and obscure as *Razvlechenie*.

After the publication of *Russian Liars*, Pisemsky ceased writing short stories for a considerable interval. Instead, he composed novels—usually lengthy ones, in the best Russian tradition—and plays. Dramaturgy had occupied a quantitatively minor place in his production up to then, although the excellence of such a work as *A Bitter Fate* made the qualitative significance of his dramatic writing relatively great. But in the mid-1860's he began writing much more extensively for the theater, and continued to do so for over ten years. Though his later plays cannot lay claim to the stature of *A Bitter Fate*, they have some value from the literary point of view. His plays of the 1860's may be divided into three categories. First are tales of unnatural sexual passion intended to be highly dramatic: *Byvye sokoly* (Former Falcons) and its sequel *Ptentsy poslednego sleta* (Fledglings of the Last Flight). In the second category appears a single play, *Boytsy i vyzhidateli* (Warriors and Temporizers), dealing with social problems. Finally, three

dramas are drawn from the Russian past: *Samoupravtsy* (The Unbridled Ones), *Poruchik Gladkov* (Lieutenant Gladkov), and *Miloslavskie i Naryshkiny* (Miloslavskys and Naryshkins).

Former Falcons was probably the first play begun by Pisemsky
after leaving *Russky vestnik*. He apparently began work on it in the
summer of 1864, for in a letter of November 19, 1864, he invited
Ostrovsky to attend a reading of his "new drama," by which he
seems to have meant *Former Falcons*.[30] Of his later plays, this one
lays the greatest claim to dramatic depth, and should probably be
ranked as the best dramatic work of that period.

The play's central situation is an incestuous relationship between
father and daughter, a fact that links it to Shelley's *The Cenci*,
where a tyrannical father is murdered by his children in retaliation
for having raped his own daughter. Though in both plays sexual
relations occur between father and daughter, in Shelley's work the
driving emotion is hatred on the part of both father and daughter,
whereas in Pisemsky's a perverted love seems to lie at the basis of
the bond. In *Fledglings of the Last Flight,* the sequel to *Former
Falcons,* it is stated that the entire fault lay with the father, who
possessed his daughter by force, almost killing a man who tried to
stop him and exiling all those who had witnessed his crime (VIII,
591). But this explanation seems to be a later interpolation and is
difficult to reconcile with certain scenes in the first play (for example, Scene 6 of Act II), in which love, however misdirected,
appears to have been responsible for the situation.

Because of its daring theme, *Former Falcons* could not possibly
have been published or staged in the 1860's. In the first version of
the play the father, Evgraf Osipych Bakreev, is a religious hypocrite,
who spends much time in prayer but is not at all averse to fleecing
his fellow man when the opportunity occurs. Bakreev has two daughters, Vera and Sofya, and one son, Boris, by his late wife. Vera, a
saintly girl, has become entangled in incest with her father. Though
it is never stated explicitly that incest has occurred, there are clear
pointers to the truth throughout the play, especially in the reference
to Lot and his daughters during the climactic scene between Boris
and Vera (VIII, 324-325). Here Boris violently accuses his sister
of the same sin; although she does not admit it in so many words,
she in effect confesses and indirectly tells her brother that a child
has been born of the liaison. The child is taken care of by Sofya's
fiancé Sashansky, who agrees to claim it as his own illegitimate offspring, so that Vera may retire to a nunnery, assured that her
child will be provided for. The play ends with a melodramatic scene

between Vera and the child next to the corpse of the elder Bakreev, who has been murdered by a serf whom he mistreated.

The main interest in *Former Falcons* lies in the gradual intensification of Boris' horror as he arrives at full consciousness of what has taken place between Vera and her father. Vera is convincingly portrayed as a truly holy woman, suffering intense mental anguish at the thought of her heinous sin; Bakreev is shown as a repulsive hypocrite, a despot who camouflages his cruelty with fraudulent religiosity but nevertheless experiences a few pangs of remorse over what he has done to his daughter. But if Boris is finally convinced of what has occurred, the reader may remain incredulous, unable to envision an incestuous link between a morally repulsive father and a daughter with a highly developed religious sense. The entire play suffers from this crucial incongruity.

Pisemsky was fully aware that this first version of *Former Falcons* would never receive the censor's approval, and he therefore wrote a markedly weaker redaction of it. In the second version the theme of incest is eliminated altogether: the father of the child is Ivan Fortunatov, a serf of Bakreev's who does not even figure in the original version. The nub of the intrigue becomes an illicit affair between Vera and Fortunatov, whose social status is far below hers. Boris' horror grows as he gradually realizes that his sister has taken a serf as a lover and borne him a child. But this horror, understandable in the first version as a response to incest, appears overdone in the second variant, where only an affair with a serf is involved. Moreover, in the second version the entire situation is lent an aura of moral legitimacy, for in the seventh scene of Act IV Vera informs her brother that she and Fortunatov had been secretly married. Also, Fortunatov had been accused of purloining a sum of money, but Vera clears his name in this regard as well, explaining that she had taken the money "as a dowry in place of the serfs whom I could no longer own after my marriage." In the second version the motif of religious hypocrisy is de-emphasized, as is the theme of the elder Bakreev's absorbing hatred for those around him. The final scene between Vera and the child beside the corpse of Bakreev is the same in both variants.

Pisemsky must have submitted this second version to the censorship, rather than the first. One of the censors was much against it, feeling that it was "unnecessary to revive among the people [the memory of] the abuses of gentry and paternal authority and instruct it only about the darker aspects of the gentry milieu." However, another censor approved, regarding the play as almost an historical drama. The censorship council as a whole sided with the second censor, requiring the author to delete only a few details.[31] This variant of the play was then published in *Vsemirny trud* (World Labor) for September 1868. At the time of publication it aroused no comment, although one may surmise that Annenkov did not care for it, since he wrote to Turgenev several years later, in 1874: "Pisemsky tells me that his new tragedy (!) [*Prosveshchennoe vremya*—An Enlightened Time] has been forbidden for the stage. I can imagine what it is like. He has already put together a tragedy out of fornication between father and daughter, between brother and sister [*Fledglings of the Last Flight*]; now it is probably a matter of fornication between sister and sister, father and son, daughter and mother or something of the sort."[32] Although these remarks refer to the first, unpublished version of the play, it is likely that Annenkov did not approve of the published variant either.

The sequel to the play, entitled *Fledglings of the Last Flight*, was first published posthumously in the 1883-1886 edition of Pisemsky's work. This delay was understandable, since it was a continuation of the first version of *Former Falcons*, not the second version; as long as the earlier play could not appear in its original form, there was no point in trying to print a sequel to it. Pisemsky probably worked on the plays more or less simultaneously, for he reported to Kraevsky in April 1865 that he had two tragedies ready to read in St. Petersburg.[33]

Fledglings of the Last Flight is unquestionably inferior to *Former Falcons*. The action takes place about twenty years after the close of the first play. The child of the incestuous union, named Mishel Krapivkin, has grown up into a hot-headed, strong-willed young man, rather like Anany Yakovlev in *A Bitter Fate*, but without his redeeming traits. Krapivkin is in love with Masha Sashanskaya, the sixteen-year-old daughter of Sashansky and Sofya Evgrafovna. In the course of the play Krapivkin discovers the truth about his parentage and realizes that he is both uncle and first cousin to the woman he loves and who is now carrying his child. The incestuous nature of the relationship bothers him less, however, than the knowledge that under the circumstances the authorities will never permit them to marry. When Sofya Evgrafovna learns of her daughter's pregnancy and attempts to discipline her, Mishel murders Sofya and then shoots both Masha and himself before the law can intervene. In the play's finale the deranged Vera Evgrafovna, now a nun with the name Angelika, visits the scene of the slayings, while the actor Erast Bogomolov pronounces speeches containing references to *Lear, Hamlet,* and *Macbeth,* and concludes with an appeal to the audience: "Gentlemen, before the grandeur of death there is no place for wrath, or love, or maledictions or benedictions: there is only prayer . . . Let us pray!" (VIII, 597). The finale, with its murders, suicides, insane nuns, and babbling actors, represents an abortive attempt by Pisemsky to achieve a sense of high tragedy springing inevitably from the original incestuous relationship between Bakreev and his daughter. This is a prime instance of his attempting to attain something greater than his powers would permit.

The play *Warriors and Temporizers* stands alone in Pisemsky's dramaturgy of the 1860's as a forerunner of his social plays of the 1870's. Apparently written in 1864, along with *Former Falcons,* it was stopped by the censorship because it dealt in an unflattering way with the higher bureaucratic spheres. Although it did not appear in its entirety until the posthumous edition of 1883-1886, A. P. Mogilyansky has recently called attention to the fact that the second act was printed separately in 1868 in the newspaper *Antrakt* (Entr'-acte).[34] This partial publication evidently passed unnoticed.

Mogilyansky, with some justification, sees in *Warriors and Temporizers* an early version of *Khishchniki* (The Plunderers, first published as *Podkopy* [Mines]), a play written in 1872 that caused its author serious difficulties with the censorship because of its attack against the morality of Russian officialdom. The most nearly positive hero of *Warriors and Temporizers* is Yakov Petrovich Obolonsky, whose sense of honor impels him to expose the misdeeds of his bureaucratic patron, Count Poltashev, in Herzen's émigré periodical *Kolokol.* It is probably not entirely coincidental that Obolonsky's first name is the same as Kalinovich's in *One Thousand Souls,* who was also guilty of personal disloyalty. After exposing the count, Obolonsky emigrates abroad, taking with him the count's beautiful daughter, who, like Nastenka, is completely devoted to him. Another important plot element, and the one linking it most intimately to *The Plunderers,* concerns the bureaucratic intrigues leading to the count's removal from high position and his replacement by yet another protégé whom he had considered loyal. In spite of the fact that the count has done many dishonorable things in the course of his career, the reader comes to feel a sympathy for him, since from the count's point of view he has been shabbily rewarded in return for years of service. As he complains bitterly to the young man replacing him, "when you have served for a long time and think that you have made yourself to a certain extent indispensable by your labors, just at that point you will be thrown out like a worthless chip and your place taken by some nonentity'' (VIII, 672).

In the course of the mid-1860's, while attempting to create tragedy, Pisemsky also entered a well-defined phase of historical play-writing. In this he was actually moving with the times. Ostrovsky had long since been using historical subjects for some of his plays, and in the latter half of the 1860's Aleksey Tolstoy was engaged in writing his great dramatic trilogy set in the period preceding the Time of Troubles in Russia at the beginning of the seventeenth century. Though Pisemsky was surely influenced by this general interest, he probably had a more personal motivation for choosing topics from times past, in his wish to avoid both the recriminations of the radical critics and the cavils of the censorship. The publication of *Troubled Seas* had vividly demonstrated the danger of stirring up political passions by writing on strictly contemporary subjects. The first indications of Pisemsky's change in approach were detectible as early as March 1862, just after the appearance of *Fathers and Sons* but long before the publication of *Troubled Seas*. The time had come, he wrote to Turgenev, ''for all of us—you and me and Ostrovsky and Goncharov—to look back and write historical things, though of course not looking so far back as Ostrovsky in his *Minin* [*Kozma Zakharich Minin-Sukhoruk*, set at the beginning of the seventeenth century], for if you do, probably about the only things you will hear will be the clang of bells and 'Lord have mercy upon us.' No, we should write about the time we have lived through ourselves— granted, what you get from this will not be fashionable, but to make up for that things will come out more deeply understood, more truthfully thought through, as well as, I must say, more needful for history.''[35] Pisemsky followed this prescription only partially, for his own historical plays were set in the late seventeenth or eighteenth centuries, although his novel *Men of the 1840's* pictured more recent times. He was correct in assuming that the radical critics would leave his historical plays in peace—but then so did almost all the other critics as well. And any hopes he may have cherished for more lenient treatment from the censors proved to be groundless.

The three plays that make up Pisemsky's historical cycle—*The Unbridled Ones, Lieutenant Gladkov,* and *Miloslavkys and Naryshkins*—have received very different evaluations from the critics. S. A. Vengerov, who held that there was nothing interesting in the first two except the author's signature, represents the extreme anti-

Pisemskian camp.[36] A much more perceptive analyst is D. S. Mirsky, who has written that Pisemsky's historical plays are "tantalizing" works which "have a strange fascination and, if revived on the stage, should prove extraordinarily effective."[37] One may easily concur with Mirsky: if Pisemsky's plays were given a starkly modern, unrealistic staging, they might be revealed as much greater creations than they have seemed up to now.

The initial play of the series, *The Unbridled Ones*, was finished by early November 1865, for it was first mentioned in a letter of November 10 to Annenkov, in which Pisemsky announced that he had temporarily rechristened it *Ekaterininskie orly* (Catherine's Eagles) and submitted it to both the censor and the Academy of Sciences for consideration for an Uvarov prize.[38] Mindful that those responsible for awarding the Uvarov prizes had originally given *A Bitter Fate* to critics generally unsympathetic to his work, Pisemsky made so bold as to suggest privately to the permanent secretary of the academy that the first reading of his play be entrusted to individuals favorably inclined toward him, namely, Annenkov and one other.[39] Possibly the secretary considered this suggestion improper; in any event, Nikitenko rather than Annenkov took responsibility for the preliminary inspection and reported his findings to the Academy on March 10, 1866. Nikitenko disapproved of the play, largely on the grounds that Pisemsky had gone too far in the direction of naturalism, defined by the critic as "blind adherence to facts in scholarship and in art."[40] Nikitenko's report was revised and published as a critical article in 1866, even before the play appeared in the February 1867 issue of *Vsemirny trud*.[41]

The Unbridled Ones reads like an eighteenth-century Russian morality play. It is set in an era when the great Russian nobles possessed absolute power of life and death over their serfs and even over the members of their own families. The central character, Prince Platon Ilarionovich Imshin, an elderly nobleman addicted to reading the Holy Scriptures, is married to a young and beautiful woman of whom he is insanely jealous. He realizes that she might be justified in betraying him in view of the difference in their ages and the fact that she had been compelled to marry him against her wishes. Indeed, Prince Platon soon discovers that his wife is having an affair with an officer named Rykov, and that the two lovers scornfully refer to him between themselves as an "old bear." The enraged prince imprisons Rykov on his own authority and then has him sewn up in a bear skin and paraded around, forcing his wife to kiss the bear. Such actions were not unthinkable for the landowning nobility of the eighteenth century. At the end of the play Rykov gains the upper hand over the prince but shows mercy to his enemy instead of wreaking revenge. The prince is so deeply moved by this that he decides to yield his wife to Rykov, and the play concludes with everyone falling on the prince's neck and blessing him as a benefactor.

This summary of the plot indicates the primitivism of the play's psychology. It is this quality that allies it to the morality play. Events and actions are interpreted in terms of abstract and fairly simple standards of good and evil, with a final abrupt transition from evil to good that in real life would be extremely improbable. If the play is judged in its own, nonrealistic terms—as a morality play —it is successful; but if mistakenly evaluated by the criteria of realism that must be applied to the bulk of Pisemsky's work, it would appear to be a failure. Nikitenko fell into precisely this error. He complained that the characters simply did nasty things to one another and nothing more. He commented in particular that, though Pisemsky had evidently attached particular importance to the scene in which Rykov is paraded around in the bearskin, this episode struck him as merely comic and devoid of deeper meaning.[42] In fact, however, this scene is very powerful, since all the prince's spurned love, wounded pride, and arrogant rage are focused in it, as well as the lovers' helplessness before the power of the irate husband. According to the author, in fact, when the scene was played in a Moscow theater, "everybody expected at this moment a laughable and scandalous thing, but instead a genuine tragic impression emerged."[43]

The second play in Pisemsky's historical series, *Lieutenant Gladkov,* was also published in *Vsemirny trud,* in March 1867. The play is set in the Russia of 1740-1741, a time of palace revolutions organized primarily by Germans vying for control of Russia after the death of the Empress Anna Ioannovna, a situation that was ultimately resolved by the Empress Elizabeth's ascension to the throne in 1741. Pisemsky engaged in extensive research on this inglorious epoch of Russian history and equipped the play with both a short historical foreword—in which he said the play encompassed the period from Peter's death in 1725 to Elizabeth's accession, although the action occurs only in 1740-1741—and copious notes referring to scholarly articles. The presence of this apparatus gives it an external resemblance to the articles upon which much of it was based.

The plot involves a young Lieutenant Gladkov, who is entirely devoted to the cause of elevating princess Anna Leopoldovna to the throne because he hopes that thereafter he will obtain supreme power, as some before him have done, by becoming the Empress' favorite. Although he remains loyal to this objective, he betrays everybody else in his path, including his father, who as a result is sentenced to life imprisonment, and his wife, whom he has married simply because she is a maid-in-waiting to Anna Leopoldovna. Anna Leopoldovna does in fact obtain power briefly, from late 1740 to late 1741, but she rewards Gladkov miserably, with a promotion merely to the rank of captain. When she is overthrown, Gladkov is killed by Saltykov, whose uncle he had betrayed in the course of his intriguings. As the play concludes, the soldiers who have participated in the latest coup d'état hasten to welcome the new Empress, Elizaveta Petrovna.

While composing *Lieutenant Gladkov* during 1866, Pisemsky sought Annenkov's advice. Annenkov made a few suggestions for revision but thought that even as it stood in unreworked form it made "enchanting reading" because of the author's skill in compressing into a small compass the essence of a considerable historical period. He expressed confidence that Pisemsky could shepherd the work through the censorship if he fought for it.[44] Nikitenko also found the play acceptable, "cleaner" than Pisemsky's other plays.[45] On the other hand, Turgenev, who ordinarily encouraged Pisemsky, violently disliked *Lieutenant Gladkov*. The play, he wrote to Annenkov after hearing Pisemsky's reading, was "absurd nonsense." Why had Pisemsky taken it into his head to dabble in history? Only the first act was even bearable, he thought.[46]

Although it was useful to have the opinions of private critics, the reaction of the censorship was more immediately significant. As usual, the censors were recalcitrant. Though the play was approved for publication easily enough, staging was another matter. The majority of the censors considered it unwise to remind the public of the ease with which coups d'état were arranged in the eighteenth century and the enormous power wielded in those days by the female sovereign's favorites. Pisemsky's advocate on the censorship committee, Goncharov, argued that matters had been satisfactorily resolved in the end and that the history of the period had already been described in minute detail in novels and historical articles. But since a play presented upon the stage may produce a much greater sensation than a discussion on the same topic buried in a scholarly journal, or even the published text of the play, Valuev, the Minister of the Interior, sided with the majority of the censors in forbidding its staging.[47]

After the announcement of this decision, Pisemsky adopted the expedient of appealing directly to Valuev to reverse his decision. There was nothing in the play, he wrote, which could be interpreted as tendentious or applicable to the present time. All he had striven for was historical accuracy. "Concealing its history from the people I consider to do more harm than good," Pisemsky maintained, adding that for the purpose of acquainting the general public with the facts of history the stage was more effective than schools or books.[48] Valuev was plainly uninterested in enlightening the public in this area, and the play was first performed only after the revolution of 1905, even though Pisemsky attempted once more to have the ban lifted in 1880, just before his death.[49]

The third of Pisemsky's historical plays, *Miloslavskys and Naryshkins,* delved even further into Russian history, back to the time of Peter the Great's accession to the throne. This totally unsuccessful drama can be read only with difficulty. Pisemsky himself recognized its weakness, and since in addition it treated a subject that was thoroughly covered in the history books, he never attempted to publish it.[50] It appeared in print for the first time in the posthumous edition of his works.

In the Bureaucracy

With the completion of *Miloslavskys and Naryshkins* Pisemsky temporarily ceased his production of plays. The fact that only one of his three latest plays had been staged may have disheartened him, and he did not return to the dramatic form until his anti-capitalist tracts of the 1870's. In the meantime he reverted to the novel, in one of those alternations between the drama and the novel that are so clearly observable in his work during the 1860's and 1870's.

Pisemsky's rupture with Katkov in 1864 had meant that he must either support himself entirely as a professional writer or else return to the civil service career he had abandoned upon joining the *Biblioteka dlya chteniya* staff. Not that his financial situation in the mid-1860's was desperate, for at some point before the middle of 1865 he constructed a spacious home in Moscow in Boris and Gleb Lane (Borisoglebsky pereulok) off Povarskaya Street. The Pisemskys' apartment, including the writer's study, was located in one wing of the house, and the rest of the building eventually contained at least four apartments, which they rented out. With the passage of time new wings were added, each of which, having been financed by monies received for a particular novel, bore the name of that novel. This wing, Pisemsky would tell visitors, is *Troubled Seas;* that one is *Men of the 1840's.*[51]

The income from renting the apartments in his Moscow home and from the sale of his novels, stories, and plays was apparently insufficient to support Pisemsky in the style he preferred, so that once again he sought civil service employment. When he learned that the post of Councillor in the Moscow Provincial Directory was available, he immediately began dispatching letters to high officials (including Valuev) who might assist him in obtaining it. After a considerable delay due to bureaucratic snarls, he was preliminarily granted the position in May of 1866. He derived little satisfaction from the success of his campaign, however, for as he wrote dispiritedly to Turgenev in the summer of 1866: "I am getting along . . . fairly well, not badly, although not very *highly:* to be a Councillor of the Provincial Directory at the age of 46 is no very great pleasure for one's self-esteem—I had the very same rank 15 years ago. But anyway I deserve this punishment: if I hadn't put my trust in Russian Literature but had stayed in the civil service instead, I wouldn't be such an unimportant individual."[52] Having no other option, Pisemsky made the best of a galling situation. He who had written so cuttingly about the bureaucratic mind now found himself awaiting a "complete uniform from the tailor, in which I shall appear before the shining eyes [of my bureaucratic superiors]."[53] Pisemsky served satisfactorily in his capacity as Councillor, and less than a year later, on February 21, 1867, Valuev confirmed his appointment to the position. About two years later, on December 25, 1868, he was promoted to the post of Senior Councillor of the Moscow Provincial Directory.[54] Concurrently he was granted a few small promotions in civil service rank: to Kollezhsky assessor (Collegiate Assessor) in June of 1866 and Nadvorny sovetnik (Court Councillor) in June of 1869.[55]

As the bureaucratic tasks to which Pisemsky was compelled to devote his time during this period afforded him little intellectual stimulation, he was always casting about for a more congenial position. In particular, he thought of becoming a censor, a post that he had earlier tried to obtain in the 1850's. In late May 1868 one of the Moscow censors resigned and Pisemsky applied for the position, writing to the head of the censorship department and also to his friend Annenkov, who acted as one of his chief St. Petersburg agents for several years after his move to Moscow.

In seeking employment as a censor, Pisemsky was clearly motivated in part by literary interests, since such a post would combine a steady income with an opportunity to supervise the literary production of the day. Some time before, in 1861, when he was asked his opinion on possible censorship reforms, Pisemsky had made several suggestions that were more radical than anything the government would presumably have allowed. He was of the opinion that translations of any books published in foreign languages should be tolerated, that people should be permitted to discuss all forms of government, that one should be able to expound any philosophical system he wished, and that satire should be given entirely free rein. The writer made these proposals because he was convinced that a contest among freely expressed opinions would in the long run be more healthy for Russian society than the muffled allusions that crept through the censorship, which actually aroused disproportionate curiosity among readers and could not be answered and rebutted clearly and effectively.[56] The attempt to impose an artificial harmony upon Russian intellectual life could only be pernicious, the novelist maintained. As he had written once to Valuev when he was seeking approval for the staging of *A Bitter Fate*, "the attempt to make of Literature a single smooth and level surface, covered merely with mutual admiration, can harm this very orientation [in literature], make it saccharine and inspire suspicions as to its sincerity."[57] Although under strain Pisemsky might depart from this view of the censorship (as when he suggested to Valuev in 1863 that the radicals be muzzled for a time), on the whole the adoption of his ideas would have been equivalent to the liquidation of the entire censorship system. The government had nothing so drastic in mind.

In view of these opinions, it is not surprising that Pisemsky was no more fortunate in obtaining a censorial post on this occasion than he had been before. Despite his protestations of loyalty to the regime and support for the existing state of things in Russia—and there is no reason to think that he was lying in his letters of application, though perhaps he was stretching the truth—his works up to that point had been extremely critical of Russian reality, and he must have enjoyed a reputation in official circles as a suspect writer. Moreover, the many occasions on which he had submitted a novel or play to the censorship in apparent confidence that it included nothing objectionable, only to see his work mutilated or forbidden altogether, demonstrate that his grasp of what was permissible from the official point of view was not very firm. As a result, those in charge of appointing censors would hardly have looked with favor upon his application.

Dull as his duties might be, Pisemsky appreciated the security of a fixed income from his civil service employment. His financial situation was further bolstered in late 1866 by an inheritance left to him by an aunt in Kostroma Province. Consequently, as he wrote to Annenkov at the time, "the material side of life is taken care of, although one cannot say the same for the spiritual side, and most of all for the literary particle in that side."[58]

Men of the 1840's

Pisemsky's relations with literary world were awkward at this point. His break with *Russky vestnik* had been so complete that apparently he could not publish there; *Biblioteka dlya chteniya* had failed in 1865; *Otechestvennye zapiski* was in the process of being taken over by the radicals; and the newly founded *Vestnik Europy* (Messenger of Europe) cherished its liberal sheen too highly to risk publishing the work of a writer with Pisemsky's reputation. Thus debarred from the principal literary journals, his entire published production for 1867 and 1868 had to appear in the obscure magazine with the "idiotic name," to use Pisemsky's phrase, *Vsemirny trud* or "World Labor." For a short while in late 1866 and early 1867 Pisemsky endeavored to persuade some of his friends, such as Ostrovsky and Almazov, to contribute to *Vsemirny trud*, but in the end even he did not remain faithful to it, for his first novel after *Troubled Seas* appeared elsewhere.

The work in question, *Men of the 1840's,* had been germinating in Pisemsky's mind since as early as 1851. It is in part an historical novel—although it might more accurately be termed a novel of reminiscence—which links it to Pisemsky's three historical plays of the 1860's. The book marked a transitional stage in his return from the more distant past of the plays to the full present of his fourth novel, *V vodovorote* (In the Whirlpool). Pisemsky first mentions *Men of the 1840's* during this period in a letter of July 12, 1868, to Almazov, in which he states that he will be reading his work to Kashpirev, the publisher of the forthcoming journal *Zarya* (The Dawn), in which it eventually appeared.[59] Pisemsky also sought advice from Annenkov while the book was in the process of composition.

By means of this new novel Pisemsky hoped to demonstrate that the generation of the 1840's in Russia had been somehow set apart and qualitatively much superior to the imitation thinkers who dominated intellectual life in the 1860's. As he phrased it in a letter to O. A. Novikova: "They say that from the very beginning old men have always praised themselves and scolded the younger generation, and in both cases, of course, unjustly; but it is hardly likely that this is so with regard to the Men of the 1840's: they were in fact better or at least more poetic than the young men of nowadays."[60] It is curious that the unpoetic Pisemsky should have equated goodness with poeticism. Some years later he remarked that his contemporaries of the 1840's had been concerned solely with aesthetic problems, to the exclusion of politics.[61] His novel was accordingly an attempt at evoking this era of a "more poetic" generation. In the same letter to Novikova, Pisemsky unleashed a tirade against the recent rise to prominence of newspapers, which in his opinion had befouled the journalistic scene. Newspapers had existed in Russia for some time, but their influence increased sharply in the mid-1860's. This gave Pisemsky yet another reason to rank the 1860's below the idealistic 1840's.

For all the "poeticism" of the group to which Pisemsky proudly proclaimed he had belonged, he himself exhibited considerable business acumen in selling *Men of the 1840's* to *Zarya*. *Zarya*, a quasi-Slavophile journal, began appearing in 1869 but lasted only until 1872. Pisemsky's friend Apollon Maykov was associated with it, as was Dostoevsky's colleague and confidant, the critic N. N. Strakhov. Though he was not a Slavophile, Pisemsky must have looked upon those planning to issue the journal as largely sharing his literary opinions. During an excursion to St. Petersburg, probably in late November 1868, Pisemsky gave a reading of the novel for the *Zarya* editorial board, which had already purchased it for the princely sum of 12,000 rubles and began printing it long before its completion in July 1869. Acquiring the novel at this price turned out to be a sad miscalculation on Kashpirev's part, for the work was very extensive and not terribly good.[62] *Zarya* nearly strangled itself in its own cradle by paying an exorbitant sum for quantity that lacked quality. To make matters worse, Pisemsky visited St. Petersburg frequently around the time of publication to ensure receipt of the installments due him.[63]

Strakhov first met Pisemsky at the time of his negotiations with the *Zarya* editorial board. The critic's initial reaction to the novel was somewhat adverse: "It is written with all Pisemsky's virtues and shortcomings. As a whole it is weak in its idea and in its execution, but in parts it is excellent and entertaining."[64] As time passed and the pernicious effect of the novel's publication on *Zarya*'s financial situation became clear, Strakhov came to dislike Pisemsky intensely. In a letter to Dostoevsky he called him a "swine," whom he would be happy to "bless out" at the first opportunity, and the "least likable of our writers."[65]

By 1869 Dostoevsky himself ranked Pisemsky quite high, despite Strakhov's sentiments and his own distaste for *One Thousand Souls* at the time of its publication. As far back as 1864 Dostoevsky had called Pisemsky a "colossal literary name."[66] By early 1869 in letters to Strakhov he was drawing comparisons between Goncharov, Turgenev, and Pisemsky, just as Pisarev had done in 1861, and arriving at roughly similar conclusions. Goncharov's *The Precipice* was "worthless," he said, as was a story of Turgenev's currently being published. That left Pisemsky's *Men of the 1840's* as the best of the three current literary offerings: "Judging by the first part of Pisemsky I conclude that there can only be very talented items in the remaining parts as well."[67]

Men of the 1840's, which came out in nine extensive installments from January through September 1869, contains a larger number of autobiographical elements than was usual for Pisemsky's novels and stories. The hero, Pavel Vikhrov, is in part based on the author. The novel is almost picaresque in character, to the extent that the story line could be cut off at nearly any point. Indeed, Pisemsky availed himself of this characteristic when the work began to grow too bulky (it is the longest of his novels): to end it, he telescoped the chronology drastically, a feeble device that he had used before. This technical shortcoming was necessitated by his continuing failure to plan his novels in advance, so as to preserve a reasonable proportion among their segments.

This novel in five parts begins with a description of the hero's childhood in the 1830's and concludes with the reforms of the 1860's, although the main concentration is upon the decade of the 1840's. In the final chapter the characters organize a feast and toast themselves for having somehow prepared the soil for the great reforms of the 1860's. One of Pisemsky's primary purposes was to demonstrate that his characters were correct in taking credit for this achievement. In the execution of this purpose, however, he proved weak.

Men of the 1840's opens with an idyllic depiction of Vikhrov's childhood. As he grows a little older, he conceives a passionate interest in the theater, reminiscent of Pisemsky's. As a student of mathematics, Vikhrov then enters Pisemsky's alma mater, Moscow University, where he does little more work than had his creator before him. After he graduates from the university, his father dies and he receives his inheritance, enabling him to write in privacy at his estate. He acquires a reputation in St. Petersburg literary circles through these efforts. During the intellectual repressions of 1848, however, Vikhrov is called to account for one of his stories and exiled to the provinces, where he is fortunate enough to obtain a civil service position under the local governor. He is, in fact, assigned responsible tasks, such as the investigation of murders and the suppression of the Old Believers. At one point he is forced to dismantle an Old Believer chapel almost entirely by himself, because the men under his command refuse to assist this religious persecution.[68] Vikhrov is on the point of encountering difficulties with the governor as the result of a denunciation accusing him of misusing the powers of his office, when the news of Czar Nicholas' death arrives; he is permitted to return home and later moves to St. Petersburg, where he spends most of his time tending to affairs of the heart and congratulating himself on the reforms of the 1860's.

Although the resemblances between Vikhrov's life and Pisemsky's are plain, even from this brief synopsis, the story of Vikhrov's adventures is primarily not an autobiography but a framework upon which to hang love intrigues. There are four main feminine characters. The most important is Mari Eysmond, married to General Eysmond and mother of one son, who indulges in an extended affair with Vikhrov, which is left unresolved at the conclusion. Vikhrov wants her to abandon her husband, but since the latter is both attractive and a military hero of the Crimean War, Mari cannot easily bring herself to take that step. A second love is Fateeva, who betrays her husband in order to commence a liaison with Vikhrov. When he rejects her, she cultivates other admirers but at heart continues to love him. A third woman, Yuliya Zakharevskaya, falls hopelessly in love with Vikhrov during the period of his provincial exile; later she is converted into a nihilist. Finally, there is Vikhrov's female serf Grunya, who attends him as both servant and mistress. Pavel becomes so involved with her that Pisemsky, at a loss to eliminate this complication, resorts to the improbable expedient of killing her accidentally when she and another peasant are playing with a gun. Of all these affairs the one between Pavel and Mari is the most serious and the most enduring.

The young man at the heart of this chronicle, though he may in some ways have been "typical" of his generation, was clearly not representative of its best intellectual and ideological traditions. To be sure, he engages in an extended conversation on Shakespeare with a colleague, discusses Victor Hugo and Balzac, attacks the inflated reputation of the now forgotten Russian playwright Nestor Kukolnik, and practically lectures on Homer to his paramour Fateeva, but most of his literary opinions, like his ruminations on contemporary society, are not especially enlightening, and in the final accounting the novel could get along handily without such interpolations. Like *Troubled Seas, Men of the 1840's* was projected as a vast historical canvas delineating the major currents of a complex and extended epoch, but Pisemsky lacked the ability to see such a project through to satisfactory fruition. His talent was not of the epic brand. The task of capturing the essence of such a decade as the 1840's in a novel would have taxed the powers of a Tolstoy, not to speak of a Pisemsky.

Men of the 1840's went surprisingly unnoticed for a novel of such length by an established author, especially a novel that the brilliant thinker Konstantin Leontev termed a "wholesome work" and recommended to a friend as an antidote to Dostoevsky.[69] One radical critic seized upon it as an excuse to publish an extended polemic on the subject of women's rights, drawing on the various heroines in Pisemsky's most recent novels as examples, and concluding that Pisemsky, the "humane defender of women's rights," actually favored doing nothing to ease woman's lot.[70] A more serious review[71] was contributed by the leftist critic N. V. Shelgunov, successor to the exiled Chernyshevsky, to both Dobrolyubov and Pisarev, who had died, and to Antonovich, by then a renegade. *Troubled Seas* had made it clear, Shelgunov claimed, that Pisemsky was incapable of rising above details and "trivialities" even when striving to encompass the higher intellectual spheres. His genuine contribution to literature—one that by then lay far in the past—had consisted in his "destruction of pseudo-literature about the common people." As for his later work, a novel like *Men of the 1840's* gave the reader not the vaguest notion of that fabled era. How was Vikhrov's career at Moscow University, say, representative of a student's path at the university which sheltered such giants as the historian Timofey Granovsky? Shelgunov proclaimed the novel a pathological product of the author's egotism and a "libel, which fails to be insulting merely because of its utter insignificance." He denied that Pisemsky was wholly a man of the 1840's: the Pisemsky who wrote "The Carpenters' Guild" truly belonged to that generation, but the author of *Troubled Seas* most certainly did not. Finally, Shelgunov lumped Pisemsky together with his old associates, Turgenev and Goncharov, as authors who had outlived their day.

The publication of *Men of the 1840's* brought to an end the most important period during which Pisemsky sought literary inspiration in the past, although in his last novel, *Masony* (The Masons), he would revert to this approach. By the end of the decade he had regained enough confidence to set his novels and plays in contemporary times once more. But the fact remained that the writer who had wanted to be a chronicler of his age in fiction had by that time been cast aside. Virtually ignored by the critics, compelled to publish for the most part in obscure newspapers and journals, he had been relegated to oblivion even while still alive.

V

Decline and Extinction

The decade of the 1870's, particularly the last half, was a period of decline, leading into the moribund 1880's, when Russian literature would devote itself principally to themes of physical, mental, and spiritual illness. To be sure, the early part of the 1870's witnessed a great deal of activity. Young radicals formed circles for discussion and action on the dominant idea of the time, populism, which held that salvation for Russia would come from the unspoiled peasantry, that they alone would supply the revolutionary force of which Russia stood in need. This notion spawned the remarkable "movement to the people" of the late 1860's and early 1870's, when young revolutionaries from the cities attempted to mix with the common people in the rural areas in order to incite them to action. In the short run, the "movement to the people" was a fiasco, for the peasants regarded their uninvited guests with suspicion and proved unreceptive to their ideas. While the radicals were attempting to incite mass political upheaval, they also continued their strategy of individual terrorism, for it seemed that if enough of them were willing to sacrifice their lives by this means, a few would almost surely penetrate the protective cordons about high government officials. Indeed, the populist revolutionary Sergey Stepniak-Kravchinsky was able to stab the chief of the St. Petersburg police on the street in broad daylight and then escape abroad. The supreme achievement of the terrorist movement was the assassination of Czar Alexander II in the middle of St. Petersburg in 1881.

Literary and intellectual life of the 1870's was more settled than the political situation. In fact, in certain areas it was so settled as to be stagnant. It is true that Dostoevsky published some of his greatest novels during the decade, primarily *The Possessed* (1871-1872), with its sweeping attack upon the radicals of the 1860's, and *The Brothers Karamazov* (1880). But this represented a final burst of creative energy before the end, for Dostoevsky died in early 1881. Turgenev continued to live abroad during the decade, harassed by melancholy and physical disability before his death in 1883. Although several years remained to Goncharov, he had practically ceased to write since the appearance of his novel *The Precipice* in 1869, and during the 1870's he became mentally unbalanced. Leskov was still working under the political cloud cast by his antinihilist novel *No Way Out* of 1864, though his achievements were beginning to be recognized. The old-line radicals remaining from the 1840's were also on the way out, leaving behind no worthy heirs. Nekrasov died a lingering, agonizing death in 1877. Herzen, the voice of honest radicalism in emigration whom Pisemsky admired almost in spite of himself, had died in 1870. Saltykov-Shchedrin was still active, writing his most important novel, *The Golovlovs*, in 1875-1876 for the most part, but his masterpiece was a tour de force of unrelieved gloom, as befitted the era. Aside from Dotoevsky, almost the only major author writing with vigor at the time was Lev Tolstoy, who published *War and Peace* in 1869 and *Anna Karenina* in 1877. But even *Anna Karenina* ends in a suicide, something that would have been unthinkable in the ultimately life-affirming *War and Peace*, and Tolstoy himself was approaching a spiritual crisis. It seemed to Pisemsky at the time that the only people who were really flourishing in the latter part of the decade were philistines, financial speculators, and entrepreneurs, who were incapable of appreciating the cultural treasures of the past and unable to create anything of worth themselves. Russia's intellectual powers had been sapped.

The 1870's were a time of depression for Pisemsky personally as well as for Russian society as a whole. In the autumn of his life he might have hoped to be respected as a representative of proud currents in the history of recent Russian literature. Instead his work was ignored by the public press, and he was surrounded by such indifference that he might actually have preferred to be the object of polemics. His health failed gradually; the tragic fates of his sons affected his morale terribly; and his hypochondria, with more to feed on now, became intensified. Though he published a fair amount in these years, he wrote with little enthusiasm: as he informed a correspondent in 1870, he found it hard to produce, "not because of various literary disgraces, but simply because a dim flame is burning within me myself."[1]

For some time after the appearance of *Men of the 1840's* Pisemsky labored over his next novel, *In the Whirlpool*, published in monthly installments in the obscure journal *Beseda* (Discourse) from January through June 1871. As there remain fewer than fifteen rather uninformative letters dating from 1870, the year of the novel's gestation, nothing is known about the stages of the book's creation and the author's feelings toward it.

In the Whirlpool reverts to the subject matter of *Troubled Seas* in dealing with nihilism, but it is not easily classified as either an antinihilist or a "nihilist" novel (one of the number of books published by radical authors for the purpose of publicizing their views on politics and society). The reader easily comprehends Pisemsky's viewpoint in *Troubled Seas*, for the nihilists shown there are little more than juvenile delinquents striving to shock decent people by their outrageous behavior. But the situation is not so clearly defined in *In the Whirlpool*, whose very title suggests helplessness in the face of uncontrollable passions or events. The novel contains three heroes, all of whom are more or less positive characters despite the fact that ideologically they are poles apart. The main heroine, a girl named Elena Zhiglinskaya, partially of Polish extraction, is a totally dedicated philosophical and political radical. She has met and fallen in love with Prince Grigorov, a nobleman who would like to tear himself from his class but who in the end is destroyed by his inability either to detach himself completely from his aristocratic background or to abandon the nihilist beliefs he has adopted. Grigorov and Elena become involved in an extended affair in spite of the prince's marriage to a woman who upholds the standards of the traditional morality and remains true to her marriage vows even after it appears that her husband has deserted her. Thus, the prince is trapped between two honorable women with diametrically opposed philosophical commitments: when he is unable to choose between them, he commits suicide, as he had early in the story threatened to do if Elena should ever reject him. Elena later dies following the moral shock of the prince's suicide.

One of Pisemsky's chief aims in writing *In the Whirlpool* was to demonstrate the way in which idealistic but frail human beings may be betrayed by their own emotions and deceived by the unscrupulous schemes of others. In the abstract their ideals may seem elevated and honest, but they are distorted in an application to real life, causing pain and grief to those who hold them. A clear example is Elena's anguish over the sufferings of her people, the Poles, under the Russian yoke. The final break between Grigorov and Elena occurs partly because the prince cannot altogether abandon his wife, but also because, having once been bilked by Polish revolutionaries, he declines to donate any more money to their cause. His refusal makes Elena so furious that she leaves him. She herself is then defrauded by a scoundrel posing as a representative of Polish revolutionaries, who relieves her of all her money. The Polish cause may have been righteous, but this rectitude did not prevent unprincipled blackguards from attaching themselves to it. To give another example of the conflict between theory and reality, after Grigorov takes Elena as his mistress, he ruminates that it would be only just for his wife to cultivate a lover, but when she pretends to do precisely this, he experiences an unexpected jealousy. By his rationalistic lights he should have welcomed his wife's dalliance, but emotional attachments prove stronger than "reason" or "theory."

Such an outcome was clearly in line with Pisemsky's respect for "common sense" and his cynical view of reality, which gave short shrift to plainly unworkable theories. Indeed, the notion of "common sense" was at the core of Pisemsky's philosophy of life. He was too practical to trust abstract theories of the right or the good and felt that in concrete circumstances the genuinely wise man would instinctively choose the proper course of action. Common sense was most frequently to be found among the common people, unspoiled by excessive cerebration. For instance, at the end of "The Petersburger" the narrator, after listening to Klementy's tale, looks at his "expressive face" and reflects that "even in his very intellect there was something broad and sprawling, and in this wise consciousness of his own missteps he has displayed much common sense, which has kept him from final ruin and which will probably support him in the future as well" (I, 610). Pisemsky by no means thought that the peasantry was the sole repository of such practical wisdom, for *In the Whirlpool* offers as mouthpiece for the author's outlook the intellectual Miklakov. Miklakov is based partially on the author himself, being not only an alcoholic but also a former journalist and literary man who has been driven from the field. He thus continues the line of autobiographical images in Pisemsky's other novels. In spite of Miklakov's no-nonsense approach to life, however, it is he who pronounces a favorable judgment on the idealistic Elena in the book's last sentence. Elena, he thought, had been true to herself though it cost her her life: "[Miklakov] considered Elena to be the only woman out of all those he knew who had *spoken* and *acted* the way she *thought* and *felt!*'' (VII, 422). At the same time the author lauds Grigorova for her faithfulness to her husband under trying conditions; after his suicide she may remarry with a clear conscience because she has done all that could have been expected of her.

It is evident, then, that Pisemsky's attitude toward his characters in this novel is more ambiguous than usual, and this quality gives the work greater psychological interest than many of his other works. Another noteworthy feature of *In the Whirlpool* is its structural spareness. The relatively uncluttered plot line can be easily followed, and Pisemsky did not introduce so many subsidiary characters, who may in themselves be entertaining but at the same time overburden his novels. In sum, the simplicity of the plot, the author's reserve in pronouncing judgment on the characters, and the psychological complexity of their relationships work together to support the claim that *In the Whirlpool* was Pisemsky's most successful novel after *One Thousand Souls.* In fact, this opinion enjoyed some currency among Pisemsky's contemporaries. After reading the separate edition of 1872, Lev Tolstoy wrote to Pisemsky that the first parts, which he had originally seen in *Beseda,* ''delighted'' him, while the third part, which he earlier missed, had proved just as good.[2] Leskov approved of the novel even more vigorously. He wrote to Pisemsky that he considered it his best work for three reasons: ''In the first place, the characters are astounding in their truthfulness and the consistency of their development; in the second place, the sketching is artistic; in the third place, economy is observed with such strictness that the novel has emerged as quite an exemplary one.''[3]

Leskov's enthusiastic reaction to *In the Whirlpool* may be taken as an indication of the two writers' affinity. They had much in common, especially their ''Russianness'' and their interest in the peasantry and its language, each being a master of the language in his own way, Pisemsky more as a reproducer, Leskov as both reproducer and creator. To a lesser degree they shared a fascination with such people as the Old Believers. For a time Leskov regarded Pisemsky as his mentor. In a letter of 1872 to Pisemsky signed ''your servant and disciple N. Leskov,'' he confessed: ''I have always respected your great intellect and talent, I have learned a great deal from you and I am bound to you by genuine bonds of discipleship of the sort which existed, for example, among artists in those days when they studied in modest studios instead of unproductive academies.''[4] Pisemsky occasionally visited the Leskov household in St. Petersburg. At those times the Leskov children were kept out of his way, since it was understood that he did not particularly care for children.[5] A recent Soviet biographer of Leskov devotes several pages to a discussion of the personal and literary relations between Leskov and Pisemsky, pointing out an interesting though not fully convincing parallel between the plot of Leskov's minor masterpiece "Lady Macbeth of the Mtsensk District" and one of the sketches from Pisemsky's *Russian Liars*.[6] Certain comments Leskov made in his later years indicate that his enthusiasm for his former teacher eventually waned, but he always respected Pisemsky highly despite his weaknesses.

The Last Plays

Over the years immediately following the publication of *In the Whirlpool* Pisemsky generally ignored the novel form and engaged in his last period of playwriting. During this time he concentrated his literary fire upon the abuses of a burgeoning Russian capitalism, which he held responsible for nearly everything that he disliked in Russian life. He gave voice to his discontent in a series of plays that Annenkov, not necessarily in reproof, aptly described as "dramatic pamphlets."[7] They are *Khishchniki* (The Plunderers) and *Vaal* (Baal), published in 1873, *Prosveshchennoe vremya* (An Enlightened Time), in 1875, and *Finansovy geniy* (The Financial Genius), in 1876.

During most of the 1870's Pisemsky was obsessed with the idea of promoting social reform through literature, an aim he had ordinarily sneered at before. A memoirist has recorded that when Goncharov once rebuked Pisemsky for betraying the ideal of "pure art" for "social art," Pisemsky brooked no criticism on this score, calling the writing of his plays a "citizen's heroic feat" and maintaining that it was the writer's duty to "expose all exploiters, concessionaires, speculators and so forth." Furthermore, he contended that his literary masterpiece was *The Financial Genius*, a tendentious work now deservedly forgotten.[8] If this information is reliable, Pisemsky had undergone a marked transformation during these years. In any case, he cast himself into the struggle against that modern-day philistine, the capitalist, with such energy that he nearly effected a reconciliation between himself and the radicals. For example, in late 1874 his old friend Ostrovsky, whom Pisemsky had described five years before as "belonging to the enemy camp,"[9] put in a word with Nekrasov in hopes of getting Pisemsky to publish in *Otechestvennye zapiski,* the leading radical journal of the day. Ostrovsky urged Nekrasov to purchase *An Enlightened Time* for his journal. On December 1, 1874, Nekrasov sent Ostrovsky an evasive reply, confiding that he feared financial overcommitment by promising to accept the play, mentioning reports that it was not especially good, and asking Ostrovsky to delay writing to Pisemsky and to keep secret what Nekrasov had said about the play.[10] Ostrovsky, blithely ignoring these requests, immediately transmitted to Pisemsky the substance of Nekrasov's remarks. Ostrovsky appears to have misread Nekrasov's answer completely and to have interpreted it as an indication of willingness to accept the play.[11]

Despite all Ostrovsky's advocacy and Pisemsky's apparent readiness to have his work appear in a journal controlled by the radicals, *An Enlightened Time* eventually came out in the conservative *Russky vestnik.* This location is surprising in view of the fact that its tone has led one recent Soviet critic to suggest that *An Enlightened Time* and *Baal* should join *A Bitter Fate* and *The Hypochondriac* in the repertory of "classical" theater in the Soviet Union.[12] As a matter of fact, two of Pisemsky's four anticapitalist "pamphlets" were published in *Russky vestnik,* and a third appeared in the well-nigh reactionary *Grazhdanin* (The Citizen). It is not easy to understand why Pisemsky should have offered his plays to these periodicals, nor why they should have been accepted.

The first of Pisemsky's four tendentious plays, *The Plunderers*—initially published under the title *Podkopy* (Mines)—was probably written during the summer of 1872. On August 20, 1872, the author informed Leskov that it had not yet been "finally reworked" and that he could not hope to have it in ultimate shape for at least another month.[13] At the end of September Pisemsky took the completed text with him to St. Petersburg, where he read it to a group at the home of A. A. Kraevsky. Among those in attendance on this occasion was A. V. Nikitenko, who commented on the play in his diary. He unexpectedly called it Pisemsky's "best work," at the same time expressing well-founded doubts as to whether it would clear the censorship unscathed.[14] For his part, Pisemsky displayed his ordinary obtuseness about what the censorship would allow and apparently submitted *The Plunderers* to the censors with no more than general apprehension. The play had actually been printed for a special collection, *Sbornik Grazhdanina* (The Citizen's Miscellany), when the censorship abruptly stopped it at the last minute and ordered it removed from the volume.

The news of this action came as a total shock to Pisemsky, who wrote to Leskov at the time that he had not slept for forty-eight hours and was concerned over the further worsening of his health.[15] When it became obvious that friends in St. Petersburg could do nothing for the play, Pisemsky journeyed to the capital once more, at the beginning of December. There the Minister of the Interior informed him that *The Plunderers* might be passed if he aimed his shafts at significantly lower ranks in the bureaucracy; in the original version Pisemsky had directed his barbs against vice-ministers and even, by implication, against the Czar himself. Pisemsky also conferred with Mikhail Longinov, head of the Censorship Committee, but received even less encouragement. When Pisemsky, despairing, asked what he should otherwise write about, Longinov is reported to have advised him that "it is better not to write at all,"[16] counsel to which an author could hardly accede. Perceiving that major concessions would have to be made, Pisemsky reworked his comedy along the required lines and obtained permission for its publication in *Grazhdanin* in 1873. Strangely enough, after all these vicissitudes Pisemsky still hoped to see his play staged, but this was manifestly impossible at the time, and *The Plunderers* was first produced only after the revolution of 1905.

The Plunderers is a slight effort, of minor significance even within the corpus of Pisemsky's dramatic writing, not to mention the entire body of his work. The original title, *Mines,* hints at the play's central idea, that everyone is intriguing against everyone else, undermining each other, for financial benefit and from pride of place. Though people may appear outwardly honest, in reality most are frauds, seething with interior corruption. Since all the characters in the play have sinned, each one is potentially a subject for blackmail by any other character. The hero, Count Zyrov, is an influential bureaucrat who, after furthering the career of his protégé Andashevsky in attaining a high post, discovers that Andashevsky has been guilty of extorting considerable sums of money from stockholders. However, the count's own daughter prevents her father from initiating any action against Andashevsky, whom she has married in the meantime, through her knowledge of his own dubious transactions. Simultaneously she and Andashevsky are involved in intrigues designed to secure the count's removal from his post and his replacement with Andashevsky. Near the play's conclusion Andashevsky is led to believe that his machinations have been successful when Count Zyrov is indeed relieved of his post, but contrary to expectations, someone else is appointed to fill the vacancy, and his efforts avail him nothing.

The entire force of the play's attack is directed against what Pisemsky considered the despicable private intrigues to which bureaucrats devoted their time, instead of promoting the public welfare. His purpose was to expose the unlovely reality behind the facade of official legality. This was clearly the task of a pamphleteer, and in many ways the play does resemble a tract. The major characters, however, are not entirely flat caricatures, but have some flesh-and-blood attributes. For instance, the count, who seems to be the play's most positive hero, is morally far from blameless, since he has illegally appropriated most of his daughter's inheritance from her mother in order to support his mistresses. Even in this play Pisemsky was not attempting to oversimplify reality. Still in all, *The Plunderers* cannot be considered an artistic success because its social purpose intrudes too obviously.

Pisemsky's problems with the bureaucracy, which cavilled at seeing itself portrayed so acidly in *The Plunderers,* led him to adopt as the setting for subsequent tendentious plays the world of non-official high finance, rather than the sphere of counts, princes, and heads of government departments. The Russian capitalists of the 1870's boasted no censorship agency to enforce a positive view of themselves. In spite of this switch, Pisemsky never thoroughly comprehended the official censorial mind, or he would also have spared himself the pointless effort of sending *The Plunderers* to the Academy of Sciences to be considered for an Uvarov prize, which he had always yearned to win once again. But dispatch the play he did, along with a covering letter, dated March 16, 1873, to the permanent secretary of the academy, K. S. Veselovsky. In the meantime, presumably at the beginning of 1873, he had produced another play, *Baal,* published in the April 1873 issue of *Russky vestnik.* Pisemsky inquired of Nikitenko whether two plays might be submitted for an Uvarov prize in the same year. After investigation Nikitenko reported back that only one prize could be given for one play in any particular year but that he might send in two plays together and receive prizes for them in consecutive years, "which I hope with all my heart will happen." Nikitenko also wrote that he had heard of *Baal,* approved of its general orientation, and was certain that it would be a "service in our literature."[17] Encouraged by this reaction, Pisemsky sent in the second play as well. But when Nikitenko was entrusted with the task of reviewing Pisemsky's two plays officially, he proved less than enthusiastic about *The Plunderers.* He reported that, while it was "not devoid of dramatic interest," it did not deserve further detailed consideration. He then recommended

Baal very highly, speaking of its "remarkable merit." Thus it seemed for a time that Pisemsky might receive another Uvarov Prize.[18]

The two plays to reach the final stage of elimination were *Razorennoe gnezdo* (The Ruined Nest), submitted anonymously by the radical poet Dmitry Minaev, and *Baal*. On the last ballot, the first drama award made in ten years was given to *The Ruined Nest*. From hindsight one can probably say that neither play should have been granted a prize, but if a selection had to be made, *Baal* would today appear to have been the better choice.

Since it did not describe the official bureaucracy, *Baal* met with no objections from the censorship and was first staged as early as October 1873 in St. Petersburg. It is probably the best of Pisemsky's last group of plays. His approach to his subject may be determined from sources outside the text itself. As he wrote in a personal letter: "Nowadays everyone is worshipping Baal, that god of money and material betterment, which, like that Fate of the Greeks once upon a time, hovers over the world and foretells all ahead of time . . . Under his oppression people accomplish abominations and great deeds, suffer and triumph."[19] Though the title alone might have suggested that Pisemsky's approach would be one-sided and that the characters in the play would be exclusively positive or negative, happily this was not quite the case. The ambiguity of the author's position is plain even in the passage just cited, for under Baal's influence people accomplish, not just abominations, but "abominations and great deeds." In *Baal* Pisemsky continued to reveal his awareness that evil is often inextricably mixed with good. Good may result from a force that is at bottom evil.

As an aside, it might be remarked that Pisemsky did not entirely agree with the conventional definitions of evil. He selected for his play an epigraph from Jeremiah, seventh chapter, ninth verse, but not in its pristine form. In the King James version the passage reads: "Will ye steal, murder, and commit adultery, and swear falsely, and burn incense unto Baal." Pisemsky's version omits the words "and commit adultery." Apparently for him adultery was hardly as heinous as the other sins listed.

Of the play's main characters, none is so corrupt as to be totally without redeeming features, and none is so pure as to be able to avoid contamination altogether. The representative of the forces of darkness is Aleksandr Burgmeyer, a rich capitalist. Burgmeyer's wife, Kleopatra, has awakened the love of the play's positive hero, Vyacheslav Mirovich, who also occupies an official position that requires him to pass upon the acceptability of a piece of work contracted to Burgmeyer, which has been done shoddily. Realizing that he cannot bribe the honest Mirovich with money, the desperate Burgmeyer considers trying to corrupt him by offering him Kleopatra as mistress. Kleopatra, aghast at her husband's cynicism, leaves him of her own will and moves in with Mirovich. The latter, after a severe crisis of conscience, accepts Burgmeyer's contract because he has taken his wife; but subsequently he loses his position and is reduced to poverty. Mirovich's struggle for material survival places an intolerable strain on his relationship with Kleopatra, who accordingly returns to her husband, leaving Mirovich with neither honor nor mistress. In the play's closing monologue Mirovich addresses Baal in hyperbolic despair: "Receive, oh Baal, two new sacrifices! Torture, rend their hearts and souls, oh bloodthirsty god, in thy fiery claws! Soon all will be worshipping thee in this age without ideals, without expectations and hopes, in this age of copper rubles and counterfeit bills" (VIII, 395). Mirovich and Kleopatra have fallen victim to the universal lust for material enrichment. In *Baal* the theme of money madness, always prominent in Pisemsky's writing, assumes a dominant role, almost overpowering all other psychological motivations except that of physical passion, which is the root of Mirovich's downfall.

One contemporary reviewer of *Baal* compared it unfavorably to *A Bitter Fate,* saying that although "freedom of emotion" was the theme of both plays, there was a marked difference between the era of the 1850's and the period of the 1870's in Pisemsky's work. In the earlier era the dramatic situation revolved about an "excess of deep, pure emotion," whereas in the later period everything depended upon an "extreme poverty and paleness of emotion."[20] The reviewer's comment was valid in that one can hardly imagine the heroes in *Baal* committing murder for the sake of emotional attachments or from a sense of honor: their love is too enmeshed with financial considerations. On the other hand, not all contemporary critics agreed that *Baal* should be ranked below *A Bitter Fate.* The French critic Jules Lemaître held that although *A Bitter Fate* was markedly inferior to Ostrovsky's *The Storm* and Tolstoy's *The Power of Darkness, Baal* was a chef-d'oeuvre that could stand comparison even with Balzac's work.[21]

In 1874 the bulk of Pisemsky's production for the theater to date was collected in a two-volume edition, *Komedii, dramy i tragedii* (Comedies, Dramas, and Tragedies). It contained the definitive versions of all his plays of consequence with the single exception of

Former Falcons, presumably excluded by the author because the text he had been allowed to print diverged too far from his original conception.

The third of Pisemsky's four tendentious plays, *An Enlightened Time,* was composed in the fall of 1874 and around the same time read privately to some of the author's friends. As usual he anticipated no trouble from the censorship but, he wrote to Annenkov, could not think where to print the work, for he "had no relationships with any journals."[22] Here Pisemsky proved to be as inaccurate a prophet as ever, for the censorship made a great deal of trouble for *An Enlightened Time,* while he experienced little difficulty in placing it in *Russky vestnik* for January 1875. The censor, though claming to find the play's purpose "praiseworthy," objected to the "series of more or less cynical scenes drawn from the family and social milieu" and would not permit it to be staged.[23] After making another excursion to St. Petersburg, Pisemsky was able to mollify the censorship by introducing certain alterations, and the play was premiered in Moscow as early as January 30, 1875.

An Enlightened Time was by no means the worst of Pisemsky's tendentious plays of the 1870's. The story line is unencumbered with the underbrush of nonessential subplots so often found in his work and leads inexorably to the play's tragic conclusion. The heroine, Sofya Mikhaylovna Daryalova, having married a man interested solely in making money, seeks affection from a handsome but flighty young man with the appropriate name of Amaturov. Amaturov indulgently humors her conviction that love should be an undying passion, which does not prevent him from pursuing other amorous flirtations as well. Although she pretends to be unconcerned, Daryalova is in fact mortally wounded by her lover's infidelity. In the play's final scene she looses her wrath upon both men who have betrayed her: her husband, who merely regarded her as a tool for the advancement of his business interests, and Amaturov, who loved her only for her "pretty face" and employed her for the satisfaction of his animal instincts. Her final speech is a raging indictment of a society in which woman is nothing but a sexual plaything and from which there is no genuine escape save death. When she then runs offstage and shoots herself, those present find her action only mildly upsetting. They are so corrupted as to be incapable of real feeling and cannot comprehend Daryalova's emotions and actions. As one of the male characters remarks at the play's conclusion, she was a "strange woman—especially in our enlightened time," a time when everyone was convinced that material well-being was the sole index of happiness.[24]

Reactions to *An Enlightened Time* were varied. Goncharov bore witness that the play aroused much negative comment. The novelist had objected to *Baal*, upbraiding Pisemsky for not "creating more powerful, sharp, i.e. typical figures" instead of his "barely outlined, pale personalities known to hardly anyone."[25] Goncharov had expected to dislike *An Enlightened Time* as well, especially after receiving adverse reports on it from friends. But upon reading it himself, he found it quite good.[26] In contrast, Pisemsky's longtime friend and supporter Boris Almazov overestimated the play's worth: he published an article extolling equally the contents of the January 1875 issue of *Russky vestnik,* which contained A. F. Pisemsky's *An Enlightened Time* and the beginning of a new novel by Lev Tolstoy, *Anna Karenina.*[27] At this remove in time the two works hardly appear comparable, but they seemed so to a contemporary.

Pisemsky was also heartened by the public's reaction to his play when staged. According to the author, the audience was so enthusiastic that it called for him to take a bow after the second act, not waiting for the conclusion.[28] Such a thing had never happened to him before, and it touched him deeply. In all probability, however, this reception was little more than a general demonstration of esteem for an author who had just celebrated his twenty-fifth anniversary of service to Russian literature.

The Financial Genius, the last of Pisemsky's anticapitalist plays, had by far the least success in print. It may have been partly in compensation for this failure that he was heard to proclaim the piece his masterwork, an assertion that he surely did not believe in his more sober moments. Submitted to the censorship by the new year 1876, *The Financial Genius* does not seem to have encountered any obstacles there, but other conditions were less favorable. It was rejected by *Russky vestnik,* where Pisemsky had expected it to appear, because some of the "younger editors had formed a party inimical" to him and considered the manuscript unfit for publication.[29] These words of Pisemsky's show that he continued to rely upon "conspiracy theories" to account for failures. The upshot of the situation was that he was forced to publish the play in the totally obscure *Gazeta Gattsuka* (Gattsuk's Newspaper) in early 1876. This established a precedent for all three of the works printed from then until his death: they first appeared in insignificant organs instead of one of the influential "thick journals."

In *The Financial Genius* Pisemsky showed himself a tendentious writer in the narrowest sense of the word, although his inborn tact would not allow him to become an utterly one-sided pamphleteer. Sosipatov, the "financial genius" of the ironic title, has amassed a considerable fortune, largely through the efforts of his partner Baron Kergof. Kergof is in love with Sosipatov's wife, a situation that was an almost inevitable ingredient of Pisemsky's later plays. He despises Sosipatov for being an "unbearable little braggart" and eventually dissolves their partnership. In the meantime Sosipatov falls under the influence of a charlatan medium and begins to display such megalomania on the subject of his financial genius that he is officially declared insane. A number of genuine and fraudulent creditors thereupon show up in the hope of receiving a portion of his assets when he enters bankruptcy. Sosipatov appears before them making wild statements, such as, "I am the high priest and judge of the entire financial world! . . . I am the Czar of trade! God himself has bestowed this crown upon me!" (VIII, 486). At the end Sosipatov and his wife are rescued from total ruin only when a number of his "creditors" are arrested for forging their promissory notes. Baron Kergof cannot resist deriving a selfish satisfaction from Sosipatov's unfortunate end.

Despite his disappointment over the play's publication, the author was comforted by the reception given by the public to its first staging. According to Pisemsky, the audience called for him many times, applauding him loudly and later thanking him for coming to the defense of public morality against dishonest operators whom the law could not reach. He looked on himself as combatting the "absurdities of spiritism, the venial and stupid press, counterfeit telegrams and worthless promissory notes,"[30] in short, all the repulsive epiphenomena of the body social that were rooted in its love of financial gain and material comfort.

Though these had been his main targets throughout his writing career, somehow in the 1870's Pisemsky's ire seemed more intense, as befitted a cranky old man who had never entrusted any of his own money to the private banks or engaged in financial speculation. In his view, certain scandals exposed at about that time provided ample justification for his actions and opinions both as a private individual and as a playwright. For example, on September 13, 1875, an important Moscow bank went bankrupt, leaving its depositors with very little. Pisemsky informed Turgenev exultingly that he had lost nothing in the crash because of his "deep detestation of all our private and so-called public institutions."[31]

The Final Years

Pisemsky's health had steadily deteriorated since his return to the civil service, with most of his troubles seeming to have sprung from a fractious digestive system. He must have obtained some gratification from his official employment, since during 1871-1872 he several times temporarily performed the duties of the Moscow Vice-Governor. Nevertheless, on May 20, 1872, he wrote an official letter to Alexander II requesting release from his duties "for domestic reasons," and he was formally permitted to retire on June 17.[32] He was only fifty-one. From that point until his death nine years later he lived in retirement. His family life during these years was not especially pleasant. True, the faithful Ekaterina Pavlovna stood firmly by his side, humoring him and easing the real and imaginary trials of his existence, and for this he had reason to be deeply grateful. But his sons were a source of unutterable grief to him—a grief that was the sharper because for a while it appeared that both Pavel and Nikolay, born in 1850 and 1852 respectively, would do outstandingly well in their chosen professions.

Pavel was very successful in his studies, graduating from the gymnasium in 1867 first in his class. The recipient of a gold medal for scholastic achievement, he entered the law faculty of Moscow University the same year. His progress aroused understandable pride in his father. In due time Pavel completed his studies and received the degree of master of civil law. He had done well enough to be sent abroad at the expense of the Ministry of Education, presumably in the fall of 1873, to continue his scholarly work in Germany. In view of his father's anticapitalist fulminations of the time, it is ironic that the topic of Pavel's researches should have been stock companies.

At first Pisemsky's younger son Nikolay was as great a joy to his parents as Pavel. Two years younger than his brother, he compiled a no less impressive school record. He too graduated from a Moscow gymnasium with a gold medal and in 1869 was admitted to Moscow University, where he majored in mathematics. He received the standard degree of "candidate" in June 1873, his deportment while at the university having been "very good" and his scholarly attainment "excellent." Leaving the paternal roof in the fall of that year, Nikolay journeyed to St. Petersburg, where he planned eventually to enter the Institut putey soobshcheniya (Communications Institute). While in the capital he served as St. Petersburg agent and correspondent for his father. He seems to have been a very intelli-

gent young man. Several of Nikolay's letters to his parents have
been preserved, in which, among other things, he reported upon the
results of his interviews with government functionaries about his
father's literary affairs and upon the reaction of St. Petersburg audiences to the staging of Pisemsky's plays.[33] Nikolay mentioned no
special personal troubles, and everything seemed to be progressing
normally.

Then the blow fell. On the fifteenth of February 1874 in the
*Vedomosti S.-Peterburgskogo gradonachalstva i S.-Peterburgskoy
gorodskoy politsii* (News of the St. Petersburg City Administration
and City Police) appeared the laconic notice:

SUICIDE

On February 13, in the fourth section of the Spassky district on
the Fontanka, building No. 101, in furnished rooms, a candidate
of mathematical sciences inflicted a revolver wound upon himself,
in the right temple, and was taken unconscious to the Obukhov hospital. The wound was a mortal one. The act was committed by him
in a fit of melancholy.[34]

The human details behind this succinct official bulletin may be
gleaned from Apollon Maykov's letters from St. Petersburg to the
distraught parents in Moscow.[35] The elder Pisemskys were probably
notified of the tragedy by telegram on February 14 but were in all
likelihood too crushed by the event to undertake a trip to St. Petersburg to attend to their son's burial. Consequently, their kinsman
Maykov assumed the burden of arranging for proper interment,
reporting to Nikolay's parents daily from the fifteenth through the
eighteenth of February.

In his first letter to them, Maykov wrote that after dinner on the
thirteenth Nikolay's roommate Andrey Lukin had gone out for a
walk, leaving Nikolay by himself. A Doctor Ostrovsky, who lived
in the apartment below, heard Pisemsky go to the piano and make
idle attempts at playing, as he often did. On this occasion, after
doodling for a while, he sounded a loud chord, after which all was
silent until the stillness was broken by the reverberation of a shot.
When Lukin returned from his walk, he found Nikolay slumped on
the sofa with a wound in the temple, revolver in hand. As he was
still alive, he was given first aid by Doctor Ostrovsky, who had been
summoned from below, and then transferred to the nearby Obukhov
hospital, where he died about 7 or 8 o'clock in the evening. The
Maykovs were not informed of his death until very early the next
morning, since it took Lukin some time to find out their address.

Maykov arranged for Nikolay Pisemsky's burial in the cemetery of the Devichy monastery, where all the Maykovs were laid to rest. This must have required a certain amount of maneuvering, since the Orthodox Church has always forbidden the interment of suicides in consecrated ground. Moreover, Nikolay was buried with all due ecclesiastical ceremony, which Maykov realized would be a comfort to his mother.

It is impossible to explain Nikolay's suicide satisfactorily, especially since even today we have no more documents on the matter than were available to Maykov in February of 1874. Racking his brain, the poet offered several differing explanations of Nikolay's action. He wrote at first: "It seems that he [Nikolay] was a hypochondriac by temperament; he had no ideals whatever, he ate a dreadful amount, and equated happiness with an income of 20,000 ... It seems to me that he devised a syllogism of this type: happiness lies in the satisfaction of our material wants. For this one must work. Is it really worth it, essentially? So he put a bullet into his brain and that was that."[36] It also appears that, if Maykov is to be believed, certain undesirable traits of character in Nikolay had been reinforced by the influence of the company he kept in St. Petersburg. He appears to have led a riotous life and reportedly said on at least one occasion that he would commit suicide should he ever contract venereal disease. Although no symptoms of any such disease were found upon him, it was established that he had talked of committing suicide to his acquaintances for some time prior to actually carrying out the intention. His father knew nothing of this.

A few days after offering this first analysis, Maykov came up with another hypothesis to explain Nikolay's suicide: he now thought that it had been occasioned by a fundamental split in his personality. Though he was by nature an idealistic sort who loved poetry and even wrote some himself, Nikolay's intellectual training had oriented him toward materialism and a lack of faith in ideals. Paradoxically, his skepticism, as Maykov aptly put it, sprang from that "belief in the papal infallibility of scholars" from which the entire age suffered. In the final accounting this had engendered a conflict within Nikolay which led to his suicide.[37]

The death of their son came as a severe shock to both Pisemsky and his wife, and as soon as they could gather their physical forces, they hastened abroad in the hope of alleviating their sorrow through both travel and a visit with their surviving son. By May 9, 1874, they had made their way to Göttingen, where Pavel Pisemsky was attending lectures. Shortly after his parents' arrival Pavel had a vacation of several days, so the entire family took the opportunity to visit Dresden for the first time. Generally speaking, Pisemsky was not nearly so impressed by Europe in 1874 as he had been during his first visit in 1862, although his negative reactions sprang mostly from crankiness. Germany seemed to him to have become a land of buyers and sellers interested in nothing but profit: guests were charged exorbitant prices in the hotels, the trains did not run on time, and conductors required compensation for offering the least assistance to the passengers. "In a word," Pisemsky decided, "we Russians may console ourselves with the thought that even if things are no better in our country, at least they are certainly no worse either."[38]

From May to July the Pisemskys based themselves in Göttingen, characterized by the writer as a "very small but at the same time very smelly town."[39] They organized excursions to nearby places and suffered from the indigestion complex travelers frequently contract when abroad. Sometime after the middle of July the entire family left Göttingen and proceeded to Baden-Baden, where they celebrated a pleasant reunion with the Annenkov family. From there the Pisemskys journeyed through Switzerland to Paris, arriving at their destination on August 10. At this stage Pavel had decided to spend the following year in Paris, so Pisemsky commended him to the care of Turgenev, who did assist him during his stay. Pisemsky managed to pay only one visit to Turgenev, who was living in a small town near Paris. As for the French capital, Pisemsky found it sadly deteriorated after the events of the years since 1862. Such things as the Paris Commune had done their work: "[Paris] seems to me to be a desolate city, as if extinct, impoverished and even rather filthy by comparison with the huge population, luxury and cleanliness with which it glistened during my first visit in 1862; and then the Parisians themselves have become somehow humble, quiet and sad; the women almost all wear modest black dresses."[40] This attitude received literary reflection in Pisemsky's later novel *Meshchane* (The Bourgeois): while in Paris the hero, Begushev, spends all his time with other Russians, and when upon his return to Russia he is asked what he did in the French capital, he replies laconically that he "slept" (III, 464). Pisemsky's approach to foreign cultures was nearly as insensitive as Begushev's: the writer was never more than a superficial observer. In any case, after a short stay of two weeks in Paris, Pisemsky and his wife hastened back to Moscow via Vienna, arriving home around the first of September.

Since Pavel Pisemsky had stayed on in Paris to continue his studies, the Pisemskys began projecting yet another journey to western Europe for the summer of 1875. In the intervening period Pisemsky wrote frequent letters to his son describing the few events of interest occurring in Moscow and scolding him for the careless composition of his official reports to the Ministry of Education. With the approach of spring final plans for the visit to western Europe were drawn up. After certain delays caused by the writer's physical indisposition, the two parents left Moscow on March 30 and proceeded via St. Petersburg to Paris, where they arrived on April 5. There they settled for five or six weeks in the Latin Quarter, not far from their son's lodgings. Most of their time in Paris seems to have been spent in battling indigestion, visiting their son, and chatting with Turgenev, who by that time had become to all intents and purposes a permanent resident of France.

The one public appearance made by Pisemsky during his three trips abroad, as far as is known, took place during this sojourn in Paris, when he agreed to participate in a "literary and musical matinee" for the benefit of the local Russian Reading Room. The event was held on May 2 at two in the afternoon at Turgenev's residence. Pisemsky contributed a reading of the second act of *An Enlightened Time*. Other participants were Turgenev, his constant companion the opera singer Pauline Viardot, her husband Paul Viardot, and Anton Rubinstein.

While in Paris on this occasion Pisemsky reportedly consulted Dr. Jean Martin Charcot, "the favorite doctor of neuropaths and alcoholics," about his alcoholism, which probably had worsened after the calamity of his son's death in 1874. The eminent doctor, with no wondrous remedies to offer, simply advised Pisemsky to give up drinking altogether. The patient must not have considered such advice very useful.[41]

Two weeks after the reading, on May 15, the Pisemskys left Paris for Baden-Baden and another reunion with Annenkov. Baden-Baden was such a popular gathering place for the Russian social and intellectual elite that Pisemsky ran into Saltykov-Shchedrin there as well.[42] It is possible that the Pisemskys returned to Russia in Annenkov's company, since he had been planning a trip home at this time. Pavel Pisemsky was dropped off in Berlin, where he was to continue his researches, and the elder Pisemskys were once more esconced in their Moscow home by early July 1875.

During the period when Pavel Pisemsky was laboring in Berlin, his parents lived in seclusion, attempting to cope with their physical infirmities and dreaming of the time when their son would be restored to them. Pavel returned to Moscow after a lonely stay in Berlin, arriving by early February 1876 at the latest. He then worked on his dissertation for a short time, defending it successfully on May 8 under the title "Aktsionernye kompanii s tochki zreniya grazhdanskogo prava" (Stock Companies from the Point of View of Civil Law). In September 1876 he joined the staff of the Moscow University law faculty as a docent, beginning his lectures at the start of the academic year.[43] Pisemsky was very proud of his son's success in the academic world.

Ultimately, however, Pavel's lot was little more enviable than Nikolay's. One memoirist has described him as a "silent and sickly analytic type,"[44] and apparently these traits of character developed to such an extreme in him that, even before his father's death, it had become clear that Pavel was mentally unbalanced. This was another blow to sadden Pisemsky's declining years. Pavel left the university in 1882 and lived the rest of his life, until his death in 1910, under the shadow of mental derangement, although precisely how his illness was manifested is not known.

Pisemsky undoubtedly would have wished to see the family line continued through his sons, but in this he was disappointed. Nikolay took his life at an early age, before he had an opportunity to marry. Pavel was almost twenty-six by the time he returned to Moscow in 1876, when he might have been expected to marry shortly, but evidently his melancholy character and then his illness prevented that outcome. He did, however, father an illegitimate daughter by an anonymous seamstress. Pisemsky lavished affection on the girl in his old age, visiting her frequently and having her call him "grandfather."[45] What became of her after her grandparents' demise is not known. In any case, with Pavel's death one entire branch of the Pisemsky family came to an end. Aleksey Feofilakto-vich's parents had produced ten children, of whom he alone reached adulthood, and Pisemsky himself fathered five children, of whom two sons survived to maturity, and both died without legitimate issue. It was as though the family were not fated to continue.

Pisemsky's last years were not as gloomy as might have been expected from these events of his personal life. For one thing, his fame beyond Russian borders began to increase at approximately the same time that it was waning most sharply at home. Turgenev, in his role as chief purveyor of Russian culture to western Europe, is to be given much of the credit for bringing him to the notice of a broader public. His work was first translated into German with a rendering of *One Thousand Souls* as early as 1870, substantially before Tolstoy and Dostoevsky had become known abroad.[46] During Pisemsky's European sojourn of 1875 he stopped off in Germany to see his translator, Dr. Leopold Kayssler, who informed him that *Troubled Seas* had also come out serially in a German newspaper about three years previously.[47] Pisemsky attempted to locate the translation, but without success. "An Old Man's Sin" appeared in German in Vienna in 1873.

Kayssler's translation of *One Thousand Souls* attracted the notice of a prominent German critic, Julian Schmidt, who in May 1870 wrote a small article comparing Pisemsky and Turgenev, in which his knowledge of Pisemsky was obviously based solely upon a reading of this novel. Schmidt was immediately impressed by Pisemsky's extraordinary "Russianness." If Turgenev as writer was only half-Russian, he commented, "this cannot be said of Aleksey Pisemsky: he is Russian through and through, and of all the authorial peculiarities that might remind one of foreign writers, he displays only the ones that derive from general world culture."[48] Pisemsky was later hampered by this very Russianness, for when he called on Schmidt during the 1875 trip, the two were unable to communicate effectively because of Pisemsky's ignorance of foreign languages.[49]

The French did not lag far behind the Germans in their appreciation of Pisemsky. Extensive remarks on his work may be found in a book of 1875 by Céleste Courrière, entitled *Histoire de la littérature contemporaine en Russie*. Courrière devoted part of one chapter to a moderately lengthy discussion of *One Thousand Souls* and an entire chapter to *Troubled Seas, Men of the 1840's, In the Whirlpool, The Plunderers,* and *Baal*. Courrière contributed to the by then solidly established tradition of comparing and contrasting Pisemsky and Turgenev as chroniclers of Russian life, remarking: "Though Turgenev is superior to Pisemsky from the point of view of the variety and subtlety of types, and also the beauty of artistic structure, to make up for that Pisemsky excels at taking nature and life alive; for this reason his creations are sometimes as ugly as reality itself."[50] It is likely that both Courrière and Schmidt, had they been forced to choose, would have agreed in placing Turgenev above Pisemsky, but they recognized Pisemsky as a worthy contender in the literary lists of contemporary Russia. For some time afterward Pisemsky occupied a modest place in western discussions of Russian literature.

If the French were slightly slower than the Germans in first discovering Pisemsky, they soon made up for the lapse by translating him energetically. His most assiduous translator was the Frenchman

Victor Derély, with whom he conducted an extensive correspondence from late 1878 until his death. Unfortunately Pisemsky did not live quite long enough to see the separate publication of Derély's initial translation, that of *In the Whirlpool* in Paris in 1881. Derély did not translate *One Thousand Souls* until 1886, but in that same year he published a French version of the novel *The Bourgeois* and three years later the two plays *A Bitter Fate* and *Baal*. "An Old Man's Sin" appeared in French in 1888.

Although Pisemsky lived a very quiet life following his retirement from the civil service in 1872, he did not sink into total obscurity in Moscow during the 1870's. He still gave occasional readings in which he displayed some of his old fire, and in 1872 Nikitenko, after hearing the author read *The Plunderers,* wrote in his diary that anybody who had witnessed Pisemsky performing his play might as well spare himself the bother of going to the theater, for it would probably be staged less competently than it had been read by the author.[51] On Wednesdays the Pisemskys received at home such visitors as the author's old friends Ostrovsky and Boris Almazov, the second-rank writers P. I. Melnikov and P. D. Boborykin, the scholars A. N. Veselovsky and N. I. Kostomarov, and the actress A. I. Shubert.[52] Pisemsky also served as literary adviser to beginning authors, most of them minor female writers like E. I. Blaramberg, who published under the pseudonym E. Ardov, and A. I. Sokolova. Sokolova's account of her dealings with Pisemsky shows that in his later years he wished to be treated with extreme respect. Sokolova had written a short story that Pisemsky had agreed to read, and accordingly she called on him at his country house in Ostankino, near Moscow. When she attempted to protest over Pisemsky's deletion of a certain passage, "he replied that this was his personal opinion and that a beginning writer could not quarrel with a literary authority."[53] Pisemsky was clinging to the shadow of his former reputation.

A high point of Pisemsky's career was his literary jubilee in 1875, celebrating twenty-five years of service to Russian literature— calculating from 1850, the year of *The Simpleton's* appearance, not from 1848, when "Nina" was published. Sponsored by the Society of Lovers of Russian Literature, to which Pisemsky had long belonged, the jubilee celebration was held on January 19 in the Moscow University library.[54] The occasion triggered such an outpouring of affection for this veteran of Russian letters that people were reportedly turned away for lack of seats. The society's temporary president, D. I. Ilovaysky, opened the meeting with a speech.

He was followed by the main speaker, Boris Almazov, who set out to survey Pisemsky's entire career but ended by concentrating on the early influences on the author and his novel *One Thousand Souls*.[55] When Almazov had finished extolling his friend, Pisemsky briefly summarized his literary credo. Various congratulatory letters and telegrams were read, including a collective telegram signed by such St. Petersburg luminaries as Maykov, Dostoevsky, Polonsky, and Strakhov. There were letters from Goncharov in St. Petersburg and Turgenev in Paris. Next, S. A. Yuryev spoke on Pisemsky's dramatic works, after which the author read selections from his latest play, *An Enlightened Time*. The occasion was capped by a dinner at which impromptu verses of dubious quality were recited. For some time after that day Pisemsky was kept busy replying to the congratulatory letters and telegrams. He professed to dislike all the fuss being made over him, but he would certainly have been deeply hurt had no one attempted to commemorate the twenty-fifth anniversary of his literary activity in an appropriate manner, since such celebrations were very much the custom in the Russia of his day.

Pisemsky's last play, *The Financial Genius*, was published in early 1876, after which he temporarily languished in the doldrums, producing little. He spent time haggling with tenants who were behind in paying their rent for the apartments in his house on Boris and Gleb Lane. He worried over his own and others' health, especially his wife's. And even when well, he frequently suffered from what he called "hypochondria," by which he presumably meant a form of ennui. "Physically I am healthy," he wrote to Turgenev in October 1876, "but the same cannot be said of my intellectual and moral sides: I am tortured by hypochondria in the most unbearable way; not only can I not write, I even experience utter revulsion at the thought of any occupation which has anything to do with the mind, so that writing this very letter is an enormous task for me which I cannot complete in fewer than three days."[56]

The Last Novels

In the same month in which the above letter was written, complaining of the difficulties of any sort of composition, Pisemsky nevertheless resumed his long interrupted work on his next novel, *The Bourgeois*, and began a new play, to be entitled *Starye schety* (Old Accounts). By December 1877 he had written only one act of the play, and he never completed the third of its projected five acts.

The Bourgeois, however, reached the public in comparatively short order. By early 1877 the author was negotiating in one or two quarters with an eye to publication. He bargained as hard as ever, demanding remuneration roughly equal to that which he had received from such journals as *Zarya* and *Beseda,* although the organs with which he was now dealing were less significant, and the earlier journals had been seriously weakened by making him excessive payments for lengthy novels. Eventually he decided to publish *The Bourgeois* in the obscure weekly *Pchela* (The Bee), where it appeared in over forty installments in the course of 1877. Considerably handier for reading was a separate edition issued in 1878 by one of *Pchela's* editors, the artist M. O. Mikeshin. A sizable fraction of Pisemsky's correspondence for 1877, which has been preserved together with most of his letters for the last few years of his life in the form of drafts kept for his own reference, concerns niggling and uninteresting problems of proofreading and his receipt of successive issues of *Pchela.* The letters do contain, however, instructions from Pisemsky to Mikeshin on illustrations to accompany the novel: these illustrations were omitted in the end, but Pisemsky's remarks cast light upon his conception of certain of the characters.

The *Bourgeois* was several years in the composition. On January 6, 1877, Pisemsky informed a correspondent that the novel had been started "some three years ago."[57] At that time he had read from it to friends. He then abandoned the book for a while, returning to it only briefly in 1875 and dropping it once more until late 1876, at which point he finally reverted to it with a determination to see it through to the end.[58] The fact that Pisemsky worked on *The Bourgeois* by fits and starts throughout the central portion of the 1870's is significant for an understanding of the work. As it was conceived at precisely the time he was engaged in writing his "pamphleteering" plays, it displays a close kinship with them. In this instance Pisemsky planned to create a positive hero. Begushev, the book's central figure, exposed by word and deed the banality of the milieu in which he was compelled to exist. As Pisemsky phrased it, Begushev was the "background against which [the new philistines] are traced . . . Without him they would not stand out so sharply."[59]

Essentially Pisemsky's vitrolic criticism of the nascent Russian capitalist class with its inborn philistinism was launched from the right, not the left. His glance was directed backward, to a time when men of noble birth were more "poetic," contemned money-grubbing, and displayed great nobility of soul. In order to bring his "knightly" ideal, as he called it on more than one occasion, into active contact with the reality of the 1870's, Pisemsky had to make his hero over fifty years old at the point when the book's action takes place. Begushev belonged to the wealthy hereditary nobility, which for all practical purposes gave him material independence from the society around him. But more important, he was in the highest degree intellectually self-reliant: "He had never been for a single moment in his life the slave and unqualified adherent of anybody else's thought, as he himself knew very well what was sensible and what not, what was beautiful and what was ugly, what was temporary and a matter of chance and what was eternal" (III, 382). Within Begushev there burned the same fire that enabled the wretched Lear, wandering on the heath, to be recognized as a king regardless of external circumstances.

The Russian prototypes of Begushev are revealed in a letter from Pisemsky to his illustrator, in which he wrote that while composing the novel, he had kept two figures in mind as exemplars of a selfless romantic spirit. They were Alexander Herzen and Bestuzhev— presumably Mikhail Aleksandrovich Bestuzhev (1800-1871), long exiled for his part in the Decembrist uprising of 1825.[60] Of these two, Herzen, who died in 1870, seems to have been substantially more important: the recollection of their strained relations in 1862-1863 did not deter Pisemsky from regarding him as the flower of all that was best in the generation of the 1840's. The Soviet scholar B. P. Kozmin has pointed out definite though not numerous coincidences in the biographies of Herzen and Begushev. More important, many of their views are essentially the same, especially their contempt for the bourgeoisie as the enemy of culture, and Pisemsky occasionally employed near quotations from Herzen's writings in his novel.[61] Herzen, however, was more conscious than Pisemsky of the dilemma faced by a supporter of the notion of a spiritual or hereditary aristocracy: the aristocrat obtains leisure to create and appreciate culture through a social inequality of which he is the beneficiary. The idea of an egalitarian aristocrat is a contradiction in terms. Begushev embodied the ideal of a spiritual aristocrat that could never be recaptured in reality.

In one of his tirades against the bourgeoisie Begushev refers to the deeds of medieval knights as examples of valor. It infuriates him to think that such men risked their lives so that the inhabitants of Taganka and Yakimanka, prosperous merchant sections of Moscow, might long afterward squeeze profits from the new lands they had annexed to the fatherland. It enrages him to think that Beethoven and Raphael "burned with their inspiration" merely for the entertainment of Taganka and Yakimanka (III, 328-329). In another oration with a Dostoevskian tinge Begushev comments that he had made a visit to Europe with some hope for civilization, but was disillusioned by what he saw, especially after viewing the London Exhibition (which contained that rationalist horror of Dostoevsky's nightmares, the Crystal Palace). He has abandoned his faith in mankind, for such immense social upheavals as the French Revolution have given rise merely to the hegemony of the "huckster, the artisan, and all sorts of filth," as well as the contemptible ideal of satisfying purely material wants. Forceful as Begushev is in condemning contemporary Russian and European society, he is nevertheless incapable of recommending any feasible correctives. When pinned down, he resorts to what may be termed an apocalyptic doctrine: " '[I want] God on earth!' Begushev exclaimed. 'Let Christ descend once more and renew our souls, or else everything decent in mankind will waste away and expire in the stench of our material well-being' " (III, 339). Unfortunately Begushev gets no further in elaborating his views, for at this point he is interrupted. Pisemsky never returned to the subject or attempted to demonstrate how a renewal of the human spirit of the type so ardently desired by Begushev could be effected by anything less cataclysmic than a Second Coming.

Despite the fact that Begushev was intended as one of the most positive characters Pisemsky had ever created, he is nevertheless entangled in degrading relationships. At the time the book opens he is a bachelor who has had a passionate affair with another man's wife, and for much of the novel's duration he is hopelessly involved in yet another adulterous liaison, with Domna Osipovna Olukhova. This might be excusable were Domna Osipovna a "chosen soul," but she is not: she indulges in financial speculation as avidly as anyone else and is only saved from ruin when she withdraws her major investment in the nick of time. When Begushev and Domna Osipovna finally part, she marries a man who is interested only in her money. At the end she loses her mind, mostly because of financial difficulties.

Meanwhile Begushev has taken in a tubercular young woman named Merova, who has loved him for some time but is now close to death. Unable to control himself, he engages in sexual intercourse with the feverish, mortally ill woman. After she dies, Begushev, feeling with some justification that everything he touches disintegrates, resolves to seek redemption through death. For this purpose he joins the army as a colonel and departs for the Caucasus, where, it is reported, he begins drinking heavily and actively courts death in battle. After he is killed, a friend of long standing muses about him: "A romantic, a romantic! He died the same sort of person he was born" (III, 629-630). Despite sordid admixtures, Begushev commands the major part of the author's sympathy, and for all his inconsistencies, he remains one of Pisemsky's most fascinating creations.

Pisemsky's literary advisors, Turgenev and Annenkov, both claimed to be pleased with *The Bourgeois* after they had read it. Turgenev, in fact, was excessively enthusiastic, perhaps partially because Pisemsky had offered an encouraging word about his recent novel *Virgin Soil*. Turgenev assured Pisemsky that *The Bourgeois* exhibited his old "power, vitality and truthfulness of talent." It was the work of a "master, even though a little weary," who could still put the younger generation of writers to shame.[62] Annenkov was more reserved in his evaluation, commenting that Pisemsky's "open, free and powerfully developed talent has been expressed well in this novel as well, although it does not grasp the interests of the day so deeply as do some of your other works."[63]

Except for a few newspapers, the press almost ignored *The Bourgeois*. The only critic of standing to discuss the novel in a major journal was N. K. Mikhaylovsky. The populist critic sympathized with Pisemsky's "intentions" but added that his designs were "noble only from the negative point of view" and objected to the "coarseness" of their execution. Mikhaylovsky felt that Begushev failed as the embodiment of what was supposedly fine in Russian society: all he did was to defend the rights of the hereditary aristocracy against the new bourgeoisie.[64] Mikhaylovsky's democratic sympathies would not allow him to applaud such an aristocratic hero. Pisemsky and Mikhaylovsky may have been against some of the same failings in contemporary society, but their positive programs were not necessarily similar.

After completing *The Bourgeois*, Pisemsky discontinued writing novels and plays on contemporary themes and turned to personal reminiscence or to history as the source of his inspiration. Although his earlier use of historical themes for the dramas of the mid-1860's, or of personal history for his novel *Men of the 1840's*, could be explained as a tactical move to avoid retaliation for "reactionary" discussions of contemporary life such as those found in *Troubled Seas*, by the late 1870's this motivation was lacking, especially since the radicals then considered him with a more neutral eye because of his anticapitalist plays.[65] Furthermore, he was by then generally ignored, so that nothing he might have published except scandalous memoirs would have aroused much furor. This being the case, the motivation for his renewed reversion to the past must be sought in his feeling that he was no longer able to observe contemporary events keenly and at first hand. He was hardly past fifty-five, but his health had been steadily deteriorating, and many of his contemporaries were passing from the scene. His close friend Almazov had died in 1876, not long after Pisemsky's jubilee. Nekrasov's life came to a close at the end of 1877, following a lingering illness. As Pisemsky wrote upon learning of this: "What's to be done? All we oldsters are in line now and it seems to me that I am the next candidate; God grant only that I don't suffer so long [as Nekrasov]."[66] A little later he commented gloomily that almost every day one heard of yet another death, though of course all the entrepreneurs were flourishing.[67] At the time of these melancholy remarks Pisemsky still had roughly three years remaining, but his attitude was one of resigned preparation for the end. Observers described him as a "ruin," who yet exhibited traces of his former grandeur. A scholar who made his acquaintance in the late 1870's described him thus: "He always astonished me with the clarity of his great intellect and by the power of his incisive wit, which was allied to that of the common people. But after a conversation with him one always experienced a generally sad and anguished feeling. You could not help recognizing that these were the remnants of former glory, that a gigantic talent had diverged from the old way but could not find a new one; that the persecution of some, the indifference of others, and the commiserating or clumsy praises of still others kept him from taking stock, infuriated him and blinded him. And the years kept on slipping away, and ever louder would resound in his soul the melancholy words: my day is done!"[68]

After 1877 only two more items by Pisemsky appeared in print during his lifetime: the sketch "Uzhe ottsvetshie tsvetki. Kapitan Rukhnev" (Faded Flowers. Captain Rukhnev) and the novel *Masony* (The Masons). "Captain Rukhnev" appeared in early 1879 in *Gazeta Gattsuka,* one of the few publishing outlets remaining to Pisemsky. In its original conception the story was to have been the first of a series based on the author's personal reminiscences, bearing the title "Faded Flowers," the implication being that the types described were no longer to be discovered in Russian life.[69] Like Pisemsky's previous projects for cycles of sketches, this plan was soon abandoned.

Nevertheless "Captain Rukhnev" is by itself an entertaining work, which compares favorably with the best of Pisemsky's writing from the 1850's. The reason lies partly in the form that it takes: the story is narrated primarily by Captain Rukhnev himself, prompted by a few questions from the author. Pisemsky's stories were most likely to be successful when cast in this mold. Rukhnev is a rascal who describes others' rascality. One of his anecdotes involves a priest who had refused to sell Rukhnev a horse at a reasonable price. Since Rukhnev occupied an official post at the time, he decided to utilize it to avenge himself. After discovering that the priest had been purchasing communion wine of much lower quality than that required by the ecclesiastical authorities, he taxed him with his misdeeds, whereupon the priest was suddenly willing to part with his horse for a much lower price than that previously demanded. At the time Rukhnev is recounting these anecdotes, he is in prison awaiting trial for conspiracy to rob. Some years later, in St. Petersburg, the narrator runs into Rukhnev again. He has managed to do quite well for himself since their last interview. "Captain Rukhnev" is thus vaguely reminiscent of "The Petersburger," although the hero's personality is of more interest in the latter, while the principal virtue of the former lies in its vivid vignettes of small-time Russian swindlers.

Pisemsky's last work, *The Masons*, incorporates the fruits of extensive historical research on the author's part. The novel is set in the Russia of the 1830's, although it contains several anachronistic references to events of an earlier period. Pisemsky had long been intrigued by unorthodox religious sects, as shown by Pavel Vikhrov's investigations of the Old Believers in *Men of the 1840's*. As for the Masons, Pisemsky had known several in his youth, though "from outside," as he put it.[70] One of them had been very close to him: Yuriy Bartenev (1792-1866), a cousin of his mother's, to whom he had dedicated his novelette *A Marriage of Passion* in 1851 and who now served as a prototype for some of the Masonic characters in the novel.[71] Pisemsky had earlier given over a chapter in *Troubled Seas* to a description of a Russian Mason.

Pisemsky first mentioned his plans for *The Masons* in a letter to his French translator of December 10, 1878, explaining that he had planned to write such a book for a long time but had only recently been able to execute his intention.[72] He plunged into his historical researches with gusto, perusing articles, histories of Masonry, and descriptions of Masonic rites, then gathering much of what he had found into a scrapbook entitled "Materialy dlya romana *Masony*" (Materials for the Novel *The Masons*), now preserved at the Institute of Russian Literature in Leningrad. This collection clearly demonstrates Pisemsky's detailed interest in the history of the

Masonic movement.[73] The author also cultivated the friendship of people in Moscow and elsewhere who could supply him with information on Masonry, including Professor Aleksandr Kirpichnikov and Vladimir Solovev.

The further Pisemsky delved into the historical background of Russian Masonry, the more competent he felt to penetrate its spiritual universe, instead of merely observing the movement "externally," as he had done in his youth. For a time he even found the Masonic frame of mind very attractive: he wrote in mid-1879 that "now, after entering their [the Masons'] interior world, I am becoming convinced that for the most part they were very cultured and honorable people who morally stood far above the people called Voltaireans at that time, who were simply coarse profligates."[74] Even though later he poked fun in the novel at some of the Masons' mystic rites, he probably continued to feel that they were fundamentally admirable people.

Though his weak eyes hindered him in reading historical materials, Pisemsky considered the trial worth enduring for the sake of becoming a genuine "historical novelist." He did most of his work at the Rumyantsev Museum, the nucleus of the present-day Lenin Library in Moscow, to which he later donated the manuscript of an early draft of the novel's ending as a token of gratitude. By October 1879 he had completed three of the five parts. Somewhat earlier—at least by July 1879—Pisemsky had commenced negotiations for the novel's publication in the journal *Ogonek* (The Flame), a magazine designed for wholesome family reading that never established itself firmly and lasted only a few years. Pisemsky not only thought the journal stable enough to complete the printing of *The Masons*, but even expected to receive as much money from it as he had from major literary journals in the halcyon days of his fame.[75] A rather favorable agreement was reached and publication begun in the first issue of *Ogonek* for 1880, although Pisemsky had not at that point completed the book and could not be sure that he would live long enough to do so. *The Masons* came out very serially indeed, in forty-three weekly issues of the magazine during 1880, and was published in a separate edition the following year. Both the *Ogonek* text and the separate edition were embellished with numerous illustrations of run-of-the-mill family-magazine quality in the spirit of the comfortably philistine 1880's in Russia—an ironic twist for the author who had recently railed against philistinism in *The Bourgeois*.

Despite the novel's title, Masonry as such is not the most important subject treated in it. *The Masons* is rather a commonplace Pisemskian work containing characteristically complicated love intrigues, which involve Masons and are placed in the historical setting of the 1830's. Several historical personages do appear in the novel under their own names, as well as numerous disguised historical figures who are sufficiently obscure that their positive identification would require a considerable amount of investigation. Many Masonic ceremonies and customs are also described. Nevertheless, the relative weight of both historical and Masonic detail in the novel is not great. Pisemsky succeeded only partially in transforming himself into a historical novelist.

As in *The Bourgeois*, the central character in *The Masons* is a man no longer young, Egor Egorich Marfin, who is a leading Mason and a bachelor. Marfin conceives an interest in a young woman named Lyudmila Ryzhova, who declines a proposal from him chiefly because she is in love with his nephew, Chentsov. Before long Lyudmila dies, after which her sister Susanna falls in love with Marfin and marries him, becoming a Mason in order to strengthen her ties with her husband. Numerous romantic subplots, some involving Susanna's struggle to remain faithful to her elderly husband, are woven into the novel, merely to flesh out the story. At the book's conclusion Marfin dies abroad, and his remains are returned to Russia for Masonic burial.

Reviews of *The Masons* were not plentiful, partly because the total number of serious intellectual journals in existence had diminished since the 1860's. Two discussions that did appear, both written before Pisemsky's death, represented divergent poles of possible reaction to Pisemsky's work. *Russky vestnik* printed an extensive and rather favorable commentary, in which the anonymous reviewer thanked the author for presenting to the public a "picture of the mores and views of an epoch which, although it is not so distant from us, still has vanished completely," and expressed the opinion that *The Masons* was one of Pisemsky's "most successful works."[76] On the other hand, a sadly negative view was aired in *Otechestvennye zapiski* by yet another anonymous reviewer. For this reader, meeting Pisemsky once more after a prolonged interval was like running into a pale and hardly recognizable ghost. Pisemsky used to be an admirable writer, but had now been transformed into a nonentity. He did not make good use of his potentially interesting subject, the reviewer declared, and his main heroes were colorless cardboard figures. "It was really sad, really sad to meet Mr. Pisemsky again."[77]

The history of the last year of Pisemsky's life is one of physical infirmity and intellectual isolation. In refusing a Paris editor's invitation to serve as a Moscow correspondent for a French paper, Pisemsky explained that his weak eyes did not permit him much reading, he did not attend public gatherings because "a crowd makes me dizzy," and at home he saw only a few selected friends. He therefore had insufficiently broad contacts to supply information for an interesting correspondence.[78] It was also during the summer of 1880 that Pavel Pisemsky became more clearly ill, a circumstance that intensified his father's melancholy.

Aside from the publication of *The Masons,* only a few events worthy of mention occurred to Pisemsky in 1880. In the late winter and early spring of that year he sat for a portrait by the eminent Russian painter Ilya Repin, which now hangs in the Tretyakov Gallery. The author was so pleased with the work as to claim that it looked more like him than he did himself.[79] Of greater moment was the Pushkin festival of 1880, which occupied several days in early June and during which the Pushkin monument in Moscow was unveiled. The Pushkin festival was a red-letter day in Russian intellectual history of the latter half of the nineteenth century. An impressive number of Russia's greatest intellectuals and writers— including Turgenev and Dostoevsky—were present. Pisemsky contributed readings of Pushkin's works at gala evenings given in the national poet's honor, and in addition, drawing on his newly acquired authority as a historical novelist, he delivered a small talk on "Pushkin as a Historical Novelist," with special reference to "The Captain's Daughter." Though the text of Pisemsky's speech has not survived, one must surmise that it was eclipsed by the grandeur of Turgenev's and especially Dostoevsky's remarks on the same occasion. Pisemsky was nothing more than a footnote in the account of the celebrations.

Toward the close of 1880 Pisemsky's health took a turn for the worse. He suffered from acute digestive disorders, rheumatism, and migraine headaches. One of his last dated letters in our possession is a short note of November 15 to his doctor imploring him to visit him that day because he felt extremely unwell.[80] Then he fell silent, and two months later, on January 21, 1881, he died.

Pisemsky was interred in an unpretentious grave within the walls of the Novodevichy monastery in Moscow; when Ekaterina Pavlovna died ten years later, in 1891, she was laid beside him. Pisemsky's funeral was modest: according to one scholar, only close relatives and about ten friends and acquaintances attended the ceremonies.[81] One friend who paid his last respects had known Pisemsky since his earliest days in Moscow—Ostrovsky. "I am very busy and ill," he wrote to a correspondent a few days later. "I caught cold at Pisemsky's funeral: I stood for a long time at the cemetery with my hat off, and the day was very cold."[82] Annenkov framed a sympathetic tribute to him: "Pisemsky is no more. Whose turn will it be next? The deceased had one great virtue which made him a dear and curious person even in his recent ruinous state. He resembled nothing and nobody. An originality wrought of bronze and a practical intellect, attached to the land, to the garden in which he lived—bestow upon him an expression which will long remain in the memories of those who knew him and which may be moderately instructive in a sensible biography."[83]

Dostoevsky died exactly one week after Pisemsky, and his funeral, a public event of major import, contrasted markedly with Pisemsky's. The coincidence of their having died within such a short time of each other gave rise to comparisons between them despite their manifest dissimilarity.[84] A year after their demise a special evening under the sponsorship of the Society of Lovers of Russian Literature was held in their honor, on January 29, 1882.[85] Two comparative obituaries written by radical scholars and critics upon the occasion of their deaths were unflattering to Pisemsky. A relatively mild one was composed by Pisemsky's old enemy A. N. Pypin, a member of the *Sovremennik* editorial board that had castigated him in 1862. After a detailed summary of the writer's career, the critic concluded: "And so Pisemsky was unsuccessful in depicting the general phenomena of our social life, and he could not have been successful because of the entire character of his concepts. He was incomparably more powerful when he took the narrower tasks of milieu vignettes and personal dramatic confrontations. In the initial period of his activity he stood in the front rank of writers who established the realistic current in our literature."[86]

The other article, published by the populist critic N. K. Mikhaylovsky and titled "O Pisemskom i Dostoevskom" (On Pisemsky and Dostoevsky), dealt primarily with Dostoevsky. Although the two were born and died at almost the same time, the critic wrote, their literary gifts were unequal. Pisemsky had written himself out long before his death, and "the grateful reader honors in his person not a live force, which one might justifiably harbor hopes and fears about—but a contribution, a completed and already evaluated contribution." With Dostoevsky the situation was quite otherwise, argued Mikhaylovsky, for his talent was so unique that he could not be compared with anyone else, least of all Pisemsky.[87] Thus, as in life Pisemsky had been continually compared to Turgenev, not always favorably, so in death he was overshadowed by a contemporary with whom almost no one could have competed successfully.

VI

On Pisemsky as Realist

It may be said that anyone wishing to comprehend the demands of realistic content completely, to attain its Pillars of Hercules, should study Pisemsky.

Apollon Grigorev (1861)

Over the more than one hundred years that have elapsed since Aleksey Pisemsky first achieved literary renown, critics of various camps have concurred in the view that he was endowed by nature with great literary "talent" but that he failed to develop this gift sufficiently to attain major status. Even when one considers that the word "talent" has been applied many times to numerous writers, the frequency of its application to Pisemsky still seems exceptional. In the course of reviewing a performance of *The Hypochondriac* in 1855, Nekrasov very early commented that "the author has no lack of talent," which engendered hope that he would eventually produce works superior to the one under consideration.[1] Thereafter the word was used many times by many critics, so that more than a century later and in another country a scholar was led to entitle his Harvard doctoral dissertation "Pisemskij's Talent as a Novelist."[2] Of all those who have spoken of Pisemsky's talent, however, Apollon Grigorev perhaps offered the most penetrating comments upon his natural abilities. Surprisingly early—in late 1852—Grigorev wrote in a general review article: "It is remarkably strange that with each new work since *A Marriage of Passion*, the author's world-view has constantly, so to speak, descended [ponizhatsya], at the same time

that all the direct indicators of talent remain the same as before.''
One page later Grigorev returned to this theme: "in everything that
has followed [*The Simpleton* and *A Marriage of Passion*] one ob-
serves merely a direct talent, as if denuded completely and deprived
of any equipment.''[3] Through the convolutions of Grigorev's style
one may perceive his drift: Pisemsky had been given the precious
gift of talent but was not channeling it rationally, not developing
intellectual guidelines that would bestow upon his work more significance than it possessed "naturally.'' It seems likely that a feeling of
this sort has prevailed among Pisemsky's readers since the time of
Grigorev's remarks, so as to prevent Pisemsky from being assigned
a higher place among Russian writers.

Pisemsky's "denuded talent'' had the peculiar quality of eliciting
metallic images from his readers in speaking of his works. Thus,
Leskov wrote of *In the Whirlpool*: "I am in ecstasy over the power
of Pisemsky's talent. The book resembles some sort of bronze sculp-
tures.''[4] Goncharov referred to *An Enlightened Time* in a remarkably similar vein in a letter to the author: "It seemed to me to be
intelligent, lively, well conceived, and extremely successfully executed, as if cast in one go from a single piece of metal.''[5] The critic
D. S. Mirsky gave a new twist to this reaction when he commented
that Pisemsky's characters "do not move about in a mellow autumnal
haze like Turgenev's, but stand out in the fierce glare of sunlight.''[6]
Nikolay Strakhov remarked that Pisemsky's stories portrayed life
"in a sort of nudity.''[7] These comments point up the fact that
Pisemsky's literary talent was intensely straightforward and occasionally simplistic, refusing to recognize gradations or shadings,
and thus producing works, characters, and situations with sharp,
clear edges. His writings display an unusual firmness.

Pisemsky's theory of artistic realism (to the extent that his atheo-
retical mind was capable of formulating a coherent creed) rested on
the uncomplicated axiom that art should be based upon life, without
any intellectual reservations. His philosophy of literary and artistic
realism approached absolute consistency in its simplicity. It differed
from the theory of realism propounded by the radical critics, who
maintained that all art should not only attack the abuses of the
existing society but also point the way to a revolutionary transformation of that society along socialist lines. Pisemsky could never bring
himself to subject his writing to such ideological demands. But
neither was he a full adherent of the "aesthetic camp'' in Russian
criticism, despite his association with Druzhinin, Botkin, and others
of their persuasion. Whereas Druzhinin emphasized the primary

importance of beauty for literature, Pisemsky could never bring himself to believe that this should be the sole criterion for judging a literary work, even a poem. In 1854, for instance, he assured Maykov that he was indisputably the best poet then writing in Russian. Afanasy Fet, Fedor Tyutchev, Nikolay Shcherbina were insignificant in comparison. Schcherbina, Pisemsky remarked sarcastically, claimed to "sing of nothing but beauty-beauty,"[8] but beauty in isolation was not enough for a poet: one had to cultivate a broad circle of interests in order to be genuinely significant. Eventually even Maykov became too aesthetic for Pisemsky. Again in 1866 Pisemsky stated his views, when describing the fashion in which his current series of dramas had been received in the two capitals. His Moscow friends had welcomed them with tearful enthusiasm, he claimed, but his St. Petersburg advisers had reacted as if he were a criminal. When he gave a reading at the home of the poet Fedor Tyutchev, he had been scolded in no uncertain terms. "All this," he wrote, "of course jarred me considerably and simply confirmed for me the conviction that I understand fiction, dramatic and even tragic art better than any of these gentlemen, and that aesthetic scrofula [zolotukha], which has penetrated them like rot, keeps them from looking at the situation as they should."[9] Being unsympathetic to both the radicals' demand for ideology and the aesthetes' demand for beauty, Pisemsky emerged as a devotee of unideological ugliness in literature, a position that brought him close to the French naturalists. He was noted for what could be termed his "merciless realism," which surveyed life boldly, without flinching before its more unpleasant aspects.

The cornerstone of Pisemsky's literary approach was attachment to real life as it was actually lived in contemporary society. As a corollary, he felt little sympathy for those who retired from the hurly-burly of everyday existence in order to write. While living in involuntary retreat at his Ramene estate in 1854, Pisemsky told his confidant Maykov that the solitude was depressing him to such an extent as to render him incapable of producing. "In the midst of many intelligent truths," he wrote, "Gogol propounded one untruth, to the effect that a writer should seek inspiration in the quiet of his study; but I, at any rate, have always drawn my inspiration from life."[10]

Because one knows one's own life better than any other, Pisemsky was naturally led to use a number of autobiographical elements in his fiction. "The Carpenters' Guild" and *One Thousand Souls* contain numerous autobiographical strands. In his autobiographical sketches Pisemsky referred the reader in particular to his novel *Men of the 1840's*, which approaches fictionalized autobiography. In *Troubled Seas* he even introduced himself as a character, under his own name. People close to him also appeared in various forms in his writings. To give only two examples, his wife Ekaterina Pavlovna served as the prototype for the faithful Evpraksiya in *Troubled Seas;* Pavel Katenin, with whom Pisemsky associated in his youth, is sketched in detail in *Men of the 1840's* under the name of Aleksandr Ivanovich Koptin. Pisemsky's friends and associates thus became important grist for his literary mill.

Once the writer had gathered his material from the flow of real life, he required some time to savor and digest it in order to make it suitable for incorporation into a literary work. For this purpose, leisure was essential. One reason for Pisemsky's revulsion against the period of the 1870's, with its rapid industrial expansion and development, was his belief that mechanization had destroyed the leisurely pace of existence. Leskov reported a conversation, probably of the early 1870's, in which Pisemsky complained that the rapidity of railroad travel had made it impossible to ingest impressions in the proper manner. The verb "ingest" is apt in this context, since according to Leskov, Pisemsky explained that these impressions "stand in you thickly, as if a 24-hour-gruel were simmering—then, of course, things come out thickly in your work as well; but now all this is done in the railroad manner—you take a plate without asking any questions; you eat, with no time to chew for a bit; clack-clack-clack and everything is set." The vital ingredient was "thickness" (*gustota*), of which railroads were the natural enemy.[11] "Thickness" demanded a patience for its preparation that nobody seemed to possess any more.

Evidently the creations of Pisemsky's imagination had a certain body for him, an independent existence verging on the hallucinatory. The memoirist A. F. Koni has recorded that Pisemsky once informed him that he drank because otherwise the creatures of his literary fantasy would allow him no rest. "They stand around me and in front of me all night and look at me—they are living beings and won't allow me to fall asleep!"[12] If this evidence is trustworthy, Pisemsky's suffering from hallucinatory visions may be linked with his mental instability. He may also be compared with Goncharov, who wrote that his literary characters sometimes seemed to inhabit the air about him and live a life independent of him. In his declining years Goncharov actually crossed the border of sanity.

Inasmuch as Pisemsky was not an intellectual in the sense of being absorbed with abstract concepts and liking to play with ideas for sheer intellectual pleasure, such theories of realism as he propounded were not intellectual and rationalistic but rather "organic" and emotional in nature. This is shown in a passage from a long letter of 1877 to the scholar F. I. Buslaev, in which the writer sets forth his view that the novel, "like any work of art, should be born, and not thought up; that, being the fruit of an author's material and spiritual organism, at the same time it should present concentrated reality, whether it be exterior, exposed reality or concealed, psychic reality."[13] In sum, the writer observed reality at his leisure and in detail, concentrated his impressions "thickly" within himself, and then produced a concentrated simulacrum of reality for his readers. This simulacrum, however, was not produced through rational analysis; it emerged from the author's subconscious as the result of a process that was irrational and unanalyzable. The catalyst of this operation was usually termed "inspiration," a factor that can never be explained in rational terms.

Pisemsky's reverence for inspiration caused him to regard with special disapproval the empty, bombastic phrases that often came out when one "composed" (sochinyat) without inspiration. During his Ramene year of 1854, when he found that he could not write in seclusion, he dreaded to force himself. It was better to write nothing than to compel oneself to produce. This he knew from experience, having already tried "composing" *A Rich Fiancé,* "which came out such trash that I was ashamed of it myself."[14] Without inspiration, no worthwhile literature could be created. Oddly enough, however, Pisemsky once argued that "compulsion" could successfully be brought into play, not directly, but at a remove. In 1855 he advised his friend Ostrovsky, "Of course art demands inspiration, but then even inspiration can be brought into being as the result of a certain forcing of oneself."[15] This remark is best interpreted as a short-lived aberration, for ordinarily he was merciless toward those who tried to accomplish something beyond their natural powers in literature. For instance, in his letter of 1877 to Buslaev, Pisemsky mocked certain writers of the 1840's who had stood straining on tiptoe in a vain attempt to analyze the "delicate feelings and exalted emotions of their characters."[16] One should recognize one's limitations and then operate as successfully as possible within them. In his clearer moments Pisemsky understood that his own talent, while genuine, was not extraordinary. It must have been for this reason that one of his characters in *Troubled Seas* said to another, the author Pisemsky: "Your flight is not lofty, not like that of the eagle, but neither is it false'' (IV, 438). Thus did the author pronounce a clear-sighted verdict upon himself. Pisemsky usually exhibited the virtue of intellectual honesty.

Pisemsky's desire to be faithful to reality prompted him to check his fiction carefully for verisimilitude, making sure that nothing ''unrealistic'' intruded. In this area Pisemsky's intellectual limitations were sometimes a handicap. A close colleague of his, Petr Veynberg, has described his ludicrous application of the yardstick of verisimilitude to the stage. Veynberg reports that Pisemsky was much better as a reader than as an actor, for when on stage in a play, he insisted on turning his back to the audience while speaking to other characters, if this seemed the natural thing to do. He justified his stance by the laws of realism, arguing, ''Do you mean to say that when I am in a room speaking to someone, I care at all about whether anyone hears me except those to whom I am addressing my words?'' To the objection that the stage has its own laws, Pisemsky retorted that ''there were no laws except one: complete realism, without any limitations or concessions!''[17] Although these words quoted in the memoir may not be exact, they express rather well Pisemsky's view that art could claim no privileges denied to ''reality.''

Two prominent elements in Pisemsky's literary style that contribute to its realism are his painstaking description of the physical milieu and his use of dialogue. To the extent that he was a ''describer of milieu [byt],''[18] he may be linked with Leskov, another leading depicter of the Russian scene. A ''describer of milieu'' is most often thought of as one who pictures his characters' physical environment in exacting detail, so as to give the reader a sense of what it was like to live and move at a given time in a given place in Russia. Pisemsky does this in such passages as the vignette of a gala evening in ''Is She To Blame?,'' where for about a page he offers brief but vivid depictions of anonymous characters, such as an old maid who was so thin that a considerable space remained between her own back and the back of her dress, or a strange gentleman who circulated through the rooms inspecting clocks, locks, drapes, and other such household items (III, 243-244). The accumulation of this type of detail creates a highly realistic atmosphere.

The use of dialogue is a characteristic of the dramatic approach to fiction, enabling the author to eschew any special omniscience that would not be granted to the ordinary observer in reality. When judging those with whom one comes in contact, one is not permitted access to their innermost thoughts, but rather must deduce them as best he can from words, gestures, and actions. The playwright, too, must rely entirely upon dialogue along with a few descriptions of external actions, leaving the analysis of his characters' motivations to the spectator. Pisemsky, a lover of the theater and a playwright, carried the theatrical approach over into his short stories and novels, relying on dialogue and plot rather more than was common for Russian fiction at the time. For instance, the short story "The Comic Actor," describing an incurable actor, contains whole pages of straight dialogue. Dialogue plays an important role in "The Old Proprietress," in which the principal characters discuss former times among themselves, subject only to occasional proddings from the narrator. "The Braggart" and "The Petersburger" are almost entirely monologues, which could with minor alterations be presented as dramatic readings: the story is narrated by a major character, assisted by a few leading questions, with some recapitulation by the author. A Soviet critic has neatly summed up Pisemsky's method in *The Simpleton,* which may be applied to a number of his other works as well: "In the structure of the work Pisemsky employs primarily images, pictures, and action, which are supposed to communicate the author's thought to the reader. The writer's role in clarifying the thoughts in the work is limited to the arrangement of the material (composition) and a minimal analysis of his heroes' moral condition at one moment of their lives or another. In this way there is achieved a feeling of unusual truthfulness in that which is depicted."[19]

Pisemsky's reliance upon dialogue relieved him to a degree of the necessity for indulging in descriptive psychological analysis. This is not to say that Pisemsky never offers a direct description of his characters' emotions, for he does so fairly often, but he exhibits a tendency to externalize situations by having the characters analyze their own feelings, either orally or in a letter. Letters, in addition to their natural function of maintaining communication between geographically separated persons, provide a "realistic" substitute for interior monologue. A prime instance is the letter from Prince Grigorov to his beloved at the beginning of *In the Whirlpool,* in which he sets down random thoughts on life and society (VII, 12-14). Again, one character in a story may use a letter to pass judgment from his limited viewpoint upon other characters, as at the conclusion of *A Marriage of Passion,* where a feminine character expresses her disillusion with both Khozarov and Mari (I, 413-414). In view of the importance Pisemsky attached to the letter in his fiction, it is somewhat surprising that he never composed an epistolary novel.

Related to Pisemsky's use of the letter is his employment of rumor and gossip, which sometimes give the reader his first hint of a character, just as in real life one may hear of a person for some time before actually meeting him. Gossip, whether founded in fact or not, serves to define the speaker's attitude toward the person or thing to which he is referring and adds to the realistic quality of the fictional work.

As a realist, Pisemsky was committed to the view that "truth" should guide the writer in the artistic reproduction of life. Of course, this aim was widespread at the time: Apollon Grigorev harped on it, the radical critics preached incessantly about it. In fact, it would be almost impossible to find a literary man of the period who seriously held that art should have no relation to truth, although there was much disagreement as to what the truth was. In the course of his career Pisemsky made several statements on the necessity for truth in art. The most prominent of them appears at the conclusion of his 1855 article on Gogol, where he exhorted writers to "tell the *truth* to the public" while at the same time adhering to exacting aesthetic standards (VII, 458). In 1867 he made another remark on the subject, in a letter to the Minister of the Interior concerning his play *Lieutenant Gladkov:* "You are personally acquainted with my literary orientation, and no matter how insignificant and feeble my works as a writer may have been, at least I have always pursued in them one single aim—*to tell the truth as far as I understand it.*"[20] Ten years later, in 1877, Pisemsky counseled Turgenev not to lose heart over the attacks on his novel *Virgin Soil,* for "an artist must first of all be objective and dispassionate and is not at all obliged to write for the pleasure of any parties whatsoever."[21] Thus, whenever Pisemsky was moved to indulge in abstract speculation on art, he clung to the banner of objectivity and truth.

An author's interpretation of "truth" or "reality," however, is of necessity subjective. Optimistic writers may choose to note only the bright sides of life. The radical authors of Pisemsky's time and later emphasized the "essential" rottenness of the existing order, which contrasted so vividly with the assumed virtues of their nascent radical social organization. Such selectivity of vision on the part of the realist was urged by *Sovremennik's* chief critic of the early 1860's, M. A. Antonovich, in an article that was fundamentally a rehash of the theories advanced in Chernyshevsky's *Aesthetic Relation of Art to Reality.* Antonovich drew a sharp distinction between "imitation" and "reproduction" of nature. It is a mistake, he wrote, to argue that the realist should transform himself into a photographer, who pictures everything mechanically, in an "imitation" of nature. In the first place, a photograph furnishes only incomplete information about the object photographed; in the second place, it may transmit with equal assiduity both important and trivial details. The true artist would not think of approaching his art in so simple-minded a fashion: "The reproducing artist, on the other hand, takes a conscious and rational attitude toward his work; he reproduces with the greatest clarity the most important and essential traits, depicts others not quite so clearly, and still others he may omit altogether; in the most essential features he does not transmit everything down to the smallest detail, but only those aspects which in his opinion characterize the object most especially."[22]

As everyone agreed that art should reproduce reality in some fashion, the disputes arose over what parts of reality were sufficiently significant to merit attention. An uncompromising realist like Pisemsky might well have argued that in theory all aspects of reality are equally important, and perhaps it was partly for this reason that he included in his fiction the masses of detail for which he was censured by some critics. As a practical matter, though, no writer could possibly describe all the details of reality. The problem of selecting facets for emphasis thus remained a central one for any writer claiming to be a realist. Pisemsky had a strong tendency to see primarily the "underside" of life. Some radical critics welcomed his work as long as the "life" he depicted was that of conventional contemporary society. According to their lights, however, he was not supposed to adopt the same approach toward the radical milieu, and when he ignored this proscription by applying his yardstick to the young progressives in *Troubled Seas*, he was abruptly condemned. At the time Saltykov-Shchedrin went so far as to deny that he was a "genuine realist" at all.[23]

On one or two occasions Pisemsky attempted to justify the jaundiced view of humankind exhibited in his stories and novels. In *The Masons*, after sketching a dreadful scene of human swinishness, he offered the following by way of apology: "The author is not recounting all this for his own enjoyment and that of the reader, but from the feeling that a describer of mores must be truthful, for the picture of human life includes, not just luminous images fragrant with a purity of the heart; rather for the most part it swarms with unattractive and repulsive figures, though at the same time nobody would deny that every author is necessarily obliged to exert all his energies in order to discover, even in a miserable group of people, certain . . . fine spiritual qualities" (VI, 264). Although in this passage he paid lip service to the necessity for picturing the good with the bad, and though he elsewhere created a number of positive characters, Pisemsky's cynical intellect instinctively sought first the unworthy motive, the selfish material interest behind human behavior. In later life this trait had developed to such an extent as to alarm his friend Leskov. In an attempt to counteract Pisemsky's pernicious influence, Leskov in 1879 published a brief foreword to an edition of his story "Odnodum" (One-Track), reporting a conversation with a "certain great Russian writer" who was "dying in his presence for the forty-eighth time" (an obvious slam at Pisemsky's hypochondria).[24] Pisemsky was bemoaning the loss of some 1000 rubles as a consequence of the censorship's suppression of one of his plays. Leskov retorted that he deserved this treatment because in his play he had chosen to depict a number of highly placed persons, "each one [of whom was] worse than the other." Pisemsky replied:

"So in your opinion, then, you should just write about good people; but, brother, I describe what I see, and I see nothing but filth."

"You are suffering from a disruption of the vision."

"Maybe so," the dying man replied, completely enraged. "But what am I to do when I see nothing but rot either in your soul or my own."

This anecdote illustrates an interesting aspect of the Pisemskian psychology: his definition of reality as the unlovely and corrupt.

An inseparable facet of Pisemsky's pessimism, noted by certain of the radical critics, was its lack of a positive ideal. His most perceptive critic, Apollon Grigorev, was repelled by this "ideallessness" when he wrote in 1852 that Pisemsky "does not have, as for example Ostrovsky does, a solid, definite, and at the same time ideal world view, which would serve him as a point of support in the exposure of everything false in seemingly noble aspirations. As a result of this, the negative approach may easily lead him into stolid indifference."[25] In after years Pisemsky was berated more than once for his "indifference" to the sin and social evil portrayed in his fiction. He has found defenders on this point as well: Strakhov, for instance, held that the fundamental note sounding in his work was "offended idealism."[26] From our vantage point it is also clear that he was not indifferent to evil. He maintained an ideal that perhaps was not exalted enough to suit Grigorev but which he nevertheless attempted to embody in such characters as Nastya in *One Thousand Souls*. By and large, he was too acutely aware of the frailty of human nature to believe that any ideal in society could long remain uncontaminated by crass, unworthy admixtures. For him any ideal was unrealistic.

Another basic tenet of Pisemsky's explicit theory of realism was that literature should eschew didacticism and tendentiousness. In his letter of 1877 to Buslaev he deals at length with the problem of didacticism. Pisemsky dissented strongly from Buslaev's view that didacticism in literature was desirable. From contemporary French, German, and English writers who had set out to instruct the public down to such novels as Chernyshevsky's *What Is To Be Done?*, Pisemsky argued, didacticism had always failed to guide people toward better ways, and "all these instructive works, I should surmise, stand in danger of falling into prompt and eternal oblivion." The classic writers of world literature—Cervantes, Smollett, Scott, even George Sand, Pushkin, Lermontov—had created with no deliberate intention of instructing their reading public. What they wrote may in fact have been instructive, at least in part, but they allowed the reader to select what was important for him. To cite Pisemsky's inelegant words, they in effect told the reader: "Here you are, put it in your sack, and when you get home you can figure out what you can use and what not!" Gogol was a sad example of a writer who had been deflected from the strait path by "various advisers" lacking any idea of what literature should accomplish. Even in *Dead Souls*, Pisemsky wrote, Gogol had attempted didactic flights, and in his *Selected Passages from Correspondence with Friends* he had reached the limit of unrelieved didacticism.[27]

It was not inconsistent for Pisemsky to express such opinions on literary didacticism in the 1850's, when in fact his own fiction was not especially tendentious and he was under the direct influence of Druzhinin, but it is curious that he should have held to this position as late as 1877, after his intervening plays and novels. Not only was his tendentious intent obvious in such books as *Troubled Seas* and *The Bourgeois*, in plays like *Baal*, *The Financial Genius*, and others of that cycle, but Pisemsky openly rejoiced at what he considered the success of his plays precisely because of their didacticism. In describing the public reception of *The Financial Genius* to Turgenev, Pisemsky reported that the audience had called him to the stage several times with applause and then verbally expressed its gratitude "because I punish all these monsters on the stage at least, since, unfortunately, the public procurator and the courts have as yet no legal means of getting at many of them."[28] Where didacticism was concerned, Pisemsky's practice sometimes diverged sharply from his theoretical views.

On occasion Pisemsky strove to be not merely didactic but prophetic. Radical literary theory of the 1860's stressed the possibility of projecting the future from the present. By selecting certain facets of reality for artistic reproduction, they held, the artist implicitly avowed his belief that these were the ones "with a future." If mankind progressed as expected, these facets would develop further, while the nonessential and thus unrecorded features of contemporary reality would be forgotten. The artist was supposed to be a species of seer, and the quality of his work had to be judged by the extent to which he succeeded in culling out those aspects of present reality that would in fact prove viable in the future. In his tendentious works of the later period Pisemsky did indeed regard himself as something of a prophet. He carried this attitude to absurdity in a personal letter of 1878 in which he claimed that his *Former Falcons* and *Fledglings of the Last Flight,* written some fourteen years before, had turned out pure prophecy. He recalled that the poet Fedor Tyutchev had protested violently against the suicides, murders, and incestuous relationships portrayed in the plays, saying that "nothing like this had ever occurred in real life and could not occur —but alas, it turned out that all my friends were mistaken and that I was prophesying something which was already in the air."[29] One is hardly convinced that cases of incest between father and daughter had been uncovered with greater frequency since the writing of *Former Falcons,* but for suicides and murders, one might recall the political assassination attempts of the period as well as the suicide of Pisemsky's own son. Whereas a prophetic interpretation of his plays of the 1860's was largely unjustifiable, he perhaps had better grounds for thinking his anticapitalist plays of the 1870's prophetic. After the crash of a large Moscow bank in 1875 Pisemsky reported to Turgenev: "Wherever I appear everybody calls me a prophet, remembering the second act of my play *An Enlightened Time.* In the Loan-bank there was discovered just the same sort of . . . villainy as in my play."[30] In sum, while feeling no compulsion to underline the positive aspects of contemporary life, Pisemsky forecast the development of certain negative features of capitalist society. He was a representative of a twisted form of "socialist realism": instead of discerning the positive aspects of a future socialist society in the present, he delineated the negative aspects of the future capitalist society in the present.

Pisemsky's objective in his fiction was to get at the true state of affairs behind the facade that human beings set up to disguise their genuine motivations, either from others or from themselves. It is for this reason that many of his works describe the destruction of illusions and expose deceit.[31] In determining the "truth," ideological schemes were more of a hindrance than a help, in Pisemsky's view: all that was required was the application of a modicum of "common sense," the standard he usually took as his final authority. Anton Chekhov, who also sought to depict reality unadorned, approved of Pisemsky's approach in general. In a letter of 1893 he first remarked that parts of Pisemsky's novels by then appeared dated because of their analyses of topical questions, which demonstrated that "the novelist who is an artist should bypass everything which has temporary significance"—a judgment that Soviet scholars customarily omit in their citation of the passage. But Chekhov went on: "In his *History* Skabichevsky accuses him of obscurantism and treason, but good Lord, out of all our contemporary writers I don't know a single one who is so passionately and with such conviction a liberal as Pisemsky. All his priests, functionaries and generals are scoundrels through and through." In sum, Pisemsky was a "great talent," who devoted his powers to the exposure of the rotten in contemporary society.[32]

The compass employed by Pisemsky in his quest for truth was the conviction that people's actions were almost invariably grounded in material self-interest or physiological urges (hunger or the sexual instinct). Though many strove to conceal this fundamental reality with lies or poses, Pisemsky stood ready to rip away the mask of pretense from the ignoble motives beneath.

Pretense could assume many forms, innocent and not so innocent. A person could pretend to be something he was not through outright lying, for example. Pisemsky's fascination with the liar and his moral world led to the creation of *Russian Liars*, in which he originally set himself the task of thoroughly investigating the prevaricator's ways. Curiously enough, most of Pisemsky's liars do not tell falsehoods with the clear intention of deceiving others for personal gain or to discomfit those who believe them. Rather, they lie for the sheer enjoyment of it. At one point in *Troubled Seas* Aleksandr is talking to Venyavin about his connection with Sonya. Aleksandr implies plainly that she is his mistress ("We have entered into a relationship of a sort from which there is no retreating") when in fact this is not the case at all. In this instance Pisemsky is inclined to be indulgent with his hero: "The reader sees quite well that the young man was lying here in ghastly, dreadful fashion! But what can you do? This was not so much a lie as overwrought fantasy" (IV, 149). In the same novel a nihilist girl, Elena Bazeleyn, concocts falsehoods from a sense of loyalty to radical ideals. She was arrested and brought to trial partly because of a diary in which she had written that she did not believe in God and despised being forced to attend church. Further, she claimed that once she had asked a student whether he had a couch with a pillow and had then gone to study in his room, the implication being that she had spent the night there as well. The sensible Varegin is certain that she has made all this up "out of obeisance before a fashionable idea," that she actually believed in God and had never visited any student. She felt that she must contrive falsehoods in order to keep up with the crowd (IV, 545).

One need not lie with words: one's appearance may be as false as any verbal untruth. A sketch from *Russian Liars*, entitled "Krasavets" (A Handsome Fellow), deals with precisely this notion. "A great many ladies," Pisemsky remarks sagely, "both old and young, are convinced to this very day that a handsome and stately man must have a beautiful soul as well, not at all suspecting, in their childish simplicity, that a man can lie with his body as well as in words, and that very frequently the coarsest sensual inclinations and most despicable traits of character may be concealed beneath a pleasant exterior" (IV, 589-590). Failure to comprehend such an elementary principle can be disastrous, as demonstrated by the fate of Iosaf Ferapontov from "An Old Man's Sin." Ferapontov is entranced by the beautiful Kostyreva, described as an "angelic blonde," with luxurious hair, a lovely complexion, blue eyes, dimples, a rather low-cut blouse, and a most attractive knee discernible through the folds of her dress (IV, 36). Ferapontov is convinced that a creature so physically exquisite must possess the most delicate moral character as well, but in reality she is a callous deceiver who discards him as soon as he is no longer useful to her. During the investigation of Ferapontov's misdeeds at the story's conclusion, Kostyreva is at a great advantage in the eyes of the investigating committee: "It would have been easier to suspect a child of a capital crime of some sort than that angelic little face!" (IV, 81). Even after she has been exposed as an impostor, the impression created by her physical beauty still lingers in the air.

Pretense based on physical beauty may be consciously reinforced by the cultivation of fine manners and appropriate attitudes, as is the case with Batmanov, who made his mark in local society "on the basis of his rather pleasant exterior, his dress brought from the capital, his manners, and a certain originality of opinion" (III, 96).

He was accepted as a worthy member of society because of his external attributes, although in fact he was a selfish individual seeking only his private advantage.

A minor character in *A Rich Fiancé* embodies pretension in its crudest form. The person in question, Aleksey Sergeich Ukhmirev, having been born neither wealthy nor handsome, makes his way in the world by putting up a front. Though quick to grovel before the rich, he snubs those less fortunate. He pretends to have a stomach so delicate that he cannot eat certain dishes and to be incapable of imbibing the local Madeiras because he has become accustomed solely to imported wines. He claims to read a great deal, although his associates who know him well sneer at this pretension, affirming that he orders books merely for show and never cuts the pages. Although his false front does not deceive everybody, it enables him to capture a wealthy widow for his wife and thus ensures his future material well-being (I, 90).

Pisemsky thought that the desire for money and for the things it could purchase was one of the main driving forces in men's lives. Financial gain is therefore the chief factor in the calculations of a large number of his heroes. Kalinovich's career graphically demonstrates that even love must yield to the thust for money, power, and comfort. In *A Marriage of Passion* Khozarov's confidante berates all male humanity in his presence, saying that men marry "as some sort of moral oldsters, incapable not only of feeling but even of understanding feelings! You have only business and money in the head!" (I, 322). Consequently, a woman who marries for love is eventually left with no recourse but to demand expensive entertainment, since her husband thinks only in those terms.

Shamaev, the corrupted hero of "The Braggart," is cognizant of the advantages of a wealthy marriage. He candidly informs his uncle that he is seeking a rich bride in order to obtain sufficient funds to live well, as he feels he has a right to (III, 179). He is also aware of the importance of appearances. When his uncle remonstrates with him for giving expensive dinners he cannot afford, Shamaev laughs off the criticisms. He readily admits having hired a cook of his own for these occasions because "decent people" cannot do without one. He looks upon his dinner parties as an investment in the future: connections can be developed and reputations established only on the basis of lavish entertainments. "Nowadays," Shamaev lectures his uncle, "the dinner plays an important role in society. Connections are established through the dinner, and after money, connections are the most important thing in life. Capital is acquired through dinners because one accumulates credit! Dinner! Dinner! That's a very deep thing, worth thinking about a bit" (III, 193).

The ladies are also aware of money's worldly importance. In *Troubled Seas* the ravishing Sonya, in the course of her training for life in an artificial society, realizes that "birth and wealth" alone are genuinely respected. The most unappealing girls are eagerly sought after if they have extensive means (IV, 179). Physical beauty itself has financial value in that it attracts rich men, as Sonya demonstrates when she takes a wealthy man as her first husband. Yet during the wedding ceremony she must strain to keep from weeping: "Her face was pale and convulsive: she realized fully that she was selling herself and wanted at least to make it worth her while: her wedding dress alone had cost about three thousand, and a diamond diadem worth five thousand burned on her forehead" (IV, 195). The irony of life, however, is that those who think they have grasped the fact that only money can bring happiness and who act on this knowledge to further their material fortunes, usually end unhappily anyway. One is discontented either with money or without it.

In the plays of the 1870's the theme of money as the source of evil becomes even more insistent. Now all emotions and all virtue are reduced to purchasable commodities. In *Baal* the positive character Mirovich argues with Kunitsyn, who dreams of embezzling a million rubles from a bank and then escaping to America. When Mirovich objects that not everything can be bought, Kunitsyn challenges him to give an example of something not subject to the power of money "in our age of steam, railroads, and electricity." Mirovich replies that one cannot purchase the genuine love of a woman, artistic talent, or an honest reputation, but Kunitsyn sneers at him, retorting that nowadays one can buy any of these things, including a love that will "flame and burn," as he puts it with thick sarcasm (VIII, 347).

Such is the outlook of a poor man who wishes he were rich. Burgmeyer, the rich man of *Baal*, has in the meantime discovered that money does not bring happiness. He reviews his personal situation in a bitter monologue inviting all who thirst for millions to gaze upon him. He hesitates to consult doctors about his illnesses, because he knows they will extend the period of his recovery in order to receive larger fees. Everywhere money stands in his path. "I have ceased even to be a man for other people," he cries. "Rather I am some sort of money-bag from which everybody hopes to extract some profit one way or another'' (VIII, 373). Emotions, feelings, aspirations, even the very quality of being human—all are vanquished by the omnipotent ruble. But Burgmeyer dreads the specter of financial ruin even more than the sufferings occasioned by the possession of wealth. He maintains that in his day poverty is far more disastrous than it was in previous ages, when one could always hope that a "kind relative or a faithful old friend or a virtuous magnate" would provide food and shelter. In the heartless era of the 1870's all human relations are so intimately dependent upon wealth that the bankrupt can anticipate nothing better than death of cold and starvation (VIII, 340).

The generalized hatred of money and its evil works permeating Pisemsky's writings of the 1850's was in the 1870's transformed into an almost unreasoning rage against Russian capitalism as the systematic utilization of money to create yet more money in the form of profit. The landed gentry of his early stories sold off their possessions to obtain funds with which to live in suitable fashion; impoverished individuals dreamed of obtaining a post with a good salary to ease their material situation. But the entrepreneur of the 1870's considered the making of money an end in itself, and he had much less idea of what to do with money after acquiring it than had his predecessors of the 1850's. His only aim in life was to keep from losing any and to obtain more if possible.

The existence of entrepreneur-capitalists was the central ill of the 1870's, in Pisemsky's opinion, and he concentrated his faded powers on the assault against them. In *Baal* an exchange takes place between Mirovich and Kleopatra Sergeevna in which Mirovich heatedly denies that a merchant can be anything other than a "parasite." Incapable of becoming an honorable man, he is of no use whatever to society. "Nowadays all the efforts of our honest and best minds," Mirovich tells his listener, "are directed toward seeing to it that there shall be no merchants and toward depriving capital of all power" (VIII, 386-387). One of Pisemsky's most sustained onslaughts against the new capitalism occurs in *The Bourgeois*, where the entrepreneur Khmurin employs a variety of illegal and unethical tactics in the course of his self-seeking speculations. Such men are perhaps the most unredeemable in the entire gallery of Pisemsky's creations.

If the possession of money does not guarantee happiness, neither do human relationships, and most especially the relationships between the sexes. Though it is possible to discover instances of an enduring passion in Pisemsky's works, such as Nastya's in *One*

Thousand Souls, love is ordinarily a temporary emotion, when it exists at all. In *An Enlightened Time* Amaturov complains about his mistress' silliness in imagining that eternal love can exist between a man and a woman. "Perhaps you could find it somewhere on a desert island between monkeys, but you certainly can't see it among people" (VIII, 404). But since Daryalova sincerely believes in this ideal, its destruction drives her to suicide in a way analogous to that in which Prince Grigorov, of *In the Whirlpool,* puts an end to his life when he realizes that Elena's love for him is not everlasting. In short, people who believe in such disastrously erroneous ideals cannot help ending badly in ordinary human society.

Although Pisemsky felt that love should be regarded as an irrational emotion almost invariably destined to fade with time, he had to admit that on occasion it exerted a bafflingly powerful influence on people. He claimed to be puzzled, for example, by the passion of Stepan Gerasimovich for Vera Pavlovna in *A Rich Fiancé.* Stepan falls so thoroughly in love with Vera Pavlovna that he is ready to marry her "just with the clothes on her back," or even to spend his own money in order to win her. The author could not comprehend what there was in Vera Pavlovna's character to captivate her swain so completely (I, 110). Love lacking a solid material or sexual motivation was beyond his understanding.

If love had any nonfiscal foundation, in Pisemsky's view, it could only be straightforward sexual passion. Though some of his heroes begin with an exalted ideal of womankind, when an actual female comes within their grasp, purely physiological factors prove more significant for the development of "love" than most of these dreamers had supposed. By comparison with other authors of his day, Pisemsky was straightforward in his depiction of sexual attraction, another trait that marks him as a great "realist." For instance, Khozarov in *A Marriage of Passion,* after receiving the longed-for acceptance of his proposal to Mari, becomes inflamed by his partner while they are dancing and, standing upon his rights as a fiancé, "set her down beside him on the couch, embraced her and began kissing her hands, cheeks, eyes, neck, and breast," until he is interrupted by the entrance of a third person into the room (I, 381). Again, Prince Grigorov of *In the Whirlpool,* while alone with his mistress-to-be, Elena, becomes overly enthusiastic, unfastens her bodice, and strips her to the waist, after which he drops to his knees in admiration of her beauty. Though at first dreadfully embarrassed, Elena then reflects that, according to her advanced principles, a man should have the right to admire the body of his beloved (VII, 46).

Later on Prince Grigorov is reproached by another character in the novel with having "worn out" Elena: in this case the verb has sexual overtones (VII, 66). Pisemsky described Sonya in *Troubled Seas* as "taller than almost all the other girls, with a fully developed breast" (IV, 152), and included in the novel a suggestive depiction of a ball: "Baklanov noted that the men were twirling the ladies very unceremoniously and seemingly intentionally trying to make their dresses rise higher. The ladies as well seemed somehow to be pressing very close to their partners" (IV, 363). Descriptions of this sort do not shock any more, but Pisemsky's cynical attitude toward love and sex seemed coarse to many readers in nineteenth-century Russia. The poet Aleksey Tolstoy, for instance, though not precisely incensed over Pisemsky's semipornography, once included in a private letter a parody of his approach to the subject, which at least indicates that Tolstoy felt Pisemsky paid excessive attention to these phenomena and depicted them with untoward relish: "Then [the parody goes] he threw her down on the bed and ripped off her silken dress with powerful hand; she vainly strove to keep her cambric chemise on her bare shoulders. In an instant it was lying in tatters on the Persian rug. His hands crept hungrily over her fresh contours. 'Lord, how beautiful you are!' he exclaimed, ripping off her underwear—and their lips came together in a divine kiss.'"[33]

Marriages of various sorts occur in Pisemsky's pages. Sometimes they are contracted involuntarily by one of the partners, usually the woman. The man, impelled by idealistic love or more often lust, makes a proposal that the woman, for one reason or another, is forced to accept, which sets the stage for a marital tragedy. This is the central situation in such stories as *The Simpleton* and "Is She To Blame?" Of course, marriages need not always be forced upon unwilling brides: the story of *A Marriage of Passion* involves the heroes' gradual discovery that neither is mature enough for the marriage which both originally desired ardently. Pisemsky may occasionally describe an outwardly successful marriage, but usually there is something wrong with it at bottom. One example of such a union is the relationship between the elderly Marfin and his much younger wife Susanna Nikolaevna in *The Masons*. Toward the end of the novel Susanna is strongly attracted to a man nearer her own age, named Uglakov. Susanna refuses to violate her matrimonial vows, however, despite the fact that her marriage has never been consummated: for an idealist like her, physical relations are an unimportant component of married life. Pisemsky explains that she "continued to love her husband, but this was a passive love, founded upon admiration for his intellect and his noble spirit,'' whereas her love for Uglakov was a ''transport of the young heart, a searching for the poesy of life, a seeking for some mysterious happiness; in a word, a purely active and more realistic feeling'' (VI, 485). As is evident from this passage, though, Susanna's feelings even for Uglakov have a tinge of unreality.

Illicit love, according to Pisemsky, usually proves as great an illusion as love sanctified by marriage. The initial charms of an irregular liaison fade rapidly. Elchaninov in *Boyarshchina* discovers as much when his former beloved, Anna Pavlovna, leaves her husband and moves in with him. After a time Elchaninov becomes indifferent to his mistress' caresses and no longer cares to spend hours in conversation with her. ''There were even moments,'' Pisemsky confides, ''when it occurred to him that it might be very good if he were completely free, not tied down with this woman'' (II, 145). Other examples of the pain endured by participants in illicit affairs—Nastya and Kalinovich in *One Thousand Souls*, Vikhrov and Mari in *Men of the 1840's*—could be adduced to support the view that Pisemsky was under no illusions about such relationships. One almost satisfactory affair—which, characteristically, is only reported, not enacted—is that between Begushev and Natalya Sergeevna in *The Bourgeois*. She had been the great love of his life and for his sake had abandoned her husband, an important general. But she died young, confessing to Begushev on her deathbed that her ambiguous position had caused her immense suffering, an admission that in turn poisoned Begushev's later life (III, 383-384). For whatever reason, unselfish love can never come to fruition in the world as it is. Man will be unhappy with or without love, just as he will be miserable with or without money. The individual is trapped by the society in which he must live.

A character of Pisemsky's could protest against this suffocating society in several ways. He could retreat into himself through drunkenness, as does Rymov in ''The Comic Actor.'' He could commit suicide, as does Ferapontov by hanging himself, or Begushev by going off to the wars to seek death actively. Like Kalinovich, he could strive to reform society by working within its already established framework in order to seize the levers of control and then fill the old forms with new moral content—though this was a senseless dream that could never be realized. Or, just as fruitlessly, he could rebel against the society by becoming a revolutionary nihilist, as in *Troubled Seas,* or by resorting to banditry, as in the first variant of *A Bitter Fate,* where Pisemsky intended to have Anany escape, become the leader of an outlaw gang, and return to murder the *burmistr,* his tormentor. Though Pisemsky discarded this ending for *A Bitter Fate,* he employed a similar one in the story "The Old Proprietress," where the husband of the granddaughter, after she has returned to her grandmother's house, disguises himself as a local bandit, breaks into the house, and makes off with his wife. The scheme ends catastrophically, however, for in the process his wife dies of terror. It seemed that there really was no way of altering Russian society or even of inflicting a limited revenge upon it: the best one could do was to try to live within it without being conformed to it. Few could manage even this much. Society is, after all, composed of individuals, and if most individuals are corrupt, as Pisemsky thought, the society will inevitably also be corrupt and oppress those few who wish to adhere to high ideals.

The foregoing analysis of Pisemsky's theoretical view of literary realism and the major aspects of his literary practice is plainly not exhaustive. It is sufficient, however, to support the contention that of the leading Russian prose-writers of his time, Pisemsky was the most thoroughgoing realist, if by "realist" is meant a writer who portrays as broadly as possible all levels of contemporary society, who employs exacting period detail, who refuses to idealize his characters or employ improbable coincidences, who deemphasizes style by not using brilliant language or recurrent and obtrusive structural devices. In other words, the more realistic a work is, the more nearly can a reader derive an accurate conception of the author's social surroundings, without distortion caused by artistic and ideological predilections. Of course, Pisemsky worked on the basis of certain assumptions, but until his final decade he exhibited little tendency toward a doctrinaire interpretation. Indeed, so undoctrinaire was he that one critic claimed his fiction aroused the same "perplexity" (*nedoumenie*) in a reader as did life itself.[34] It is instructive to compare his type of realism with that of his contemporaries now considered as classics of Russian literature.

Pisemsky's literary approach is most nearly akin to that of his master Gogol, who influenced him powerfully for years. Apollon Grigorev once wrote that "Pisemsky is a direct, though somewhat coarse, consequence of Gogol, and Goncharov is an indirect one."[35] Pisemsky not only devoted his most important critical article to Gogol, he also mentioned him frequently in his private correspondence (though it does not appear that the two ever met) and made direct references to him in his fiction, as in the discussion of Chichikov and *Dead Souls* in *One Thousand Souls* (II, 534). Although the relationship between the two has attracted scholarly attention, it still has not been analyzed satisfactorily.[36]

The Soviet scholar N. I. Prutskov has isolated the most important single element common to the two writers: their concern with what he calls the "mechanism" of society.[37] According to Prutskov, a character like Kalinovich is depicted not so much as a psychological entity but as a social one, constantly interacting with his social milieu. It is precisely this predilection for analyzing society as a whole that was Gogol's most sweeping legacy to his followers, including Pisemsky. As a matter of fact, on two important occasions Pisemsky borrowed from Gogol the structural device of successive visits by his hero to individual representatives of local society, by which means he could present an array of allegedly typical Russians.

Another link between the two writers is their "dramatism." In fact, Pisemsky's early enthusiasm for the stage was sustained by his interest in Gogol, and one of his favorite dramatic roles was that of Podkolesin in *The Marriage*. Although it would be an exaggeration to explain Pisemsky's playwriting ambitions as the result of any-one's "influence," they must at least have been nourished by his admiration for Gogol's achievements in this genre. Furthermore, there is unquestionably a resemblance between the "dramatism" of Pisemsky's stories and novels—his avoidance of extensive psycho-logizing, his emphasis upon the words and outward actions of his characters, his predilection for dialogue and monologue—and the Gogolian method in literature.

Yet a third bond between Pisemsky and Gogol is their detailed description of the milieu in which their heroes move, as a means of creating an illusion of reality. A number of examples could be cited from *One Thousand Souls* alone: the charming vignette of morning in the provincial town (II, 260-263), the less than charming description of St. Petersburg as seen through the eyes of the newly arrived Kalinovich (II, 474-475), the cameo of the provincial evening party (II, 542-543). In each of these passages Pisemsky introduces several characters, usually nameless, who come to life only for an instant in order to create an effect, thereafter subsiding into oblivion and never reappearing. Gogol utilized this approach often, as, for example, in his celebrated description of the Nevsky Prospect. There is, however, an important difference in their realization of the device: as I. V. Kartashova phrases it, Gogol's episodic characters possess "no individual differentiation, no individual psychology," whereas in Pisemsky the "milieu *always* consists of a number of completely defined individual personages."[38] This in turn points to one of the major divergences between the two writers: Pisemsky depicts rather ordinary, even humdrum individuals in such scenes, whereas Gogol transforms his characters into surrealistic beings, "noses" and "hats" instead of genuine people. When he does so, Gogol is the greater writer, but Pisemsky is the better realist. Pisemsky could not have followed Gogol in his flights of fancy even had he wished to. Moreover, Gogol was a magnificent stylist; the reader constantly admires the intricacy and verbal brilliance of his writing and therefore is always conscious that he is dealing with a literary artifact. This rarely happens with Pisemsky, whose aim was merely to write reasonably clearly and who wasted little effort on polishing and revising his prose.

Pisemsky's dislike for abstract theories set him apart from the radical prose-writers of his day, who in their later work carried on Gogol's interest in the little man oppressed by his social superiors. By and large the radicals took it for granted that the society they were describing was hopelessly corrupt and therefore inevitably destined to disintegrate. Although Pisemsky agreed that contemporary society was far from ideal, his pessimism did not reach the absolute depths displayed in the works of a Saltykov-Shchedrin, for example. In comparing Pisemsky and Saltykov-Shchedrin as satirists, one of their contemporaries remarked that a drawing of Shchedrin would show him without the remotest semblance of a smile on his face. But, "Pisemsky I would sketch smiling—smiling with apparently gay, pleasant laughter; but from every note would project a sharp sting, which would usually cause shivers to run up and down the spines of those whom they stung."[39] In a novel like *The Golovlovs* Shchedrin's humor is bitterly sardonic; his characters are thoroughly base. It was because Shchedrin approached life abstractly and often negatively—as in certain of his later novels, which he said were written against the principles of the family, property, and the state—that he in 1863 asserted that Pisemsky was wrongly considered a realist. Today it seems clear that Shchedrin himself was not being faithful to reality in applying so black a brush to its depiction: instead, he was a dedicated satirist who had to be unfair to reality in order to write effective satire. Pisemsky, on the other hand, though he displayed a satirical bent, tried to present a more objective picture. Moreover, he exhibited considerably greater toleration for human weakness and even corruption. He was indulgent toward scoundrels whom a Shchedrin would have condemned outright on the basis of a priori concepts of justice and morality. A consistent satirist, after all, cannot be more than a fitful realist, since he declines to see the admixture of good that reality usually contains.

In their realistic approach to literature Pisemsky and Tolstoy had a great deal in common. Both were interested in the peasantry as the repository of much that was good in contemporary society, and perhaps both somewhat idealized the peasantry. Both were known for the pitiless honesty of their approach: they attempted to get behind the facade of deception in order to discover true motivations and emotions. Tolstoy even more than Pisemsky was concerned with the problem of working out a transparent prose style to transmit his ideas with the minimal distortion. On the other hand, Pisemsky was unconcerned by the immense, sometimes epic problems that fascinated Tolstoy, with which he dealt in such novels as *War and Peace* and *Anna Karenina*. Except in the 1870's, Pisemsky usually did not utilize fiction to illustrate his theories of life, as Tolstoy did, and certainly he never attempted to describe the thoughts of animals and even plants. Tolstoy's use of interior monologue and internal psychologizing, though not unrealistic, was not so easily checked against reality as was Pisemsky's more external brand of realism. Also, Tolstoy employed structural devices and repetitive phrases for the characterization of his heroes much more consciously than did Pisemsky. In almost all these areas, then, Tolstoy is no more consistent a realist than Pisemsky, and in some cases less so.

Critics have often drawn parallels between the work of Turgenev and Pisemsky. Indeed, for a time it was intellectually fashionable to compare the two. They do have certain points of literary contact. Like Tolstoy, both wrote of the peasantry; both often used love intrigues as the core of their works; and both investigated the characteristics of contemporary or near-contemporary society in their fiction, which therefore may be read with profit even by historians. Traces of Turgenevian influence may be discovered in Pisemsky's writings, most especially in "Is She To Blame?" a tale of idealized love. An instructive contrast between the two writers may be obtained by comparing the opening paragraph of "The Petersburger" with the introduction to Turgenev's "Hor and Kalinych," by which it was clearly inspired. Both passages describe particular regions in the provinces, but whereas Turgenev emphasizes the natural landscape and ends by discussing the advantages to the hunter of different areas, Pisemsky gives a detailed description of the houses to be found there, the people, and the peculiarities of their speech. Pisemsky is more exclusively interested in man's artifacts and his social

relationships than is Turgenev. Pisemsky never felt any desire to
emulate Turgenev by meditating on abstract questions of existence,
such as the meaninglessness of life and the indifference of nature,
and he rarely attempted anything like Turgenev's remarkable nature
descriptions. In his social novels Turgenev strove to distil the essence
of an historical epoch and embody it in his Rudin, Insarov, or
Bazarov, so that they would become emblematic of their time without ceasing to be believable as individuals. In contrast, Kalinovich,
though he expresses certain attitudes prevalent in his epoch, does
not rise to the same high level of generalization. He stands only for
himself, whereas Bazarov represents an entire segment of his generation. Turgenev was far more concerned with complex ideas and the
effect they produced in society than was the nonideological Pisemsky.
Turgenev's heroes are chosen spirits, whereas Pisemsky's are commonplace and therefore in a sense truer to life.

Only the chance occurrence of their deaths within a week of each
other led to serious comparisons between Pisemsky and Dostoevsky.
One can occasionally discover Dostoevskian themes in Pisemsky's
fiction, such as the description in "An Old Man's Sin" of Ferapontov's father, who is painted with Dostoevskian power. But
Dostoevsky was immeasurably more subtle and resourceful a writer
than Pisemsky, who could never pretend to his metaphysical depth
or match his sheer force of invention and genius. Pisemsky was not
so torn by ideological, particularly religious, conflicts as was Dostoevsky; his heroes did not ordinarily revel in the laceration of their emotions; and he did not place the same stress on extraordinary events
(murders, madness, frenzies), nor utilize his characters as mouth-
pieces for philosophical doctrines. He did not write for the purpose
of working out problems of personal and social morality. His characters do not live with the one-sided intensity of Dostoevsky's heroes.
Both Gogol and Dostoevsky, after all, were no more than partial
realists, for they were so closely involved in their own viewpoints
as to want to take from reality only those aspects that fitted their
viewpoints. Pisemsky, however, tried seriously to depict reality as it
was, without excessive distortion in an artistic prism.

Considered strictly as a realist, Goncharov was closest to Pisemsky
of all the great Russian prose writers of the mid-nineteenth century.
Goncharov tended to select heroes who were not extraordinary and to
describe everyday events; consider, for instance, the title of his
first novel, *A Common Story*. He wrote in a style that did not attract
attention to itself. He also had a sharp eye for detail, which enabled him to become one of Russia's greatest travel writers even

when he wrote without special knowledge of the areas he visited. His greatest novel, *Oblomov,* is a remarkably thorough investigation of a small area of human life, with concentration upon the psychological states of the hero under ordinary circumstances. It reveals much about a particular individual insulated from the society about him, having retreated from the struggle for existence into the warmth of his apartment, there to contemplate his spiritual impulses and dream of action. By contrast, Pisemsky's heroes all face the unpleasantnesses of life; they are busy coping with their problems rather than trying to avoid them.

Perhaps, as Claude Backvis has suggested in a thought-provoking comparison between Pisemsky and the greatest Russian fabulist Ivan Krylov,[40] if Pisemsky had lived at the end of the eighteenth century rather than the middle of the nineteenth, and if he had possessed a stronger poetic inclination, he might have found his niche as a writer of fables. His cynically realistic view of life, coupled with his understanding indignation over human weakness and his humorous vein, would have fitted him well to produce the sort of social satire in which fable writers usually specialized.

These, then, are the grounds for regarding Pisemsky as the most genuine realist of his time. Not so oblivious of the good in human beings as was Saltykov-Shchedrin, not so hampered by a prodigious artistic fancy as were Gogol and Dostoevsky, having no desire to prove philosophical points such as Tolstoy's, more concerned with the over-all workings of society than was Goncharov, lacking the idealizing vision of a Turgenev—Pisemsky, because of the very practicality of his mind, came nearer to creating an unbiased picture of his times than any of his colleagues, even while remaining inferior to them as a literary artist. Convinced that society, as well as the bulk of the individuals constituting it, were corrupted beyond redemption, Pisemsky aimed to describe, as realistically and therefore negatively as he could, the Russian world in which he lived. He offered no program of social reform and lacked any desire to contrive one. Though temporary political passions and an abstract thirst for justice sometimes caused him to abandon the anchor of objective "truth," which in his theoretical statements he claimed always to employ, in his best works Russian and human reality have been fixed as with corrosive acid, in a manner peculiarly Pisemsky's own.

Bibliography

Notes

Index

Bibliography

This bibliography makes no claim to completeness. Rather, it lists the most important Russian editions of Pisemsky's works, all the translations of his writings into European languages that could be located, and the most significant critical, scholarly, and memoir pieces on him. Anyone requiring more detailed references may consult the bibliographies cited in the first section. In an attempt to make the bibliography as accurate as possible, I have sought to check every entry *de visu*, but because such verification is out of the question for the rarer editions of Pisemsky's works, many translations, and certain of the scholarly articles, in these cases I have relied upon bibliographical sources alone.

Within each section except the last (memoir literature) the arrangement of entries is chronological, by date of first publication, even though the item may be more accessible elsewhere and may be cited from another source in the notes to this study. In the section on individual works the bibliography is organized around each piece, so as to facilitate its investigation.

BIBLIOGRAPHICAL GUIDES

Anon. "Bibliografiya A. F. Pisemskogo," in V. V. Zelinsky, ed., *Polnoe sobranie sochineniy A. F. Pisemskogo*, 2nd ed. St. Petersburg, 1895, vol. I, pp. VII-XIV.

Yazykov, D. D. *Obzor zhizni i trudov pokoynykh russkikh pisateley*, no. 1 (St. Petersburg, 1885), pp. 39-41. Supplements: no. 9 (Moscow, 1905), p. 93; no. 11 (St. Petersburg, 1909), p. 221; no. 12 (St. Petersburg, 1912), p. 246.

Vengerov, S. A. *Sobranie sochineniy S. A. Vengerova.* St. Petersburg, 1911, V, 254-275.

Berkov, P. N., and M. K. Kleman. "Bibliografichesky ukazatel proizvedeniy A. F. Pisemskogo," in A. F. Pisemsky, *Izbrannye proizvedeniya.* Moscow-Leningrad, 1932, pp. 628-633.

Kleman, M. K. "Sudba literaturnogo naslediya Pisemskogo," in A. F. Pisemsky, *Pisma.* Moscow-Leningrad, 1936, pp. 3-20.

Krendel, R. N., and B. A. Peskina, eds. *Russkie pisateli vtoroy poloviny XIX—nachala XX vv (do 1917 goda): Rekomendatelny ukazatel literatury.* Moscow, 1958, I, 189-203.

Alekseev, A. D. "Pisemsky Aleksey Feofilaktovich," in K. D. Muratova, ed., *Istoriya russkoy literatury XIX veka: Bibliografichesky ukazatel.* Moscow-Leningrad, 1962, pp. 544-548.

EDITIONS OF WORKS AND LETTERS

Povesti i rasskazy A. F. Pisemskogo. Moscow, 1853, 3 vols.

Reviews

K. P. [K. A. Polevoy] "Pchelka," *Severnaya pchela,* no. 94 (April 30, 1853).

Anon. *Biblioteka dlya chteniya,* no. 2 (February 1854), section V, pp. 41-70.

Sochineniya A. F. Pisemskogo. St. Petersburg: Stellovsky. Vols. I-III, 1861; Vol. IV, 1867.

Komedii, dramy i tragedii. Moscow, 1874, 2 vols.

Review

A. [V. G. Avseenko] "Komediya obshchestvennykh nravov," *Russky vestnik,* no. 10 (October 1874), pp. 883-922.

Sochineniya: posmertnoe polnoe izdanie. St. Petersburg-Moscow: Volf, 1883-1886, 20 vols.

Polnoe sobranie sochineniy, 2nd ed. St. Petersburg-Moscow: Volf, 1895-1896, 24 vols.

Polnoe sobranie sochineniy, 3rd ed. St. Petersburg: Marks, 1910-1911, 8 vols. Reprinted St. Petersburg: Volf, 1912.

Izbrannye proizvedeniya, ed. P. N. Berkov and M. K. Kleman. Moscow-Leningrad, 1932.

Pisma, ed. M. K. Kleman and A. P. Mogilyansky. Moscow-Leningrad, 1936.

Izbrannye proizvedeniya, ed. I. A. Martynov. Moscow-Yaroslavl, 1940.

Meylakh, B. S., ed. *Russkie povesti XIX veka: 40-50-kh godov.* Moscow, 1952, II, 359-614.

Rasskazy. Moscow, 1955.

Sochineniya, ed. M. P. Eremin. Moscow, 1956, 3 vols.

Uchenye zapiski Azerbaydzhanskogo gosudarstvennogo instituta russkogo yazyka i literatury, no. 2 (1957), pp. 79-92 (letters).
Pesy, ed. M. P. Eremin. Moscow, 1958.
Sobranie sochineniy, ed. A. P. Mogilyansky and M. P. Eremin. Moscow, 1959, 9 vols.
Review
Gin, M. M. "Sobranie sochineniy A. F. Pisemskogo," *Voprosy literatury,* no. 10 (October 1960), pp. 211-217.
"Pitershchik" i drugie rasskazy. Moscow, 1960.
"Pisma A. F. Pisemskogo (1855-1879)," in I. I. Anisimov et al., eds., *Literaturnoe nasledstvo.* Moscow, 1964, LXXIII, bk. 2, pp. 138-194.

INDIVIDUAL WORKS

"Nina: Epizod iz dnevnika moego priyatelya"
(Nina: An Episode from My Friend's Diary)

Journal publication
Syn Otechestva, no. 7 (July 1848), section III, pp. 3-30.

Translation
"Nina. A. Pisemski. Epizoda iz dnevnika moga prijatelja," trans. Vera Nikolić. *Domaćica,* XXXI, no. 8 (August 1910), pp. 28-33; no. 9 (September 1910), pp. 25-31 (Serbian).

Tyufyak (The Simpleton)

Journal publication
Moskvityanin, October 1850, bk. 1, section I, pp. 161-244; October 1850, bk. 2, section I, pp. 255-292; November 1850, bk. 1, section I, pp. 3-93.

Reviews
O. [A. N. Ostrovsky] *Moskvityanin,* April 1851, bk. 1, pp. 374-382.
Anon. *Biblioteka dlya chteniya,* no. 5 (May 1851), section VI, pp. 1-13.

Separate editions
Moscow, 1850.
St. Petersburg, 1861.

Translations
Nemotora, trans. E. G. Valečka. *Album Slovanských listův* (Jičín), I (1875), pp. 10-13, 26-29, 43-45, 93-96, 123-127, 141-143, 172-175, 187-191, 202-205, 210-216, 225-232, 241-250, 257-263, 273-278, 289-293.
Hňup—Bojarština, trans. Vilém Mrštík, in Jaromír Hrubý, ed., *Spisy Alekseja Feofilaktoviče Pisemského.* Prague, 1898, III (Russian Library, 28).

Nekňuba, trans. Vojtěch Gaja. Prague, 1950.
The Simpleton, trans. Ivy Litvinov. Moscow [1959].

Article
Pisarev, D. I. "Stoyachaya voda," *Russkoe slovo,* no. 10 (October 1861), section II, "Russkaya literatura," pp. 1-39.

Sergey Petrovich Khozarov i Mari Stupitsyna. Brak po strasti
(Sergey Petrovich Khozarov and Mari Stupitsyna.
A Marriage of Passion)

Journal publication
Moskvityanin, February 1851, bk. 2, pp. 457-493; March 1851, bk. 1, pp. 21-51; March 1851, bk. 2, pp. 139-189; April 1851, bk. 1, pp. 317-365.

Review
Anon. *Otechestvennye zapiski,* no. 1 (January 1852), section V, pp. 15-36.

Separate edition
St. Petersburg, 1861.

Translations
Ženidba iz ljubavi, trans. Laza Lazarević. 1906 (Serbian).
Manželství z vášně, trans. S. Minařík. Prague, 1919.
Manželstvo z vášne, trans. Hana Kostolanská. Bratislava, 1965.

"Komik" (The Comic Actor)

Journal publication
Moskvityanin, November 1851, bk. 1, pp. 23-104.

Separate edition
St. Petersburg, 1861.

Bogaty zhenikh (A Rich Fiancé)

Journal publication
Sovremennik, no. 10 (October 1851), section I, pp. 251-292; no. 11 (November 1851), section I, pp. 31-68; no. 12 (December 1851), section I, pp. 91-130; no. 1 (January 1852), section I, pp. 107-140; no. 2 (February 1852), section I, pp. 215-248; no. 3 (March 1852), section I, pp. 111-146; no. 4 (April 1852), section I, pp. 261-280; no. 5 (May 1852), section I, pp. 39-64.

Review
Anon. *Otechestvennye zapiski,* no. 1 (January 1852), section V, pp. 15-36.

Separate editions
St. Petersburg, 1861.

Moscow, 1955.
Cherkessk, 1960.

Translations
Der reiche Bräutigam, trans. L. Hauff. Berlin, 1890.
Bohatý ženich, trans. S. Minařík. Rokycany, 1915.
Nekňuba, trans. Vojtěch Gaja. Prague, 1950.
Bohatý ženich, trans. Jozef Vavro. Bratislava, 1957.

Ipokhondrik (The Hypochondriac)

Journal publication
Moskvityanin, January 1852, bk. 1, section I, pp. 3-120.

Separate edition
St. Petersburg, 1861.

Translation
Hypochondr, trans. Karel Martínek and Zdeněk Digrin. Prague, 1960.

"M-r Batmanov" (M. Batmanov)

Journal publication
Moskvityanin, September 1852, bk. 1, section I, pp. 1-52; September 1852, bk. 2, section I, pp. 53-112.

Separate edition
St. Petersburg, 1861.

Translations
"Pan Batmanov," trans. E. G. Valečka, *Jitřenka* (Polička), IV (1885), pp. 33-35, 49-51, 81-84, 97-100, 113-116, 129-132, 145-148, 161-164, 177-180, 193-196, 227-231.
Mr. Batmanov, trans. Vincenc Červinka. Prague, 1921.

"Pitershchik" (The Petersburger)

Journal publication
Moskvityanin, December 1852, bk. 1, section I, pp. 93-128.

Review
P. A-v [P. V. Annenkov]. "Po povodu romanov i rasskazov iz prostonarodnogo byta," *Sovremennik*, no. 2 (February 1854), section III, pp. 53-70; no. 3 (March 1854), section III, pp. 1-22.

Separate edition
St. Petersburg, 1861.

Translation
"Petrohraďan," trans. František Mach, *Slavia*, II (1876), no. 22, pp. 603-606; no. 23, pp. 633-635; no. 24, pp. 661-664.

Razdel (The Division)

Journal publication
Sovremennik, no. 1 (January 1853), section I, pp. 79-155.

Separate edition
St. Petersburg, 1861.

"Leshiy: Rasskaz ispravnika"
(The Wood Demon: The Story of a District Police Officer)

Journal publication
Sovremennik, no. 11 (November 1853), section I, pp. 7-52.

Review
P. A-v [P. V. Annenkov]. "Po povodu romanov i rasskazov iz
prostonarodnogo byta," *Sovremennik,* no. 2 (February 1854),
section III, pp. 53-70; no. 3 (March 1854), section III, pp. 1-22.

Separate edition
St. Petersburg, 1861.

Translation
"Der Waldteufel," trans. Claire von Glümer, in *Novellenschatz des*
Auslandes. Munich [1925?], XIV, 41-124.

"Fanfaron: Odin iz nashikh snobsov"
(The Braggart: One of Our Snobs)

Journal publication
Sovremennik, no. 8 (August 1854), section I, pp. 121-182.

Separate editions
Dlya legkogo chteniya, St. Petersburg, 1859, IX, 256-351.
St. Petersburg, 1861.

Veteran i novobranets: Dramatichesky sluchay iz 1854 goda
(The Veteran and the New Recruit: A Dramatic Incident of 1854)

Journal publication
Otechestvennye zapiski, no. 9 (September 1854), section I, pp. 97-122.

Separate edition
St. Petersburg, 1861.

"Vinovata li ona?" (Is She To Blame?)

Journal publication
Sovremennik, no. 2 (February 1855), section I, pp. 217-304.

Separate edition
Moscow, 1955.

Translations
"Est-ce bien sa faute?", in A. F. Pisemsky, *Mille âmes,* trans. Victor Derély. Paris, 1886, II, 235-352.
Är hon skyldig? trans. Eugenie Packendorff. Stockholm, 1914.
Čím se provinila? trans. Vincenc Červinka. Milotice, 1918 (new edition 1923).
"Este ea oare vinovată?" in *Este ea oare vinovată?,* trans. Cornelia Dichter and Iulia Constantinescu, Bucharest, 1955, pp. 3-140.
Byla Lydie vinna? Stará milostpaní, trans. Darja Podlipská. Prague, 1958.

"Plotnichya artel: Derevenskie zapiski"
(The Carpenters' Guild: Country Notes)

Journal publication
Otechestvennye zapiski, no. 9 (September 1855), section I, pp. 1-54.

Separate edition
St. Petersburg, 1861.

Translation
Nekňuba, trans. Vojtěch Gaja. Prague, 1950.

"Sochineniya N. V. Gogolya, naydennye posle ego smerti:
Pokhozhdeniya Chichikova, ili Mertvye dushi, Tom vtoroy"
(Works of N. V. Gogol Found After His Death: *Chichikov's
Adventures, or Dead Souls,* Volume Two)

Journal publication
Otechestvennye zapiski, no. 10 (October 1855), section III, pp. 57-76.

Ocherki iz krestyanskogo byta (Sketches of Peasant Life)

Separate edition
St. Petersburg, 1856.

Reviews
S. S. D. [S. S. Dudyshkin] *Otechestvennye zapiski,* no. 12 (December 1856), section III, pp. 71-77.
[Druzhinin, A. V.] *Biblioteka dlya chteniya,* no. 1 (January 1857), section V, pp. 1-36.
[Chernyshevsky, N. G.] *Sovremennik,* no. 4 (April 1857), section IV, "Bibliografiya," pp. 38-50.

Article
Malkin, V. A. "*Ocherki iz krestyanskogo byta* A. F. Pisemskogo," *Naukovi zapysky Lvivskogo pedagogichnogo instytutu,* III, no. 1 (1953), pp. 41-62.

"Staraya barynya" ("The Old Proprietress")

Journal publication
Biblioteka dlya chteniya, no. 2 (February 1857), sec. I, pp. 237-270.

Review
[Chernyshevsky, N. G.] "Zametki o zhurnalakh," *Sovremennik*, no. 3 (March 1857), section V, pp. 200-202.

Separate editions
Dlya legkogo chteniya, St. Petersburg, 1857, VII, 118-173.
St. Petersburg, 1861.

Translations
"The Old Proprietress," excerpted in Leo Wiener, ed., *Anthology of Russian Literature*. New York-London, 1903, II, 311-319.
"O bătrînă boieroaică," in *Este ea oare vinovată?*, trans. Cornelia Dichter and Iulia Constantinescu. Bucharest, 1955, pp. 141-198.
Byla Lydie vinna? Stará milostpaní, trans. Darja Podlipská. Prague, 1958.

Boyarshchina

Journal publication
Biblioteka dlya chteniya, no. 1 (January 1858), pp. 1-81; no. 2 (February 1858), pp. 82-166.

Review
Anon. *Syn Otechestva*, no. 12 (March 23, 1858), pp. 346-350.

Separate editions
St. Petersburg, 1861.
Moscow, 1959.

Translations
Förnämt Folk. Wiborg, 1890.
Hohe Herrschaften, trans. L. Hauff. Berlin, 1890.
Manowsky. Helsinki, 1890 (Swedish).
Hňup-Bojarština, trans. Vilém Mrštík, in Jaromír Hrubý, ed., *Spisy Alekseja Feofilaktoviče Pisemského*. Prague, 1898, III (Russian Library, 28).

Article
Silaev, N. "A. F. Pisemsky (1820-1881)," in A. F. Pisemsky, *Boyarshchina*. Moscow, 1959, pp. 177-190.

Tysyacha dush (*One Thousand Souls*)

Journal publication
Otechestvennye zapiski, no. 1 (January 1858), section I, pp. 1-106; no. 2 (February 1858), section I, pp. 389-440; no. 3 (March 1858), section I, pp. 1-52; no. 4 (April 1858), section I, pp. 455-530; no.

5 (May 1858), section I, pp. 1-68; no. 6 (June 1858), section I, pp. 553-664.

Reviews

S. R. *Russky vestnik*, XVII, no. 20 (October 1858), pp. 304-308.

Dudyshkin, S. S. *Otechestvennye zapiski*, no. 1 (January 1859), section II, pp. 1-21.

Edelson, E. N. *Russkoe slovo*, no. 1 (January 1859), section II, pp. 49-66.

Annenkov, P. V. "O delovom romane v nashey literature," *Ateney*, no. 1 (January-February 1859), pp. 242-266.

Druzhinin, A. V. *Biblioteka dlya chteniya*, no. 2 (February 1859), section IV, pp. 1-15.

De-Pule, M. F. *Russkaya beseda*, no. 2 (1859), section "Kritika," pp. 1-16.

[Kotlyarevsky, A. A.] *Moskovskoe obozrenie*, no. 2 (1859), section II, pp. 42-107, 262-268.

Akhsharumov, N. D. *Vesna*. St. Petersburg, 1859, pp. 291-344.

Delaveau, Henri. "Le roman satirique en Russie," *Revue des deux mondes*, XXV (January 15, 1860), 425-453.

Separate editions

St. Petersburg, 1858.

St. Petersburg, 1861.

Moscow, 1949.

Petrozavodsk, 1955.

Moscow, 1958.

Moscow, 1965.

Translations

Tausend Seelen, trans. Leopold Kayssler. Berlin, 1870.

Duizend zielen, trans. G. Wörrheide. Alkmaar [1871].

Tisíc duší, trans. Coelestin Frič. Prague, 1883.

Tusend sjaele, trans. Johannes Magnussen. Copenhagen, 1885.

Mille âmes, trans. Victor Derély. Paris, 1886.

Den öfvergifna. Stockholm, 1891.

Tisíc duší, trans. Vilém Mrštík, in Jaromír Hrubý, ed., *Spisy Alekséja Feofilaktoviče Pisemského*. Prague, 1905, IV (Russian Library, 43). New edition 1924.

Xiljadu duša, trans. Zorka Velimirovićka. Belgrade [1921].

Tusen sjeler, trans. Nicolai Henriksen. Oslo, 1948.

Tisíc duší, trans. Prokop Voskovec. Prague, 1952.

O mie de suflete. Bucharest, 1953.

Tysiąc dusz, trans. Zofia Kaczorowska. Warsaw, 1953.

Tausend Seelen, trans. Woldemar Feysack. Berlin, 1955.

One Thousand Souls, trans. Ivy Litvinov. Moscow, 1958.

One Thousand Souls, trans. Ivy Litvinov. New York, 1959.

Tisíc poddaných, trans. Rudolf Klačko. Bratislava, 1961.

Articles

Schmidt, Julian. "Turgenjew und Pisemski," in *Characterbilder aus der zeitgenössischen Literatur*, vol. IV of *Bilder aus dem geistigen Leben unserer Zeit*. Leipzig, 1875, pp. 250-267.

Prodanović, Jaša. "Pisemski," *Srpski književni glasnik*, XIII (September-December 1924), 217-224.

Martynov, I. A. "Posleslovie," in A. F. Pisemsky, *Tysyacha dush*. Moscow, 1949, pp. 472-495.

Mogilyansky, A. P. "Ob izdanii romana *Tysyacha dush*," *Novy mir*, no. 4 (April 1950), pp. 274-276.

Gin, M. M. "A. F. Pisemsky i ego roman *Tysyacha dush*," in A. F. Pisemsky, *Tysyacha dush*. Petrozavodsk, 1955, pp. 475-493.

Mogilyansky, A. P. "Novoe izdanie *Tysyachi dush*," *Na rubezhe*, no. 1 (1956), pp. 182-184.

Tyunkin, K. I. "Posleslovie," in A. F. Pisemsky, *Tysyacha dush*. Moscow, 1958, pp. 481-492.

Kartashova, I. V. "Ideyno-khudozhestvennoe svoeobrazie romana A. F. Pisemskogo 'Tysyacha dush.' " Unpub. diss., Kazan, 1963.

———. "Khudozhestvennoe svoeobrazie romana A. F. Pisemskogo *Tysyacha dush*," *Uchenye zapiski Kazanskogo universiteta*, vol. 123, bk. 8 (1963), pp. 35-92.

Tyunkin, K. I. "Roman Pisemskogo o geroe vremeni," in A. F. Pisemsky, *Tysyacha dush*. Moscow, 1965, pp. 3-14.

Pustovoyt, P. G. "K istorii romana A. F. Pisemskogo *Tysyacha dush*," *Vestnik moskovskogo universiteta*, series X: Philology, no. 6 (November-December 1966), pp. 80-90.

———. "Stroki, ne uvidevshie sveta," *Voprosy literatury*, no. 9 (September 1966), pp. 249-253.

Gorkaya sudbina (A Bitter Fate)

Journal publication
Biblioteka dlya chteniya, no. 11 (November 1859), pp. 1-70.

Reviews

Dudyshkin, S. S. "Dve novye narodnye dramy," *Otechestvennye zapiski*, no. 1 (January 1860), section III, pp. 37-57.

Mikhaylov, M. L. *Russkoe slovo*, no. 2 (February 1860), section II, pp. 1-9.

Kushelev-Bezborodko, G. A. *Russkoe slovo*, no. 11 (November 1860), section II, pp. 1-11.

Akhsharumov, N. D. "Mnenie N. D. Akhsharumova o drame g. Pisemskogo: *Gorkaya sudbina*," *Otchet o chetvertom prisuzhdenii nagrad grafa Uvarova 25 sentyabrya 1860 goda*. St. Petersburg, 1860, pp. 53-64.

Khomyakov, A. S. "Otzyv A. S. Khomyakova o drame g. Pisemskogo *Gorkaya sudbina*," *Otchet o chetvertom prisuzhdenii nagrad grafa Uvarova 25 sentyabrya 1860 goda.* St. Petersburg, 1860, pp. 50-52.

Pletnev, P. A. "Mnenie Akademika P. A. Pletneva," *Otchet o chetvertom prisuzhdenii nagrad grafa Uvarova 25 sentyabrya 1860 goda.* St. Petersburg, 1860, pp. 33-41.

[Saltykov-Shchedrin, M. E.] "Peterburgskie teatry," *Sovremennik*, no. 11 (November 1863), section II, pp. 90-106.

Separate editions
St. Petersburg, 1860.
St. Petersburg, 1861.
Dramatichesky sbornik, no. 3 (1862), pp. 1-84.
Moscow, 1923.
Moscow, 1939.
Moscow-Leningrad, 1951.

Translations
Une amère destinée, in A. F. Pisemsky, *Théâtre choisi*, trans. Victor Derély. Paris, 1889, pp. 1-126.

Hořký osud, trans. Vincenc Červinka. Prague, 1908.

Das bittere Los, trans. Arthur Luther, in Arthur Luther, ed., *Meisterwerke der russischen Bühne*. Leipzig [1922], pp. 291-363.

Hořký osud, trans. Vincenc Červinka. Prague, 1926. Later edition, no date.

A Bitter Fate, trans. Alice Kagan and George Noyes, in George Noyes, ed., *Masterpieces of the Russian Drama*. New York, 1933, pp. 407-456.

Girka dolya, trans. D. Bobir. Kiev, 1955.

Articles
Ivanov, A. [A. I. Urusov] "Teatr. Zametki i vpechatleniya," *Poryadok*, no. 56 (February 26, 1881).

Milovidov, I .V. "Dve chukhlomskikh dramy: osnova *Gorkoy sudbiny* A. F. Pisemskogo," *Russkaya starina*, no. 11 (November 1889), pp. 335-360.

Annensky, I. F. "Tri sotsialnykh dramy," *Kniga otrazheniy*. St. Petersburg, 1906, pp. 77-146.

Loboda, A. M. "*Gorkaya sudbina* Pisemskogo i ee literaturny prototip," *Universitetskie izvestiya* (Kiev), no. 9 (September 1906), pp. 1-12.

Mogilyansky, A. P. "Drama A. F. Pisemskogo 'Gorkaya sudbina.' Izobrazhenie krestyanstva v russkoy dramaturgii epokhi krepostnichestva—ot Lukina do Pisemskogo." Unpub. diss., Herzen Pedagogical Institute (Leningrad), 1944.

Jenkins, Maya. "Pisemsky's 'Bitter Fate': The First Outstanding Drama of Russian Peasant Life," *Canadian Slavonic Papers*, III (1958), 76-88.

"Starchesky grekh: Sovershenno romanicheskoe priklyuchenie" (An Old Man's Sin: A Completely Romantic Adventure)

Journal publication
Biblioteka dlya chteniya, no. 1 (January 1861), pp. 1-90.

Reviews
De-Pule, M. F. *Russkaya rech,* no. 22 (March 16, 1861).
Svedentsov, N. *Svetoch,* no. 3 (1861), section III, pp. 1-20.

Translations
"Ferapontov," *Moravská orlice,* nos. 247, 249-253, 255-259 (1873).
"Alter schützt vor Thorheit nicht," in *Nordische Nachtstücke,* trans. H. von Lankenau. Vienna-Budapest-Leipzig, 1873, pp. 87-160.
"Den gamle Bogholder," *Nyt dansk Maanedsskrift,* V (1873), 313-331, 373-409.
"Alderdom og Klogskab følges ei altid ad," in *Udvalgte fortaellinger af russiske novellister,* trans. V. Möller. Copenhagen, 1875, pp. 101-174.
Le péché de vieillesse, trans. Victor Derély. Paris, 1888.
"Stařecký hřích," trans. Ervín Kačer, in *Národní listy večerní,* LXXIII (1933), nos. 18-20, 23, 25-27, 30-34, 37-41, 43-48, 51-55, 58-62, 65-69, 72-73.

"Batka" (The Father)

Journal publication
Russkoe slovo, no. 1 (January 1862), section I, pp. 1-34.

Review
[Grigorev, A. A.] *Svetoch,* no. 3 (March 1862), section III, pp. 1-13.

Separate editions
St. Petersburg, 1866.
Leningrad, 1926.

Vzbalamuchennoe more (Troubled Seas)

Russky vestnik, no. 3 (March 1863), pp. 93-184; no. 4 (April 1863), pp. 481-570; no. 5 (May 1863), pp. 43-114; no. 6 (June 1863), pp. 561-636; no. 7 (July 1863), pp. 5-86; no. 8 (August 1863), pp. 571-644.

Reviews
[Grigorev, A. A.] *Yakor,* nos. 18-25, 28 (1863).
Zotov, V. R. "Kak okanchivayut nekotorye pisateli," *Severnoe siyanie,* III (1864), 621-640.

Zaytsev, V. A. "Vzbalamuchenny romanist," *Russkoe slovo*, no. 10 (October 1863), section II, pp. 23-44.

Annenkov, P. V. *Sankt-Peterburgskie vedomosti*, no. 250 (November 9, 1863).

Milyukov, A. P. "Mertvoe more i Vzbalamuchennoe more," *Golos*, no. 317 (November 29, 1863).

E. E-n [E. N. Edelson] *Biblioteka dlya chteniya*, no. 11 (November 1863), section "Russkaya literatura," pp. 1-26; no. 12 (December 1863), section "Russkaya literatura," pp. 1-21.

Anon. *Otechestvennye zapiski*, no. 12 (December 1863), section II, "Literaturnaya letopis," pp. 83-115.

Antonovich, M. A. "Sovremennye romany," *Sovremennik*, no. 4 (April 1864), section II, pp. 201-238.

Separate editions
Moscow, 1863.
St. Petersburg, 1866[?].

Translation
Rozbouřené moře, trans. Vilém Mrštík, in Jaromír Hrubý, ed., *Spisy Alekséja Feofilaktoviče Pisemského*. Prague, 1894, I-II (Russian Library, 17-18).

Boytsy i vyzhidateli (Warriors and Temporizers)

Apparently written 1864, first published in posthumous edition of 1883-1886.

Russkie lguny (Russian Liars)

Journal publication
Otechestvennye zapiski, no. 1 (January 1865), pp. 88-116; no. 2 (February 1865), pp. 483-496; no. 4 (April 1865), pp. 501-524.

Translations
"Krasavec," trans. Vilém Mrštík, in *Hlas národa*, nos. 223, 230, 237 (1893).

"Rytíř řádu 'pour le mérite,' " trans. Karel Frypés, in *Národní listy*, LII (1912), no. 20.

"Bohatí lháři a chudý," trans. Vladimír Sokolov, in *Národní listy*, LII (1912), no. 318.

Ruští lháři a jiné povídky, trans. Karel Frypés and Vincenc Červinka, in Jaromír Hrubý, ed., *Spisy Alekséja Feofilaktoviče Pisemského*. Prague, 1926, VI (Russian Library, 98).

Samoupravtsy (The Unbridled Ones)

Journal publication
Vsemirny trud, no. 2 (February 1867), pp. 1-82.

Review
Nikitenko, A. V. *Tri literaturno-kriticheskie ocherka*. St. Petersburg, 1866, pp. 1-16.

Separate editions
St. Petersburg, 1867.
Moscow, 1955.

Article
Sergeev, Vsevolod. "A. F. Pisemsky i ego tragediya *Samoupravtsy*," in A. F. Pisemsky, *Samoupravtsy*. Moscow, 1955, pp. 60-64.

Poruchik Gladkov (Lieutenant Gladkov)

Journal publication
Vsemirny trud, no. 3 (March 1867), pp. 1-95.

Separate edition
St. Petersburg, 1872.

Miloslavskie i Naryshkiny (Miloslavskys and Naryshkins)
(Composed 1866-1867, first published in posthumous edition of 1883-1886.)

Byvye sokoly (Former Falcons)

Journal publication
Vsemirny trud, no. 9 (September 1868), pp. 1-71.

Separate edition
St. Petersburg, 1918.

Ptentsy poslednego sleta (Fledglings of the Last Flight)

First published in the posthumous edition of 1883-1886.

Separate edition
St. Petersburg, 1919.

Lyudi sorokovykh godov (Men of the 1840's)

Journal publication
Zarya, no. 1 (January 1869), pp. 1-165; no. 2 (February 1869), pp. 1-117; no. 3 (March 1869), pp. 119-197; no. 4 (April 1869), pp. 1-90; no. 5 (May 1869), pp. 91-190; no. 6 (June 1869), pp. 1-102; no. 7 (July 1869), pp. 103-205; no. 8 (August 1869), pp. 1-74; no. 9 (September 1869), pp. 75-157.

Reviews
N. Sh. [N. V. Shelgunov] "Lyudi sorokovykh i shestidesyatykh godov," *Delo*, no. 9 (September 1869), "Sovremennoe obozrenie," pp. 1-29; no. 10 (October 1869), "Sovremennoe obozrenie," pp.

1-38; no. 11 (November 1869), "Sovremennoe obozrenie," pp. 1-51; no. 12 (December 1869), "Sovremennoe obozrenie," pp. 1-51.

Tsebrikova, M. K. "Gumanny zashchitnik zhenskikh prav (Po povodu romana g. Pisemskogo *Lyudi sorokovykh godov*)," *Otechestvennye zapiski*, no. 2 (February 1870), "Sovremennoe obozrenie," pp. 209-228.

Separate editions
St. Petersburg, 1869.
Moscow-Leningrad, 1928.
Irkutsk, 1957.

Article
Skatov, N. "Ob odnom epizode romana A. F. Pisemskogo *Lyudi sorokovykh godov*," *Russkaya literatura*, no. 3 (1964), pp. 201-203.

V vodovorote (In the Whirlpool)

Journal publication
Beseda, no. 1 (January 1871), pp. 13-80; no. 2 (February 1871), pp. 5-74; no. 3 (March 1871), pp. 5-81; no. 4 (April 1871), pp. 5-73; no. 5 (May 1871), pp. 110-187; no. 6 (June 1871), pp. 5-91.

Separate editions
Moscow, 1872.
Kursk, 1959.

Translations
Dans le tourbillon, trans. Victor Derély. Paris, 1881.
Im Strudel, trans. Wilhelm Lange. Berlin, 1882.
Im Strudel, trans. Wilhelm Lange. Leipzig, 1885.
I Malstrømmen. Kristiania, 1889-1890.
Ve víru, trans. Vincenc Červinka, in Jaromír Hrubý, ed., *Spisy Alekšěja Feofilaktoviče Pisemského*. Prague, 1919, V (Russian Library, 71).

Article
Gruzinskaya, N. N. "Khudozhestvennoe svoeobrazie romana A. F. Pisemskogo *V vodovorote*," *Voprosy metoda i stilya* ("Uchenye zapiski Tomskogo gosudarstvennogo universiteta imeni V. V. Kuybysheva," no. 62). Tomsk, 1966, pp. 261-274.

Podkopy (Khishchniki) (Mines [The Plunderers])

Journal publication
Grazhdanin, 1873, no. 7, pp. 191-197; no. 8, pp. 227-232; no. 9, pp. 259-265; no. 10, pp. 295-308.

Separate edition
St. Petersburg, 1873.

Article
Mogilyansky, A. P. "Tsenzurnaya istoriya pesy Pisemskogo *Khishchniki*," *Russkaya literatura*, no. 2 (1965), pp. 167-172.

Vaal (Baal)

Journal publication
Russky vestnik, no. 4 (April 1873), pp. 482-567.

Separate edition
Moscow, 1873.

Translations
Baal, trans. Victor Derély, in A. F. Pisemsky, *Théâtre choisi*. Paris, 1889, pp. 127-290.
Démon zlata, trans. Bořivoj Prusík. Prague, 1920.

Article
Lemaître, Jules. "Pisemsky," *Impressions de théâtre*, fifth series. Paris, 1891, pp. 69-81.

Prosveshchennoe vremya (An Enlightened Time)

Journal publication
Russky vestnik, no. 1 (January 1875), pp. 68-139.

Finansovy geniy (The Financial Genius)

Journal publication
Gazeta Gattsuka, no. 3 (1876), pp. 38-54; no. 4 (1876), pp. 62-73.

Separate editions
Moscow, 1876.
St. Petersburg, 1876.

Meshchane (The Bourgeois)

Journal publication
Pchela, 1877, no. 18, pp. 274-275; no. 19, pp. 282-283; no. 20, pp. 298-299; no. 21, pp. 314-315; no. 22, pp. 330-331; no. 23, pp. 346-347; no. 24, pp. 362-366; no. 25, pp. 378-382; no. 26, pp. 394-395; no. 27, pp. 410-411; no. 28, pp. 426-427; no. 29, pp. 442-446; no. 30, pp. 458-462; no. 31, pp. 474-475; no. 32, pp. 490-491; no. 33, pp. 506-510; no. 34, pp. 522-526; no. 35, pp. 538-542; no. 36, pp. 554-558; no. 37, pp. 570-574; no. 38, pp. 586-590; no. 39, pp. 607-610; no. 40, pp. 624-625; no. 41, pp. 634-638; no. 42, pp. 650-653; no. 43, pp. 666-671; no. 44, pp. 686-690; no. 45, pp. 702-706; no. 46, pp. 722-730; no. 47, pp. 742-750; no. 48, pp. 762-767; no. 49, pp. 782-789.

Review
N. M. [N. K. Mikhaylovsky] "Literaturnye zametki," *Otechestvennye zapiski*, no. 5 (May 1878), section II, pp. 146-152.

Separate editions
St. Petersburg, 1878.
St. Petersburg, 1904.

Translations
Měšťané, trans. Ant. Kumpera. Prague, 1883.
Les faiseurs, trans. Victor Derély. Paris, 1886.
Měšťáci, trans. Vincenc Červinka, in Jaromír Hrubý, ed., *Spisy Alekseja Feofilaktoviče Pisemského.* Prague, 1927, VII (Russian Library, 105).

Article
Gruzinskaya, N. N. "Sredstva raskrytiya kharaktera glavnogo geroya v romane A. F. Pisemskogo *Meshchane,*" *Voprosy literatury i yazyka* ("Uchenye zapiski Tomskogo gosudarstvennogo univer- siteta," no. 54). Tomsk, 1965, pp. 29-38.

Starye schety (Semeyny omut) (Old Accounts [A Domestic Pool])

Begun in 1877 and left incomplete; first published in posthumous edition of 1883-1886.

"Uzhe ottsvetshie tsvetki: Kapitan Rukhnev" (Faded Flowers: Captain Rukhnev)

Journal publication
Gazeta Gattsuka, no. 2 (1879), pp. 21-26; no. 3 (1879), pp. 37-39.

Translations
"Le capitaine Roukhneff," trans. Victor Derély, *Le Télégraphe* (Paris), November 25-28, 1879.
"Setník Ruchněv," trans. V. Č. [Vincenc Červinka], *Cesta,* II (1920), nos. 49-50.
Setník Ruchněv, trans. Vincenc Červinka. Kolín, 1921.

Masony (The Masons)

Journal publication
Ogonek, III (1880), no. 1, pp. 2-10; no. 2, pp. 25-31; no. 3, pp. 49-56; no. 4, pp. 69-77; no. 5, pp. 89-95; no. 6, pp. 109-117; no. 8, pp. 150-158; no. 9, pp. 165-173; no. 10, pp. 185-193; no. 11, pp. 205-213; no. 12, pp. 225-233; no. 13, pp. 245-251; no. 14, pp. 265-272; no. 15, pp. 285-292; no. 16, pp. 305-313; no. 17, pp. 321-325; no. 18, pp. 337-342; no. 19, pp. 353-361; no. 20, pp. 373-377; no. 21, pp. 394-399; no. 22, pp. 414-417; no. 23, pp. 433-438; no. 24, pp. 450-454; no. 25, pp. 466-470; no. 26, pp. 486-489. Vol. IV (1880), no. 27, pp. 502-505; no. 28, pp. 522-526; no. 29, pp. 538-542; no. 30, pp. 554-557; no. 31, pp. 570-573; no. 32, pp. 590-594; no. 33, pp. 606-613; no. 34, pp. 626-631; no. 35, pp. 642-648; no. 36, pp. 658-662; no. 37, pp. 674-683; no. 38, pp. 694-700; no. 39, pp. 710-717; no.

40, pp. 726-733; no. 41, pp. 746-753; no. 42, pp. 762-768; no. 43, pp. 778-781.

Reviews

Anon. *Russky vestnik*, no. 1 (January 1881), pp. 438-465.

Anon. "Novye knigi," *Otechestvennye zapiski*, no. 1 (January 1881), section II, pp. 77-81.

[Pypin, A. N.] *Vestnik Evropy*, no. 2 (February 1881), pp. 882-888.

Separate edition
St. Petersburg, 1881.

Articles

Červinka, Vincenc. "Zednářství na Rusi i Pisemského román o 'Zednářích,'" *Topičův sborník*, no. 9 (June 1922), pp. 412-422.

Roshal, A. A. "Iz nablyudeniy nad tvorcheskoy istoriey romana A. F. Pisemskogo *Masony*," *Russkaya literatura*, no. 1 (1963), pp. 180-184.

―――. "Istoricheskie i dokumentalnye istochniki romana A. F. Pisemskogo *Masony*," *Uchenye zapiski Azerbaydzhanskogo pedagogicheskogo instituta yazykov*, no. 17 (1963), pp. 75-97.

GENERAL STUDIES OF PISEMSKY

Miller, O. F. "A. F. Pisemsky," *Russkie pisateli posle Gogolya*, St. Petersburg, 1874, pp. 72-95.

Vengerov, S. A. *Pisemsky* (1884), in *Sobranie sochineniy S. A. Vengerova*. St. Petersburg, 1911, V, 97-213.

Skabichevsky, A. M. *A. F. Pisemsky, ego zhizn i literaturnaya deyatelnost*. St. Petersburg, 1894.

Zelinsky, V. V. "Aleksey Feofilaktovich Pisemsky: ego zhizn, literaturnaya deyatelnost i znachenie ego v istorii russkoy pismennosti," in A. F. Pisemsky, *Polnoe sobranie sochineniy*. St. Petersburg, 1895, vol. I, pp. XV-CLX.

Ivanov, I. I. *Pisemsky*. St. Petersburg, 1898. Also published serially in *Mir Bozhy*, nos. 7-12, 1896.

Mrštík, Vilém. *A. F. Pisemskij*. Prague, 1908.

Izmaylov, A. A. "A. F. Pisemsky," *Ezhemesyachnye literaturnye i populyarno-nauchnye prilozheniya k "Nive,"* no. 11 (November 1909), cols. 439-472.

Vetrinsky, Ch. (V. E. Cheshikhin). "Aleksey Feofilaktovich Pisemsky," in D. N. Ovsyaniko-Kulikovsky, ed., *Istoriya russkoy literatury XIX v.* Moscow, 1911, III, 232-252.

Berkov, P. N. and M. K. Kleman. "Literaturny put Pisemskogo," in A. F. Pisemsky, *Izbrannye proizvedeniya*. Moscow-Leningrad, 1932, pp. 3-22.

Martynov, I. A. "A. F. Pisemsky," in A. F. Pisemsky, *Izbrannye proizvedeniya*. Moscow-Yaroslavl, 1940, pp. 7-48.

Evnin, F. I. *A. F. Pisemsky*. Moscow, 1945.

Backvis, Claude. "Un témoin négligé d'une grande époque: le romancier Pisemskij," *Revue des études slaves*, XXXII, nos. 1-4 (1955), pp. 42-55.

Martynov, I. A. "Pisemsky," in *Istoriya russkoy literatury*. Moscow-Leningrad, 1956, VIII, pt. 1, pp. 462-483.

Eremin, M. P. *A. F. Pisemsky*. Moscow, 1956.

———. "A. F. Pisemsky," in A. F. Pisemsky, *Sochineniya*. Moscow, 1956, I, 5-47.

———. "Vydayushchiysya realist," in A. F. Pisemsky, *Sobranie sochineniy v devyati tomakh*. Moscow, 1959, I, 3-52.

Steussy, R. E. "The Bitter Fate of A. F. Pisemsky," *Russian Review*, XXV, no. 2 (April 1966), pp. 170-183.

MISCELLANEOUS STUDIES OF PISEMSKY

Grigorev, A. A. "Russkaya izyashchnaya literatura v 1852 godu," *Moskvityanin*, January 1853, bk. 1, section V, pp. 27-33.

Anon. "Zhurnalistika," *Otechestvennye zapiski*, LXXXVI (1853), section V, pp. 87-108.

[Nekrasov, N. A.] "Zametki o zhurnalakh za oktyabr 1855 goda," *Sovremennik*, no. 11 (November 1855), section V, pp. 78-81.

Grigorev, A. A. "Realizm i idealizm v nashey literature (Po povodu novogo izdaniya sochineniy Pisemskogo i Turgeneva)," *Svetoch*, no. 4 (1861), section III, pp. 8-22.

[Strakhov, N. N.] "Neskolko slov o g. Pisemskom po povodu ego sochineniy," *Vremya*, no. 7 (July 1861), "Kriticheskoe obozrenie," pp. 13-19.

Pisarev, D. I. "Pisemsky, Turgenev i Goncharov," *Russkoe slovo*, no. 11 (November 1861), section II, "Russkaya literatura," pp. 1-48.

Skabichevsky, A. M. "Russkoe nedomyslie," *Otechestvennye zapiski*, no. 9 (September 1868), section II, pp. 1-46.

A. [V. G. Avseenko] "Praktichesky nigilizm," *Russky vestnik*, no. 7 (July 1873), pp. 389-427.

Boborykin, P. D. "Pamyati A. F. Pisemskogo," *Russkie vedomosti*, no. 32 (February 1, 1881).

A. V. [A. N. Pypin] "Literaturnoe obozrenie. F. M. Dostoevsky—A. F. Pisemsky. Nekrolog," *Vestnik Europy*, no. 3 (March 1881), pp. 429-436.

Derély, Victor. "Préface," in A. F. Pisemsky, *Théâtre choisi*. Paris, 1889, pp. I-XIII.

Polevoy, P. N. "A. F. Pisemsky, po ego sobstvennym avtobiograficheskim zametkam," *Istorichesky vestnik*, no. 11 (November 1889), pp. 276-295.

Maksimov, S. V. "Literaturnaya ekspeditsiya (Po arkhivnym dokumentam i lichnym vospominaniyam)," *Russkaya mysl*, no. 2 (February 1890), pp. 17-50.

Rusakov, Viktor [S. F. Librovich]. "Literaturny zarabotok Pisemskogo," *Nov*, XXXII, no. 5 (January 1, 1890), pp. 36-44.

Ginisty, Paul. *Choses et gens de théâtre*. Paris, 1892, pp. 76-92.

Kirpichnikov, A. I. *Dostoevsky i Pisemsky: opyt sravnitelnoy kharakteristiki*. Odessa, 1894.

Tikhomirov, N. "Znachenie Pisemskogo v istorii russkoy literatury," *Nov*, no. 20 (1894).

Lobov, L. P. "Slavyanofilstvo i ego literaturnye predstaviteli: Pisemsky," *Slavyanskie izvestiya*, no. 7 (1905), pp. 567-575.

Anon. "A. F. Pisemsky, kak dramaturg," *Ezhegodnik imperatorskikh teatrov*, season 1905-1906, appendix, pp. 83-101.

Vinogradov, N. A. "Melochi dlya biografiy A. F. Pisemskogo i A. A. Potekhina," *Izvestiya Otdeleniya russkogo yazyka i slovesnosti Imperatorskoy akademii nauk*, XIII, bk. 3 (1908), pp. 322-327.

N. [N. V. Drizen] "Novye dannye o A. F. Pisemskom," *Ezhegodnik imperatorskikh teatrov*, no. 1 (1909), pp. 9-14.

Anon. "A. F. Pisemsky kak dramaturg," *Biblioteka teatra i iskusstva*, no. 1 (January 1916), pp. 3-18.

Vinogradov, N. A. "A. F. Pisemsky (Materialy dlya ego biografii i vyyasneniya protsessa tvorchestva)," *Izvestiya Otdeleniya russkogo yazyka i slovesnosti Imperatorskoy akademii nauk*, XXI, bk. 2 (1916), pp. 123-151.

Prutskov, N. I. "Tvorchestvo Pisemskogo 40-50-kh godov i gogolevskoe napravlenie," *Uchenye zapiski Omskogo pedagogicheskogo instituta*, no. 1 (1941), pp. 3-54.

Chicherin, A. V. "Pisemsky i staraya Kostroma," *Kostromskoy almanakh*. Kostroma, 1946, pp. 192-202.

Mogilyansky, A. P. "Novye dokumenty o Pisemskom," *Leningradskaya pravda*, no. 82 (April 6, 1946).

Roshal, A. A. "Tvorchestvo Pisemskogo v 40-50 gody (Pisemsky v *Moskvityanine*)." Unpub. diss., Leningrad State University, 1948.

Kozmin, B. P. "Pisemsky i Gertsen: k istorii ikh vzaimootnosheniy," *Zvenya*. Moscow, 1950, VIII, 103-151.

Kastorsky, V. V. *Pisateli kostromichi (XVIII-XIX vv.)*. Kostroma, 1958, pp. 49-69.

Roshal, A. A. "A. F. Pisemsky v Baku," *Uchenye zapiski Azerbaydzhanskogo instituta russkogo yazyka i literatury*, no. 7 (1958), pp. 49-64.

Eremin, M. P. "Pisemsky-dramaturg," in A. F. Pisemsky, *Pesy*. Moscow, 1958, pp. 5-35.

Steussy, R. E. "Pisemskij's Talent as a Novelist." Unpub. diss., Harvard University, 1959.

Lakshin, V. Ya. "Spor o Pisemskom-dramaturge," *Teatr*, no. 4 (April 1959), pp. 94-97.

Oganyan, N. S. "K voprosu otsenki tvorchestva A. F. Pisemskogo russkoy literaturnoy kritikoy," *Nauchnye trudy (Erevansky universitet)*, no. 70 (1960), pp. 93-124.

Mogilyansky, A. P. "Pisemsky pro Marka Vovchka," *Radyanske literaturoznavstvo*, no. 2 (1960), pp. 117-120.

Urban, A. A. "Iz nablyudeniy nad stanovleniem realizma v tvorchestve A. F. Pisemskogo," *Uchenye zapiski Leningradskogo gosudarstvennogo pedagogicheskogo instituta imeni A. I. Gertsena*, no. 219 (1961), pp. 121-150.

Mogilyansky, A. P. "Iz nachala novykh ocherkov 'Svishchi,' " *Literaturny arkhiv*, no. 6 (1961), pp. 19-24.

Chopyk, Dan. "The Plays of Alexei Feofilaktovich Pisemsky," Unpub. master's thesis, University of Colorado, 1962.

Moser, Charles. "Pisemskij's Literary Protest: An Episode from the Polemics of the 1860's in Russia," *Etudes slaves et est-européennes*, VIII, no. 1-2 (Spring-Summer 1963), pp. 60-72.

Ledovoy, Peter. "Gogol's Influence on Pisemski's Dramaturgy." Unpub. master's thesis, New York University, 1963 (in Russian).

Urban, A. A. "Materialy k izucheniyu zhizni i tvorchestva A. F. Pisemskogo," *Uchenye zapiski Leningradskogo gosudarstvennogo pedagogicheskogo instituta imeni A. I. Gertsena*, no. 245 (1963), pp. 237-259.

Brown, Deming. "Pisemskij: The Aesthetics of Scepticism," *American Contributions to the Fifth International Congress of Slavists*, vol. II: *Literary Contributions*. The Hague, 1963, pp. 7-20.

Gruzinskaya, N. N. "Ob izuchenii mirovozzreniya i metoda A. F. Pisemskogo v sovetskom literaturovedenii," *Uchenye zapiski Tomskogo universiteta*, no. 48 (1964), pp. 106-115.

Lotman, L. M. "Pisemsky-romanist," in A. S. Bushmin et al., eds., *Istoriya russkogo romana*. Moscow-Leningrad, 1964, II, 121-148.

Millet, Yves. "Predislovie," *Literaturnoe nasledstvo*. Moscow, 1964, LXXIII, bk. 2, pp. 125-128.

Tyunkin, K. I. "Pisemsky i Turgenev v ikh perepiske," *Literaturnoe nasledstvo*. Moscow, 1964, LXXIII, bk. 2, pp. 129-137.

Mogilyansky, A. P. "Novye dannye dlya kharakteristiki otnosheniya Pisemskogo k Gertsenu," *Russkaya literatura*, no. 1 (1966), pp. 165-169.

Pustovoyt, P. G. "K voprosu ob otnoshenii A. F. Pisemskogo k A. I. Gertsenu," *Russkaya literatura*, no. 1 (1967), pp. 154-160.

———. "Sposoby motivirovki v romanakh Pisemskogo 50-60-kh

godov," *Nauchnye doklady Vysshey shkoly: filologicheskie nauki,* no. 2 (1967), pp. 3-13.

———. "Esteticheskie vzglyady A. F. Pisemskogo v 50-60-kh godakh," *Vestnik Moskovskogo universiteta,* series X: Philology, no. 3 (May-June 1967), pp. 14-25.

MEMOIR LITERATURE RELATING TO PISEMSKY

Almazov, B. N. "Aleksey Feofilaktovich Pisemsky i ego dvadtsati-pyatiletnyaya literaturnaya deyatelnost," *Russky arkhiv,* no. 4 (1875), pp. 453-467.

Annenkov, P. V. "Khudozhnik i prostoy chelovek (Iz vospominaniy ob A. F. Pisemskom)," *Vestnik Evropy,* no. 4 (April 1882), pp. 623-660.

Ardov, E. [E. I. Apreleva] "U A. F. Pisemskogo," *Russkie vedomosti,* no. 97 (April 10, 1905); no. 101 (April 14, 1905).

Avseenko, V. G. "Kruzhok," *Istorichesky vestnik,* no. 5 (May 1909), pp. 444-446.

Boborykin, P. D. *Za polveka.* Moscow-Leningrad, 1929.

Gorbunov, I. F. "Iz moego dnevnika. 1855," in I. F. Gorbunov, *Sochineniya.* St. Petersburg, 1907, III, pt. 1, pp. 50-52.

Grigorovich, D. V. *Literaturnye vospominaniya.* Leningrad, 1928.

Koni, A. F. *Na zhiznennom puti.* St. Petersburg, 1913, vol. II.

Librovich, S. F. *Na knizhnom postu.* Petrograd-Moscow, 1916.

Maksimov, S. V. "Za A. F. Pisemskogo (Po literaturnym vospominaniyam)," *Novoe vremya,* no. 4880 (September 29, 1889).

Nikitenko, A. V. *Dnevnik.* 3 vols. Leningrad, 1955-1956.

Panaeva, A. Ya. *Vospominaniya (1824-1870).* Moscow, 1956.

Potekhin, A. A. "Iz teatralnykh vospominaniy," *Sochineniya A. A. Potekhina.* St. Petersburg, 1904, XII, 321-338.

Shtakenshneyder, E. A. *Dnevnik i zapiski (1854-1886).* Moscow-Leningrad, 1934.

Shubert, A. I. *Moya zhizn.* Leningrad, 1929.

Stakheev, D. I. "Gruppy i portrety," *Istorichesky vestnik,* no. 3 (March 1907), pp. 846-854.

Veynberg, P. I. "Literaturnye spektakli (Iz moikh vospominaniy)," *Ezhegodnik imperatorskikh teatrov.* Season 1893-1894. Appendices, no. 3, St. Petersburg, 1895, pp. 96-109.

Notes

CHAPTER I. The Provincial in the Provinces

1. See P. N. Polevoy, "A. F. Pisemsky, po ego sobstvennym avtobiograficheskim zametkam," *Istorichesky vestnik*, XXXVIII (1889), 283n.

2. See N. M. Karamzin, *Istoriya gosudarstva rossiyskogo* (St. Petersburg, 1852), IX, 420-427.

3. What we know of Pisemsky's formative years must be gleaned primarily from the small autobiographical sketches he wrote in later years in response to requests for details about his early life. His first known biographical sketch, written in 1854 for a biographical dictionary of Moscow University graduates, was published only recently in A. F. Pisemsky, *Sobranie sochineniy v devyati tomakh* (Moscow, 1959), IX, 602-605. Another sketch may be found in Pisemsky, *Polnoe sobranie sochineniy*, 3rd edition (St. Petersburg, 1910-1911), I, 3-6. In the present study all references to Pisemsky's writings given in parentheses within the text are to this edition. Although further biographical information may be obtained from certain of his fictional works, particularly those that he occasionally mentioned as containing autobiographical elements, such sources must be used with caution. They may suggest the author's psychological state at a given time as he recalled that state years later, and in some instances they may furnish useful scraps of factual detail, but they nonetheless remain fiction and are therefore not entirely reliable.

4. Pisemsky's account of his parents' marriage (I, 3-4) suffers from chronological difficulties. In his autobiography he states that his father, having served about thirty years in the military, married when he was about forty-five and his wife was thirty-seven. Elementary calculations demonstrate that this cannot be correct. Since Pisemsky was born in 1821 after four other children, by the closest reckoning his parents could not

have been married later than 1817. Pisemsky's mother was thus only about thirty at the time of her marriage, and her husband roughly thirty-six. Perhaps Pisemsky confused his parents, so that it was his father who was thirty-seven at the time of marriage, not his mother. From this it would follow that his father did not serve much more than twenty years in the army, and the rest of the chronology would fit fairly well into place. For the birth dates of Pisemsky's parents, I rely on information in A. F. Pisemsky, *Pisma* (Moscow-Leningrad, 1936). This important collection of letters and other materials is cited hereafter as *Pisma*.

5. Pisemsky always maintained that his birth date was March 10, 1820, but recent investigations have shown him to be in error. See A. P. Mogilyansky, "Novye dokumenty o Pisemskom," *Leningradskaya pravda*, no. 82 (April 6, 1946) (unavailable to me).

6. On Pisemsky's secondary and university education, see A. A. Urban, "Materialy k izucheniyu zhizni i tvorchestva A. F. Pisemskogo," *Uchenye zapiski Leningradskogo gosudarstvennogo pedagogicheskogo instituta imeni A. I. Gertsena*, vol. 245 (Leningrad, 1963), pp. 249-255.

7. Pisemsky, *Sobranie sochineniy v devyati tomakh* (Moscow, 1959), IX, 604.

8. Ya. P. Polonsky, "Moi studencheskie vospominaniya," *Ezhemesyachnye literaturnye prilozheniya k Nive*, no. 12 (December 1898), p. 665.

9. *Pisma*, p. 366.

10. Letters of December 3-5, 1877, and April 24, 1880, to S. A. Usov, *Pisma*, pp. 369-370, 464.

11. B. N. Almazov, "Aleksey Feofilaktovich Pisemsky i ego dvatsatipyatiletnyaya literaturnaya deyatelnost," *Sochineniya B. N. Almazova* (Moscow, 1892), III, 404-405.

12. V. N. Orlov, "Katenin," in *Istoriya russkoy literatury*, USSR Academy of Sciences (Moscow-Leningrad, 1953), VI, 53.

13. Almazov, "Pisemsky," p. 403.

14. Letters of August 13/25, 1859, to Ivan Turgenev, *Literaturnoe nasledstvo* (Moscow, 1964), LXXIII, bk. 2, p. 159.

15. Letter of March 13, 1847, to S. P. Shevyrev, *Pisma*, p. 24.

16. For a detailed discussion of "Nina," see A. A. Urban, "Iz nablyudeniy nad stanovleniem realizma v tvorchestve A. F. Pisemskogo," *Uchenye zapiski Leningradskogo gosudarstvennogo pedagogicheskogo instituta imeni A. I. Gertsena*, vol. 219 (Leningrad, 1961), pp. 121-150.

17. P. P. Svinin was also an artist of sorts, who wrote and illustrated rather inaccurate travel books. From 1811 to 1813 he served in Philadelphia as secretary to the Russian general consul, publishing a book entitled *Sketches of Moscow and St. Petersburg* (Philadelphia, 1813). Upon his return to Russia he founded *Otechestvennye zapiski*, which he guided from 1820 to 1830. After 1830 he retreated to his estate near Galich, Kostroma Province, where Pisemsky presumably first met his wife. See the article on Svinin in *Russky biograficheский slovar* (St. Petersburg, 1896-1918).

18. E. I. Ardov (Apreleva), "U Alekseya Feofilaktovicha Pisemskogo," *Russkie vedomosti*, no. 97 (April 10, 1905).

19. P. D. Boborykin, *Za polveka* (Moscow-Leningrad, 1929), p. 153.

20. I. F. Gorbunov, "Iz moego dnevnika," *Sochineniya I. F. Gorbunova* (St. Petersburg, 1907), III, 50.

21. A. F. Pisemsky, "Biografiya Alekseya Feofilaktovicha Pisemskogo," *Sobranie sochineniy v devyati tomakh*, IX, 605.

22. *Pisma*, pp. 25-27.

23. Several articles have been written on the subject of the *molodaya redaktsiya*. The most informative is perhaps S. A. Vengerov, "Molodaya redaktsiya *Moskvityanina*," *Vestnik Evropy*, no. 2 (February 1886), pp. 581-612.

24. *Pisma*, pp. 27-28.

25. Nikolay Barsukov, *Zhizn i trudy M. P. Pogodina* (St. Petersburg, 1897), XI, 89.

26. *Pisma*, p. 27.

27. For a detailed discussion of this work, see Urban, "Iz nablyudeniy nad stanovleniem realizma," pp. 121-150.

28. "Pisma inogorodnogo podpischika," *Sobranie sochineniy A. V. Druzhinina* (St. Petersburg, 1865), VI, 406.

29. Review of the separate edition of *The Simpleton* by O. [Ostrovsky] in *Moskvityanin* (April 1851), bk. 1, pp. 374-382. The text is more easily accessible in A. N. Ostrovsky, *Polnoe sobranie sochineniy* (Moscow, 1952), XIII, 150-158.

30. Unsigned review of the separate edition of *The Simpleton* in *Biblioteka dlya chteniya*, CVII, pt. 1 (May 1851), section VI (Literaturnaya letopis), pp. 1-13.

31. [A. D. Galakhov] "Russkaya literatura v 1850 godu," *Otechestvennye zapiski*, LXXIV, no. 1 (January 1851), section V, p. 25.

32. Letter of August 17, 1851, to A. A. Kraevsky, *Pisma*, p. 41.

33. Letter of December 1, 1850, to Galakhov, *Pisma*, pp. 30-31.

34. Letter of December 26, 1850, to Ostrovsky, *Pisma*, p. 31.

35. *Raut na 1851 god*, pp. 17-43.

36. Letter of February 8, 1851, from Ostrovsky to Pogodin, in Ostrovsky, *Polnoe sobranie sochineniy* (Moscow, 1953), XIV, 20.

37. See text of the letter in Ostrovsky, *Polnoe sobranie sochineniy*, XIV, 20.

38. On the literary evening of February 12, see Barsukov, *Zhizn i trudy M. P. Pogodina*, XI, 338-339.

39. The text of the agreement is published in *Pisma*, pp. 592-593.

40. *Moskvityanin* began publishing the story without delay, commencing it in the second issue for February (the journal put out two issues a month) and completing it in the first issue for April.

41. An exception to this rule was *Bogaty zhenikh*, which appeared in *Sovremennik*.

42. Barsukov, *Zhizn i trudy M. P. Pogodina*, XI, 380.

43. Letter of June 2, 1853, to A. N. Maykov, *Pisma*, p. 59.

44. Article in the regular column "Pchelka," *Severnaya pchela*, no. 94 (April 30, 1853).

45. Review of *Raut* published in *Sovremennik*, no. 5 (1851); also in N. A. Nekrasov, *Polnoe sobranie sochineniy i pisem* (Moscow, 1950), IX, 235.

46. Semyon Vengerov cites P. D. Boborykin, without precise reference,

to the effect that Pisemsky began publication before completing the story. Vengerov, *Pisemsky*, in *Sobranie sochineniy S. A. Vengerova* (St. Petersburg, 1911), V, 146. Since Boborykin was only about fifteen in 1851, he could hardly have had first-hand knowledge of the situation, but the assertion is certainly reasonable.

47. Letter of October 21, 1852, to Turgenev, in Nekrasov, *Polnoe sobranie sochineniy*, X, 179.

48. Letter of August 18, 1855, to D. V. Grigorovich, in Nekrasov, *Polnoe sobranie sochineniy*, X, 234.

49. Letter of December 1, 1850, to A. D. Galakhov, *Pisma*, p. 31.

50. This ending is reprinted in the notes to *A Marriage of Passion* in Pisemsky, *Sochineniya v devyati tomakh*, II, 552.

51. Letter of April 15, 1854, to Nekrasov, *Pisma*, p. 66.

52. Letter of October 7, 1854, to Nekrasov, *Pisma*, pp. 78-79.

53. Article of January 1852 in *Sobranie sochineniy A. V. Druzhinina*, VI, 589-590.

54. Letter of February 21, 1852, to Pogodin, *Pisma*, pp. 536-537.

55. Letter of August 12, 1852, to Nekrasov, *Pisma*, p. 53.

56. Unsigned article "Zhurnalistika," *Otechestvennye zapiski*, LXXXVI (1853), section V, p. 100.

57. Letter of April 21, 1850, to Ostrovsky, *Pisma*, pp. 27-28. *Woe from Wit* was Aleksandr Griboedov's classic play.

58. Ostrovsky, *Polnoe sobranie sochineniy*, XIV, 28.

59. Column of March 1851 in *Sobranie sochineniy A. V. Druzhinina*, VI, 539. In a fascinating article, Korney Chukovsky contends that Druzhinin, though at heart a humorless person, was constantly striving to cultivate gaiety and joy in others, as if these qualities were hothouse plants. Chukovsky, "Druzhinin i Lev Tolstoy," *Lyudi i knigi* (Moscow, 1960), pp. 44-97.

60. Column of December 1851 in *Sobranie sochineniy A. V. Druzhinina*, VI, 568.

61. Anon., "Russkaya literatura v 1852-m godu," *Otechestvennye zapiski*, LXXXVI, no. 1 (January 1853), section IV, p. 15.

62. Letter of August 12, 1852, to Nekrasov, *Pisma*, pp. 52-53.

63. N. V. Drizen, *Dramaticheskaya tsenzura dvukh epokh: 1825-1881* (Petrograd, 1917), p. 76.

64. Letter of January 20, 1853, to Pogodin, *Pisma*, p. 56.

65. For information on these amateur theatricals, see Nikolay Vinogradov, "Melochi dlya biografiy A. F. Pisemskogo i A. A. Potekhina," *Izvestiya Otdeleniya russkogo yazyka i slovesnosti Imperatorskoy akademii nauk*, XIII, bk. 3 (1908), pp. 322-327.

66. A. A. Potekhin, "Iz teatralnykh vospominaniy," in *Sochineniya A. A. Potekhina* (St. Petersburg, 1904), XII, 336.

67. Letter of May 8, 1854, *Pisma*, p. 68.

68. Letter of June 17, 1854, to Ostrovsky, *Pisma*, p. 75. The Ramene spring is evoked in an idyllic, autobiographical light in the first section of "The Carpenters' Guild." The narrator describes the wondrous spring, mentions his children Nikolay and Pavel (almost two and four), and motivates the plot by expressing his desire to build something on the estate, not because it is needed but because he wishes to observe the construction.

69. Letter of October 1, 1854, to A. N. Maykov, *Pisma*, p. 77.

70. Letter of December 1853 to Maykov, *Pisma*, p. 62.

71. Vinogradov, "Melochi," p. 326.

CHAPTER II

1. P. V. Annenkov, "Khudozhnik i prostoy chelovek (Iz vospominaniy ob A. F. Pisemskom)," *Polnoe sobranie sochineniy A. F. Pisemskogo* (St. Petersburg, 1911), VIII, 753. Annenkov was an excellent memoirist, and many of his remarks about Pisemsky's character are perceptive, although he tends to round off the rougher edges. However, as his memoir was written after Pisemsky's death and thus was based on recollection, some of the details are inaccurate. Another of Pisemsky's close friends even described Annenkov's essay as a "portrait with a barely detectible hint at the features of the original." Sergey Maksimov, "Za A. F. Pisemskogo (Po literaturnym vospominaniyam)," *Novoe vremya*, no. 4880 (September 29/October 11, 1889).

2. A. F. Koni, *Na zhiznennom puti* (St. Petersburg, 1913), II, 131.

3. Letter of December 29, 1856, from Annenkov to Turgenev, in *Trudy publichnoy biblioteki SSSR imeni Lenina* (Moscow, 1934), III, 62.

4. P. D. Boborykin, *Za polveka* (Moscow-Leningrad, 1929), p. 154.

5. Letter of October 22, 1854, from Nekrasov to Turgenev, in N. A. Nekrasov, *Polnoe sobranie sochineniy i pisem* (Moscow, 1952), X, 211.

6. Avdotya Panaeva, *Vospominaniya: 1824-1870* (Leningrad, 1929), p. 225.

7. N. F. Shcherbina, "Sonnik sovremennoy russkoy literatury," in *Polnoe sobranie sochineniy N. F. Shcherbiny* (St. Petersburg, 1873), p. 333.

8. D. V. Grigorovich, *Literaturnye vospominaniya* (Leningrad, 1928), p. 225. A letter of February 28, 1857, from Annenkov to Turgenev (*Trudy publichnoy biblioteki*, p. 67) gives a slightly different version of the incident. According to Annenkov, Pisemsky told Grigorovich he would be more successful if he wrote his peasant stories in French, implying that Grigorovich was too citified to produce accurate descriptions of the Russian peasant.

9. D. I. Stakheev, "Gruppy i portrety," *Istorichesky vestnik*, CVII (1907), 847-848.

10. The article by L. P. Lobov, "Slavyanofilstvo i ego literaturnye predstaviteli: Pisemsky," *Slavyanskie izvestiya*, no. 7 (1905), pp. 567-575, is a serious attempt to cull Slavophile notions from the texts of several of Pisemsky's works. These notions were often placed in the mouths of his fictional characters, however, and the author would by no means have subscribed to all of them himself.

11. Letter of May 25, 1867, to Turgenev, *Pisma*, p. 219.

12. Letter of March 3/15, 1880, to Victor Derély, *Pisma*, p. 451.

13. Letter of May 8, 1854, to A. N. Maykov, *Pisma*, p. 68.

14. Pisemsky, "Priem chernomortsev v Astrakhani," VII, 582-585 (dated February 27, 1856).

15. E. I. Ardov (Apreleva), "U Alekseya Feofilaktovicha Pisemskogo," *Russkie vedomosti*, no. 101 (April 14, 1905).

16. Letter of August 18, 1878, to P. A. Pisemsky, *Pisma*, p. 389.

17. Letter of May 8, 1854, to A. N. Maykov, *Pisma*, pp. 68-69.

18. Letter of December 9, 1864, to A. A. Kraevsky, *Pisma*, pp. 179-180.

19. The message was first published in the newspaper *Golos*, April 21, 1866; see text in *Pisma*, p. 670.

20. P. N. Polevoy, "A. F. Pisemsky, po ego sobstvennym avtobiograficheskim zametkam," *Istorichesky vestnik*, XXXVIII (1889), 291.

21. Letter of April 6, 1857, from E. Ya. Kolbasin to Turgenev, in P. I. Zisserman et al., eds., *Turgenev i krug Sovremennika* (Moscow-Leningrad, 1930), pp. 332-333.

22. Stakheev, "Gruppy i portrety," pp. 848-849.

23. Letter of January 16, 1858, from E. Ya. Kolbasin to Turgenev, *Turgenev i krug Sovremennika*, p. 347.

24. Louis Léger, *Souvenirs d'un Slavophile (1863-1897)* (Paris, 1905), pp. 104-105. Léger probably errs in thinking this episode occurred in Moscow, for the period of Pisemsky's most boisterous drunkenness occurred during the 1850's, when he was residing in St. Petersburg.

25. For further information on this aspect of Kostrov's career, see the piece on him in *Russky biografichesky slovar* and also P. O. Morozov, "E. I. Kostrov: ego zhizn i literaturnaya deyatelnost," *Filologicheskie zapiski*, III (1875), 13-20.

26. Letter of May 1, 1855, from Annenkov to Turgenev, *Trudy publichnoy biblioteki*, p. 54.

27. Letter of September 29, 1856, from Botkin to Turgenev, in V. P. Botkin and I. S. Turgenev, *Neizdannaya perepiska (1851-1869)* (Moscow-Leningrad, 1930), p. 92.

28. Grigorovich, *Literaturnye vospominaniya*, pp. 225-226.

29. Koni, *Na zhiznennom puti*, II, 131.

30. I. F. Gorbunov, "Otryvki iz vospominaniy," in Gorbunov, *Polnoe sobranie sochineniy* (St. Petersburg, 1904), II, 403-404.

31. Letter of April 20, 1880, to K. A. Shapiro, *Pisma*, p. 462.

32. Annenkov, "Khudozhnik i prostoy chelovek," VIII, 757.

33. See the passage quoted at length in Semyon Vengerov, *Pisemsky, Sobranie sochineniy S. A. Vengerova* (St. Petersburg, 1911), V, 127.

34. Letter of September 1864 to Kraevsky, *Pisma*, p. 173.

35. Aleksandra Shubert, *Moya zhizn* (Leningrad, 1929), p. 178.

36. Letter of October 12-15, 1876, to Turgenev, *Pisma*, p. 335.

37. Boborykin, *Za polveka*, p. 143.

38. Gorbunov, "Otryvki iz vospominaniy," II, 403.

39. Letter of December 26, 1856, from Druzhinin to Turgenev, *Turgenev i krug Sovremennika*, p. 201.

40. Letter of January 19/31, 1863, from Turgenev to Annenkov, in I. S. Turgenev, *Polnoe sobranie sochineniy i pisem: Pisma* (Moscow-Leningrad, 1963), V, 88.

41. Annenkov, "Khudozhnik i prostoy chelovek," pp. 756-757n.

42. From external evidence it seems that Pisemsky did not invariably blame society for the fate of individuals. In 1861, when entering his most conservative period, he made the following statement, which should not be taken entirely at face value because of its context, but which is indicative of a more individualistic approach: "Every person, whether because of his

foul temperament or because of his ignorance, is always to blame [*vinovat*] for what people do to him" (VII, 614).

43. Letter of March 30, 1855, to Ostrovsky, *Pisma*, p. 80.

44. I. F. Gorbunov, "Iz moego dnevnika: 1855 god," *Sochineniya I. F. Gorbunova* (St. Petersburg, 1907), III, 50.

45. Letter of July 26, 1855, to Ostrovsky, *Pisma*, p. 82.

46. Gorbunov, "Iz moego dnevnika," pp. 51-52.

47. N. A. Nekrasov, *Polnoe sobranie sochineniy i pisem* (Moscow, 1950), IX, 571-573.

48. See, for instance, his discussion of Turgenev's "The Inn" (Postoyaly dvor) in a letter of April 29, 1855, to the author, or his thoughts on Turgenev's "Yakov Pasynkov" in a letter to him of May 30, 1855, in I. I. Anisimov et al., eds., *Literaturnoe nasledstvo* (Moscow, 1964), LXXIII, bk. 2, pp. 138, 141.

49. Letter of mid-March 1852 to Pogodin, *Pisma*, pp. 537-538.

50. Letter of March 20, 1852, to Ostrovsky, *Pisma*, p. 49.

51. Nekrasov, "Zametki o zhurnalakh za oktyabr 1855 goda," *Polnoe sobranie sochineniy*, IX, 341-345.

52. Letter of September 14, 1855, from Botkin to Nekrasov, in V. E. Evgenev, "N. A. Nekrasov i lyudi 40 gg. IV. Pisma V. P. Botkina," *Golos minuvshego*, no. 10 (October 1916), pp. 85-88.

53. Botkin and Turgenev, *Neizdannaya perepiska*, p. 72.

54. Nekrasov, *Polnoe sobranie sochineniy*, X, 247-248.

55. Evgenev, "N. A. Nekrasov i lyudi 40 gg.," p. 89.

56. Letter of September 16, 1855, from Nekrasov to Botkin, in Nekrasov, *Polnoe sobranie sochineniy*, X, 248.

57. Letter of November 27, 1856, to Turgenev, *Literaturnoe nasledstvo*, LXXIII, bk. 2, p. 148.

58. N. A. Nekrasov, "Zametki o zhurnalakh za sentyabr 1855 goda," *Sovremennik*, October 1855; also in Nekrasov, *Polnoe sobranie sochineniy*, IX, 313-314.

59. Review of *Sketches of Peasant Life* in *Sobranie sochineniy A. V. Druzhinina* (St. Petersburg, 1865), VII, 257-286.

60. Review of the *Sketches* in N. G. Chernyshevsky, *Polnoe sobranie sochineniy* (Moscow, 1948), IV, 564.

61. V. E. Evgenev-Maksimov and N. K. Piksanov, eds., *Nekrasovsky sbornik* (Petrograd, 1918), p. 100.

62. Letter of April 19, 1856, from Botkin to Nekrasov, in Evgenev, "N. A. Nekrasov i lyudi 40 gg.," pp. 92-93.

63. For a detailed account of this episode, see V. E. Evgenev-Maksimov, "Neudavshayasya koalitsiya: Iz istorii *Sovremennika* 1850-kh godov," *Literaturnoe nasledstvo* (Moscow, 1936), XXV-XXVI, 357-380.

64. Letter of March 9/21, 1857, from Turgenev to Annenkov, in Turgenev, *Polnoe sobranie sochineniy i pisem: Pisma*, III, 109.

65. Letter of January 16, 1858, from E. Ya. Kolbasin to Turgenev, *Turgenev i krug Sovremennika*, p. 347.

66. Letter of November 11, 1857, to Turgenev, *Literaturnoe nasledstvo*, LXXIII, bk. 2, p. 150.

67. On Pisemsky and Turgenev, see the foreword by Yves Millet to

"Pisma A. F. Pisemskogo," and K. I. Tyunkin, "Pisemsky i Turgenev v ikh perepiske," both in *Literaturnoe nasledstvo*, LXXIII, bk. 2, pp. 125-137.

68. Letter of August 5, 1855, from Botkin to Turgenev, in Botkin and Turgenev, *Neizdannaya perepiska*, p. 69.

69. Letter of November 10, 1856, from Botkin to Turgenev, *Neizdannaya perepiska*, p. 103.

70. Letter of January 3-8, 1857, from Botkin to Turgenev, *Neizdannaya perepiska*, pp. 112-113.

71. Druzhinin's diary entry of February 9, 1856, in *Pisma k A. V. Druzhininu, Letopisi gosudarstvennogo literaturnogo muzeya* (Moscow, 1948), IX, 242. I have amended the third noun, printed *yudoitizm*, to *idiotizm*, since I can discover no such word as *yudoitizm* in Russian.

72. This account of the literary expeditions is based on Sergey Maksimov, "Literaturnaya ekspeditsiya (Po arkhivnym dokumentam i lichnym vospominaniyam)," *Russkaya mysl*, no. 2 (February 1890), pp. 17-50.

73. Letter of March 30, 1855, to Ostrovsky, *Pisma*, p. 80.

74. Maksimov, "Ekspeditsiya," pp. 23-24.

75. *Literaturnoe nasledstvo*, LXXIII, bk. 2, p. 146.

76. Letter of February 19-21, 1856, to E. P. Pisemskaya, *Pisma*, pp. 91-92.

77. Letter of February 28, 1856, to Ostrovsky, *Pisma*, pp. 94-95.

78. Letter of March 25, 1856, to E. P. Pisemskaya, *Pisma*, p. 95.

79. Letter of July 6, 1856, to Kraevsky, *Pisma*, p. 99.

80. Letters of May 17, 1856, to Druzhinin, and June 2, 1856, to Kraevsky, *Pisma*, pp. 97-98.

81. Letter of June 1856 to Shevchenko, *Pisma*, p. 99.

82. Maksimov, "Ekspeditsiya," pp. 33-34. See also letter of October 13, 1856, from Druzhinin to Turgenev, *Turgenev i krug Sovremennika*, p. 190.

83. Letter of Oct. 2, 1856, to E. P. Pisemskaya, *Pisma*, p. 100.

84. Letter of November 27, 1856, to Turgenev, *Literaturnoe nasledstvo*, LXXIII, bk. 2, p. 147.

85. "Astrakhan" was published in the February 1857 issue; "Biryuchya kosa," "Poezdka v Baku" (Journey to Baku) and "Tyuk-Karagansky poluostrov i Tyuleni ostrova" (The Tyuk-Karagan Peninsula and the Tyulen Islands) in the April 1857 issue.

86. Letter of June 2, 1856, to Kraevsky, *Pisma*, p. 98.

87. Letter of January 5, 1857, from Tolstoy to Ostrovsky, in L. N. Tolstoy, *Polnoe sobranie sochineniy* (Moscow, 1949), LX, 148.

88. Letter of January 3-8, 1857, from Botkin to Turgenev, in Botkin and Turgenev, *Neizdannaya perepiska*, p. 113.

89. Letter of April 18/30, 1857, from Turgenev to D. Ya. and E. Ya. Kolbasin, in Turgenev, *Polnoe sobranie sochineniy i pisem: Pisma*, III, 120.

90. Chernyshevsky, *Polnoe sobranie sochineniy*, IV, 722.

91. His disagreements with Chernyshevsky did not prevent Pisemsky from heeding certain criticisms of both an ideological and literary nature made by him in his review of the *Sketches*. Thus, in reworking "The Wood Demon" for the Stellovsky edition of 1861, Pisemsky made minor alterations in some passages singled out by Chernyshevsky (see Pisemsky, *Sobranie sochineniy v devyati tomakh*, II, 557-558).

92. Letter of March 12, 1854, to Maykov, *Pisma*, pp. 63-64.

93. Letter of November 24, 1856, to Almazov, *Pisma*, p. 103.

94. Letter of November 25, 1855, to Nikitenko, *Pisma*, p. 90.

95. Letter of October 6, 1857, to Ostrovsky, *Pisma*, pp. 110-111.

96. Letter of November 18, 1857, from Grigorev to M. P. Pogodin, in Vladimir Knyazhnin [V. N. Ivoylov], ed., *Apollon Aleksandrovich Grigorev: Materialy dlya biografii* (Petrograd, 1917), pp. 189-190.

97. *Pisma*, p. 832.

98. Letter of December 18, 1857, to Edelson, *Pisma*, pp. 114-115.

99. Letter of September 19, 1858, from Druzhinin to Turgenev, *Turgenev i krug Sovremennika*, p. 216.

100. Letter of March 30, 1857, to Ostrovsky, *Pisma*, p. 109.

101. *A Rich Fiancé* in particular had borrowed heavily from the earlier story, and the similarity between it and *Boyarshchina* remained noticeable even after the later story had been redone. For details on *Boyarshchina's* creation, see Pisemsky, *Sobranie sochineniy v devyati tomakh*, I, 473-477.

102. Letter of February 28, 1857, from Annenkov to Turgenev, *Trudy publichnoy biblioteki*, p. 67.

CHAPTER III

1. The most comprehensive single study of *Tysyacha dush* is I. V. Karta-shova, "Khudozhestvennoe svoeobrazie romana A. F. Pisemskogo *Tysyacha dush*," *Uchenye zapiski Kazanskogo gosudarstvennogo universiteta imeni V. I. Ulyanova-Lenina*, vol. 123, no. 8 (1963), pp. 35-92.

2. At one time Pisemsky considered characterizing his hero directly by means of his title: "Umny chelovek" (An Intelligent Man). Letter of March 12, 1854, to A. N. Maykov, *Pisma*, p. 63.

3. *Pisma*, p. 83.

4. *Literaturnoe nasledstvo*, LXXIII, bk. 2 (Moscow, 1964), p. 149.

5. Letter of October 1, 1854, to Maykov, *Pisma*, pp. 77-78.

6. "Primechanie ot redaktsii," *Russkaya beseda*, no. 2 (1859), section "Kritika," p. 19.

7. See text in Pisemsky, *Sobranie sochineniy v devyati tomakh*, III, 475.

8. A. P. Mogilyansky, "Ob izdanii romana *Tysyacha dush*," *Novy mir*, no. 4 (April 1950), pp. 274-275.

9. S. S. Dudyshkin, Review of *Tysyacha dush*, *Otechestvennye zapiski*, CXXII (January 1859), section "Russkaya literatura," 1-21.

10. Evgeny Edelson, Review of *Tysyacha dush*, *Russkoe slovo*, no. 1 (January 1859), section "Kritika," p. 56.

11. Review published in *Biblioteka dlya chteniya*, February 1859. See text in *Sobranie sochineniy A. V. Druzhinina* (St. Petersburg, 1865), VII, 514-527.

12. *Sobranie sochineniy A. V. Druzhinina*, VII, 515.

13. P. V. Annenkov, "O delovom romane v nashey literature," *Ateney*, no. 2 (1859), pp. 242-266.

14. M. F. de-Pule, Review of *Tysyacha dush, Russkaya beseda*, no. 2 (1859), section "Kritika," pp. 1-16.

15. Nikolay Aksharumov, Review of *Tysyacha dush, Vesna: Literaturny sbornik na 1859 god* (St. Petersburg, 1859), pp. 291-344.

16. Letter of May 31, 1858, to M. M. Dostoevsky, in F. M. Dostoevsky, *Pisma* (Moscow-Leningrad, 1928), I, 237.

17. N. A. Dobrolyubov, Review of the almanac *Vesna, Sovremennik,* June 1859; also in his *Sobranie sochineniy* (Moscow-Leningrad, 1962), IV, 375-376.

18. Letter of January 29, 1859, from Shchedrin to Annenkov, in M. E. Saltykov-Shchedrin, *Polnoe sobranie sochineniy* (Moscow, 1937), XVIII, 143.

19. Letter of February 3, 1859, from Shchedrin to Annenkov, in Saltykov-Shchedrin, *Polnoe sobranie sochineniy,* XVIII, 144.

20. Henri Delaveau, "Le roman satirique en Russie," *Revue des deux mondes,* XXV (January 15, 1860), 425-453. Turgenev once wrote that Delaveau was "such a Russophile as is hard even to imagine. For him Russia is the summit of perfection—I don't disillusion him." Letter of October 25/November 6, 1856, to V. P. Botkin, in I. S. Turgenev, *Polnoe sobranie sochineniy i pisem: Pisma* (Moscow-Leningrad, 1961), III, 24.

21. Nikolay Barsukov, *Zhizn i trudy M. P. Pogodina* (St. Petersburg, 1902), XVI, 213.

22. Cited in A. G. Tseytlin, *I. A. Goncharov* (Moscow, 1950), p. 400.

23. See text of memoir in the notes to Pisemsky, *Sobranie sochineniy v devyati tomakh,* IX, 607-608.

24. *Literaturnoe nasledstvo,* LXXIII, bk. 2, p. 157.

25. Letters of August 7, 1859, to Ostrovsky and Druzhinin, *Pisma,* pp. 130-131.

26. Letter of August 7, 1859, to Ostrovsky, *Pisma,* p. 130.

27. Letter of October 19, 1859, from Annenkov to Turgenev, in *Trudy publichnoy biblioteki SSSR imeni Lenina* (Moscow, 1934), III, 86. For extracts from official documents pertaining to this entire episode, see *Pisma,* pp. 634-635.

28. A. V. Nikitenko, *Dnevnik* (Leningrad, 1955), II, 100.

29. Goncharov must have approved of Pisemsky's toning down the violent ending, for on August 28 he had written him in distress over a rumor to the effect that Anany was to smash the head of his wife's illegitimate child. In his usual irresolute way, Goncharov ventured the opinion that this might be excessive, although then again it might not be so bad. Letter of August 28/September 9, 1859, in I. A. Goncharov, *Sobranie sochineniy* (Moscow, 1955), VIII, 326.

30. In 1865, speaking of a later play of his, Pisemsky offered some interesting observations on the subject of tragedy. Only the Russians and the English, he said, were worthy heirs of the tragic tradition. The French tragic hero seemed "theatrical and windy (*frazisty*), while the German is excessively thoughtful (*dumchivy*) and reflective." English literature had long since given birth to genuine tragic heroes, whereas Russia still bore "in its organism and in its history the seeds of genuine tragedy." Although such early Russian tragedians as Knyazhnin, Sumarokov, and Ozerov had not succeeded in raising satisfactory literary fruit from these "seeds," in recent times writers like Ostrovsky had finally begun to realize the potentialities of the Russian tragic spirit. Letter of November 11, 1865, to K. S. Veselovsky, *Pisma,* pp. 190-191. He did not mention it explicitly, but

Pisemsky undoubtedly thought of *A Bitter Fate* as a major contribution to Russian tragedy.

31. For a general discussion of the play, see Maya Jenkins, "Pisemsky's *Bitter Fate*: The First Outstanding Drama of Russian Peasant Life," *Canadian Slavonic Papers*, III (1958), 76-88.

32. Ivan Milovidov, "Dve chukhlomskie dramy: osnova 'Gorkoy sudbiny' A. F. Pisemskogo," *Russkaya starina*, LXIV, no. 11 (November 1889), pp. 335-360.

33. A. M. Loboda, " 'Gorkaya sudbina' Pisemskogo i ee literaturny prototip," *Universitetskie izvestiya* (Kiev), no. 9 (September 1906), pp. 1-12.

34. Innokenty Annensky, "Tri sotsialnykh dramy," *Kniga otrazheniy* (St. Petersburg, 1906), pp. 77-111.

35. My view is at variance with that of K. S. Stanislavsky, who ranked *A Bitter Fate* below *Power of Darkness*, though he thought both good. Stanislavsky, *Moya zhizn v iskusstve*, 3rd ed. (Moscow-Leningrad, 1936), p. 166.

36. Letter of December 20, 1859, from Tolstoy to Druzhinin, in Tolstoy, *Polnoe sobranie sochineniy*, LX, 317.

37. N. A. Dobrolyubov, *Sobranie sochineniy* (Moscow-Leningrad, 1963), VI, 335-337.

38. N. Shchedrin, "Peterburgskie teatry," *Sovremennik*, no. 11 (1863); also in Saltykov-Shchedrin, *Polnoe sobranie sochineniy*, V, 161-175.

39. This discussion is based on, and all unidentified quotations come from, the official report of the Uvarov prize committee, *Otchet o chetvertom prisuzhdenii nagrad grafa Uvarova, 25 sentyabrya 1860 goda* (St. Petersburg, 1860).

40. Pisemsky was partially cognizant of his debt to Pletnev. In the fall of 1860 he wrote twice to thank him for his support. Moreover, at the end of November he wrote to Ostrovsky urging him also to express his gratitude to Pletnev, adding, "To tell the truth, it was by his grace that we received the prize at all." *Pisma*, pp. 140-141. Pisemsky should have said "I" rather than "we," for there was never any doubt that Ostrovsky would receive a prize.

41. N. M. Lisovsky, *Russkaya periodicheskaya pechat (1703-1900 gg.)* (Petrograd, 1915), p. 40.

42. Letter of January 17, 1861, to Turgenev, *Literaturnoe nasledstvo*, LXXIII, bk. 2, p. 167.

43. Letter of September 1860 to Druzhinin, *Pisma*, pp. 136-137.

44. Letter of October 10, 1860, from Druzhinin to Turgenev, in P. I. Zisserman et al., eds., *Turgenev i krug Sovremennika* (Moscow-Leningrad, 1930), pp. 221-222.

45. Letter of November 1860 to Druzhinin, *Pisma*, p. 140.

46. Letter of August 13, 1859, to Turgenev, *Literaturnoe nasledstvo*, LXXIII, bk. 2, p. 159.

47. E. A. Shtakenshneyder, *Dnevnik i zapiski (1854-1866)* (Moscow-Leningrad, 1934), pp. 270-271.

48. Shtakenshneyder, *Dnevnik*, p. 281.

49. Petr Veynberg, "Literaturnye spektakli (Iz moikh vospominaniy),"

Ezhegodnik imperatorskikh teatrov, season 1893-1894, Appendices, bk. 3 (St. Petersburg, 1895), pp. 96-100.

50. The edition was supplemented by a fourth volume, printed in 1867, incorporating most of his production since 1861.

51. Sergey Maksimov, "Za A. F. Pisemskogo (Po literaturnym vospominaniyam)," *Novoe vremya,* no. 4880 (September 29/October 11, 1889).

52. *Russkoe slovo,* October 1861; also in D. I. Pisarev, *Sochineniya* (Moscow, 1955), I, 160-191.

53. *Russkoe slovo,* November 1861; also in Pisarev, *Sochineniya,* I, 192-230.

54. *Russkoe slovo,* December 1861; also in Pisarev, *Sochineniya,* I, 231-273.

55. Letter of March 14/26, 1862, from Turgenev to Botkin, in Turgenev, *Polnoe sobranie sochineniy i pisem: Pisma,* IV, 356.

56. Cited in *Pisma k A. V. Druzhininu (1850-1863), Letopisi gosudarstvennogo literaturnogo muzeya* (Moscow, 1948), IX, 262, n. 7. Nikolay Grech and Faddey Bulgarin were prominent conservative journalists of Nicholas I's time, whose names were usually coupled in the public mind.

57. N. A. Nekrasov, *Polnoe sobranie sochineniy i pisem* (Moscow, 1952), X, 448-449.

58. For a fuller account of this incident, see C. A. Moser, "Pisemskij's Literary Protest. An Episode from the Polemics of the 1860's in Russia," *Etudes slaves et est-européennes,* VIII, no. 1-2 (Spring-Summer 1963), pp. 60-72.

59. *Pisma,* p. 149.

60. Undated letter written before February 20, 1862, to Turgenev, *Literaturnoe nasledstvo,* LXXIII, bk. 2, p. 171.

61. L. R. Kogan, *Letopis zhizni i tvorchestva A. N. Ostrovskogo* (Moscow, 1953), pp. 114-115.

62. *Literaturnoe nasledstvo,* LXXIII, bk. 2, p. 172.

63. P. S. Usov, "Iz moikh vospominaniy," *Istorichesky vestnik,* VIII (1882), 322.

64. *Pisma,* p. 150.

65. See Ostrovsky's letter of May 19/31, 1862, to P. M. Sadovsky and friends in his *Polnoe sobranie sochineniy* (Moscow, 1953), XIV, 102.

66. These statements are based on the oblique evidence in Herzen's article of December 15, 1863, "Vvoz nechistot v London." *Polnoe sobranie sochineniy i pisem* (St. Petersburg, 1920), XVI, 554-558. On the subject of Pisemsky and Herzen, see B. P. Kozmin, "Pisemsky i Gertsen. K istorii ikh vzaimootnosheniy," *Zvenya,* no. 8 (Moscow, 1950), pp. 103-151. Recently A. P. Mogilyansky has tried revising the traditional view, arguing that Pisemsky and Herzen were never far apart, but his points have been effectively rebutted by P. G. Pustovoyt. Mogilyansky, "Novye dannye dlya kharakteristiki otnosheniya Pisemskogo k Gertsenu," *Russkaya literatura,* no. 1 (1966), pp. 165-169; Pustovoyt, "K voprosu ob otnoshenii A. F. Pisemskogo k A. I. Gertsenu," *Russkaya literatura,* no. 1 (1967), pp. 154-160.

67. *Literaturnoe nasledstvo,* LXXIII, bk. 2, p. 177.

68. In a letter of the latter part of January 1863 to Almazov (*Pisma,* p. 154), Pisemsky wrote that he was "leaving" for Moscow on January 31.

Evidently this was just a business trip, however, for when he sent the letter of February 19 to Turgenev cited above, Pisemsky was not only still in St. Petersburg but had not even quite made up his mind about moving to Moscow. In his next missive to Turgenev, dated June 4, 1863 (*Literaturnoe nasledstvo*, p. 177), Pisemsky announces his settlement in Moscow. Thus, he moved sometime between February 19 and June 4.

CHAPTER IV

1. So far as is known, Pisemsky had no personal financial stake in the journal, but evidently at the time he was leaving he assisted the publisher Pechatkin in his campaign to persuade the young staff member Petr Boborykin to purchase it and become editor and publisher simultaneously. Boborykin claims that he was misinformed as to the journal's situation: it was already shaky when he took it over, and he made a fatal error in accepting Leskov's antinihilist novel *Nekuda* (No Way Out) for publication in 1864. *Biblioteka dlya chteniya* failed in 1865, leaving its owner burdened with debts. The desire to recoup his losses may have been the economic motive for Boborykin's subsequently becoming one of the most prolific of Russian writers. See Boborykin's account in P. D. Boborykin, *Za polveka* (Moscow-Leningrad, 1929).

2. Letter of June 4/16, 1863, to Turgenev, *Literaturnoe nasledstvo*, LXXIII, bk. 2, p. 177.

3. Letter of August 25, 1864, to A. A. Kraevsky, *Pisma*, p. 170.

4. Letter of May 8, 1866, to Turgenev, *Pisma*, p. 203.

5. For a discussion of this subject, see C. A. Moser, *Antinihilism in the Russian Novel of the 1860's* (The Hague, 1964).

6. Letter of November 1, 1862, to Katkov, *Pisma*, pp. 151-152.

7. Letter of December 29, 1862, to A. V. Druzhinin, *Pisma*, p. 153.

8. P. D. Boborykin, *Za polveka* (Moscow-Leningrad, 1929), pp. 150-151.

9. Letters of November 1 and 15, 1862, to B. N. Almazov, *Pisma*, pp. 151, 153.

10. Letter of the end of November or beginning of December 1869 to Turgenev, *Literaturnoe nasledstvo*, LXXIII, bk. 2, 183-184.

11. P. V. Annenkov, "Russkaya belletristika v 1863 godu—Pisemsky," *Vospominaniya i kriticheskie ocherki* (St. Petersburg, 1879), II, 313-314.

12. Letter of April 12, 1871, *Pisma*, p. 245.

13. Entry of January 15, 1864, in A. V. Nikitenko, *Dnevnik* (Leningrad, 1955), II, 396.

14. Review by N. B. [N. M. Pavlov], *Den*, no. 32 (August 8, 1864).

15. Review by the editor [Grigorev], *Yakor*, no. 24 (August 17, 1863), p. 465.

16. A. P. Milyukov, "Mertvoe more i Vzbalamuchennoe more," *Otgoloski na literaturnye i obshchestvennye yavleniya* (St. Petersburg, 1875), pp. 193-197.

17. "Literaturnaya letopis," *Otechestvennye zapiski*, CL (October 1863), section "Sovremennaya khronika," 201.

18. Armand Coquart, *Dmitri Pisarev (1840-1868) et l'idéologie du nihilisme russe* (Paris, 1946), p. 296.

19. Published in *Sovremennik*, April 1864, also in M. A. Antonovich, *Literaturno-kriticheskie stati* (Moscow-Leningrad, 1961), pp. 135-173.

20. See N. [N. V. Drizen], "Novye dannye o A. F. Pisemskom," *Ezhegodnik imperatorskikh teatrov*, I (1909), 9-14.

21. Letter of around August 4, 1863, to A. M. Borkh, *Pisma*, p. 158.

22. *Dnevnik P. A. Valueva, ministra vnutrennikh del* (Moscow, 1961), I, 79, 215.

23. Letter of August 4, 1863, to Valuev, *Pisma*, pp. 159-161.

24. Letter of November 19, 1863, to M. M. Dostoevsky, in F. M. Dostoevsky, *Pisma* (Moscow-Leningrad, 1928), I, 341.

25. Letter of January 10, 1864, to Valuev, *Pisma*, p. 164.

26. Letter of late March 1864 to Maykov, *Pisma*, p. 167.

27. Letter of August 25, 1864, to A. A. Kraevsky, *Pisma*, p. 170.

28. S. I. S-v-ky, "Russkie sovremennye belletristy. II. Novy fazis deyatelnosti g. Pisemskogo," *Odessky vestnik*, no. 147 (July 8, 1865).

29. D. I. Pisarev, *Sochineniya* (Moscow, 1956), III, 258-259.

30. Letter of November 19, 1864, to Ostrovsky, *Pisma*, p. 177.

31. N. V. Drizen, *Dramaticheskaya tsenzura dvukh epokh: 1825-1881* (Petrograd, 1917), p. 194.

32. Letter of December 24, 1874, from Annenkov to Turgenev, in *Trudy publichnoy biblioteki SSSR imeni Lenina* (Moscow, 1934), III, 128.

33. Letter of April 25, 1865, to Kraevsky, *Pisma*, p. 182.

34. *Antrakt*, no. 12 (March 24, 1868). See A. P. Mogilyansky, "Tsenzurnaya istoriya pesy Pisemskogo *Khishchniki*," *Russkaya literatura*, no. 2 (1965), p. 168.

35. Letter of March 8, 1862, to Turgenev, *Literaturnoe nasledstvo*, LXXIII, bk. 2, p. 175.

36. S. A. Vengerov, *Pisemsky, Sobranie sochineniy S. A. Vengerova* (St. Petersburg, 1911), V, 193.

37. D. S. Mirsky, *A History of Russian Literature* (New York, 1949), p. 241.

38. Letter of November 10, 1865, to Annenkov, *Pisma*, p. 189.

39. Letter of December 3, 1865, to K. S. Veselovsky, *Pisma*, pp. 192-193.

40. A. V. Nikitenko, *Dnevnik*, III, 18.

41. A. V. Nikitenko, *Tri literaturno-kriticheskie ocherka* (St. Petersburg, 1866), pp. 1-16.

42. Nikitenko, *Tri literaturno-kriticheskie ocherka*, pp. 3-4, 8.

43. Letter of May 8, 1866, to Turgenev, *Pisma*, p. 204.

44. Letters of November 15 and December 11, 1866, from Annenkov to Pisemsky, *Nov*, XXIII, no. 20 (August 15, 1888), pp. 200-201.

45. Entry of January 29, 1867, in Nikitenko, *Dnevnik*, III, 72.

46. Letter of March 21, 1867, from Turgenev to Annenkov, in Turgenev, *Polnoe sobranie sochineniy i pisem: Pisma*, VI, 189.

47. Drizen, *Dramaticheskaya tsenzura*, p. 173.

48. Letter of May 8, 1867, to Valuev, *Pisma*, pp. 216-217.

49. Letter of September 19, 1880, to A. A. Kraevsky, *Pisma*, pp. 502-503.

50. Letter of June 29, 1872, to M. Ya. Kittary, *Pisma*, pp. 247-248.

51. V. G. Avseenko, "Kruzhok," *Istorichesky vestnik*, CXVI (1909), 445.

52. Letter of June 19, 1866, to Turgenev, *Pisma*, p. 206.

53. Letter of May 11, 1866, to Annenkov, *Pisma*, p. 206.

54. *Pisma*, pp. 669-670.

55. See official report published in *Pisma*, pp. 692-693.

56. Letter of summer 1861 to A. A. Kraevsky, *Pisma*, p. 146.

57. Letter of August 4, 1863, to Valuev, *Pisma*, p. 160.

58. Letter of November 7, 1866, to Annenkov, *Pisma*, p. 210.

59. Letter of July 12, 1868, to Almazov, *Pisma*, p. 231.

60. Letter of April 12, 1869, to Novikova, *Pisma*, p. 236.

61. Letter of November 1, 1878, to Victor Derély, *Pisma*, p. 395.

62. V. G. Avseenko, "Kruzhok," *Istorichesky vestnik*, CXVI (1909), 444-445.

63. Leskov noted in early 1871 that Pisemsky had visited him "to moan and complain about how difficult it was for him to get his money from K[ashpire]v." Letter of January 14, 1871, to P. K. Shchebalsky, in N. K. Piksanov and O. V. Tsekhnovitser, eds., *Shestidesyatye gody: materialy po istorii literatury i obshchestvennomu dvizheniyu* (Moscow-Leningrad, 1940), p. 307.

64. Letter of November 24, 1868, from Strakhov to Dostoevsky, *Shestidesyatye gody*, p. 260.

65. Letter of February 22, 1871, from Strakhov to Dostoevsky, *Shestidesyatye gody*, p. 270.

66. Letter of September 20, 1864, to Turgenev, in Dostoevsky, *Pisma*, I, 378.

67. Letter of February 26/March 10, 1869, to Strakhov, in Dostoevsky, *Pisma*, II, 169.

68. During Pisemsky's service as a special agent in Kostroma, he had experienced some contact with the Old Believers and had been in charge of pulling down at least one of their chapels. Nikolay Vinogradov, "Aleksey Feofilaktovich Pisemsky (Materialy dlya ego biografii i vyyasneniya protsessa tvorchestva)," *Izvestiya Otdeleniya russkogo yazyka i slovesnosti*, XXI, bk. 2 (1916), pp. 123-151.

69. Quoted in notes to Konstantin Leontev, *Moya literaturnaya sudba*, *Literaturnoe nasledstvo* (Moscow, 1935), XXII-XXIV, 494.

70. M. K. Tsebrikova, "Gumanny zashchitnik zhenskikh prav (Po povodu romana g. Pisemskogo *Lyudi sorokovykh godov*)," *Otechestvennye zapiski*, CLXXXVIII (February 1870), section "Sovremennoe obozrenie," pp. 209-228.

71. N. V. Shelgunov, "Lyudi sorokovykh i shestidesyatykh godov," *Delo*, no. 9 (September 1869), pp. 1-29; no. 10 (October 1869), pp. 1-38; no. 11 (November 1869), pp. 1-51; no. 12 (December 1869), pp. 1-51.

CHAPTER V

1. Letter of February 13, 1870, to V. G. Avseenko, *Pisma*, p. 241.

2. Letter of March 3, 1872, from Tolstoy to Pisemsky, in Tolstoy, *Polnoe sobranie sochineniy*, LXI, 273.

3. Letter of May 17, 1871, from Leskov to Pisemsky, in N. S. Leskov, *Sobranie sochineniy* (Moscow, 1958), X, 320.

4. Letter of March 3, 1872, in Leskov, *Sobranie sochineniy*, X, 341-342.
5. A. N. Leskov, *Zhizn Nikolaya Leskova* (Moscow, 1954), p. 262.
6. B. M. Drugov, *N. S. Leskov* (Moscow, 1957), pp. 36-39.
7. B. N. Almazov, "Aleksey Feofilaktovich Pisemsky i ego dvadtsatipya-tiletnyaya literaturnaya deyatelnost," *Sochineniya B. N. Almazova* (Moscow, 1892), III, 405n.
8. S. F. Librovich, *Na knizhnom postu* (Petrograd-Moscow, 1916), pp. 25-26.
9. Letter of December 26, 1869, to V. G. Avseenko, *Pisma*, p. 239.
10. N. A. Nekrasov, *Polnoe sobranie sochineniy i pisem* (Moscow, 1952), XI, 344.
11. Letter of December 3-4, 1874, from Ostrovsky to Pisemsky, in A. N. Ostrovsky, *Polnoe sobranie sochineniy* (Moscow, 1953), XV, 46-47.
12. V. Ya. Lakshin, "Spor o Pisemskom-dramaturge," *Teatr*, no. 4 (April 1959), p. 97.
13. Letter of August 20, 1872, to Leskov, *Pisma*, p. 248, where the letter is mistakenly dated July 20; see Leskov, *Sobranie sochineniy*, X, 558.
14. Entry of October 5, 1872, in A. V. Nikitenko, *Dnevnik* (Leningrad, 1956), III, 254.
15. Letter of November 29, 1872, to Leskov, *Pisma*, pp. 250-251.
16. Entry of December 6, 1872, in Nikitenko, *Dnevnik*, III, 262.
17. "Pismo akademika Nikitenko k A. F. Pisemskomu. S zametkoyu Viktora Rusakova," *Nov*, XXXVII, no. 3 (December 1, 1890), pp. 177-178.
18. See the documents published in *Pisma*, pp. 700-703.
19. Letter of March 16, 1873, to Nikitenko, *Pisma*, p. 252.
20. A. [V. G. Avseenko], "Komediya obshchestvennykh nravov," *Russky vestnik*, CXIII (October 1874), 907.
21. Jules Lemaître, *Impressions de théâtre*, 5th series (Paris, 1891), pp. 69-81.
22. Letter of October 20, 1874, to Annenkov, *Pisma*, p. 273.
23. N. V. Drizen, *Dramaticheskaya tsenzura dvukh epokh: 1825-1881* (Petrograd, 1917), p. 256.
24. Daryalova's "abnormality" would perhaps have been too nakedly exposed had Pisemsky selected an early possibility as his final title: "Sumas-shedshaya zhenshchina" (A Mad Woman). Letter of October 12, 1874, to V. A. Kulikova, *Pisma*, p. 272.
25. Letter of April 18, 1873, from Goncharov to Pisemsky, in I. A. Goncharov, *Sobranie sochineniy* (Moscow, 1955), VIII, 451.
26. Letter of February 5, 1875, to Pisemsky, in Goncharov, *Sobranie sochineniy*, VIII, 476.
27. B. N. Almazov, "Yanvarskaya knizhka *Russkogo vestnika* 1875 g.," *Sochineniya B. N. Almazova*, III, 447-452.
28. Letter of January 31, 1875, to P. A. Pisemsky, *Pisma*, p. 292.
29. Letter of February 8, 1876, to Annenkov, *Pisma*, p. 331.
30. Letter of February 7, 1876, to Turgenev, *Pisma*, pp. 330-331.
31. Letter of October 29, 1875, to Turgenev, *Pisma*, pp. 326-327.
32. *Pisma*, pp. 246, 692-693.
33. *Pisma*, pp. 570-580.
34. *Pisma*, p. 846.
35. *Pisma*, pp. 581-586.

36. Letter of February 15, 1874, from A. N. Maykov to the Pisemskys, *Pisma*, p. 581.

37. Letter of February 18, 1874, from Maykov to the Pisemskys, *Pisma*, p. 585.

38. Letter of May 1874 to A. A. Egorov, *Pisma*, p. 262.

39. Letter of May 1874 to S. A. Usov, *Pisma*, p. 263.

40. Letter of August 14, 1874, to Annenkov, *Pisma*, p. 269.

41. Louis Léger, *Souvenirs d'un Slavophile (1863-1897)* (Paris, 1905), pp. 105-106.

42. Letter of May-July 1875 from Saltykov to Pisemsky, in M. E. Saltykov-Shchedrin, *Polnoe sobranie sochineniy* (Moscow, 1939), XIX, 61. Dostoevsky claimed to have seen Annenkov and Pisemsky when they were on their way back to St. Petersburg. Letter of July 6, 1875, in F. M. Dostoevsky, *Pisma* (Moscow-Leningrad, 1934), III, 196.

43. *Pisma*, pp. 742-743.

44. A. F. Koni, *Na zhiznennom puti* (St. Petersburg, 1913), II, 137.

45. E. I. Ardov (Apreleva), "U Alekseya Feofilaktovicha Pisemskogo," *Russkie vedomosti*, no. 101 (April 14, 1905).

46. *Tausend Seelen*, trans. Dr. Leopold Kayssler (Berlin, 1870). One Russian investigator wrote in 1890 that the 1859 (1858?) edition of *One Thousand Souls*, published in 2000 copies, was not yet out of print (which seems incredible), whereas by 1884 the German translation of 1870 had been through two printings of 3000 each. Viktor Rusakov (S. Librovich), "Literaturny zarabotok Pisemskogo," *Nov*, XXXII, no. 5 (January 1, 1890), p. 44.

47. Letter of August 19, 1875, to Turgenev, *Pisma*, p. 317.

48. Julian Schmidt, "Turgenjew und Pisemski," in *Characterbilder aus der zeitgenössischen Literatur*, vol. IV of *Bilder aus dem geistigen Leben unserer Zeit* (Leipzig, 1875), p. 250.

49. Letter of August 19, 1875, to Turgenev, *Pisma*, p. 317.

50. Céleste Courrière, *Histoire de la littérature contemporaine en Russie* (Paris, 1875), p. 311.

51. Entry of October 5, 1872, in Nikitenko, *Dnevnik*, III, 254.

52. Ardov (Apreleva), "U A. F. Pisemskogo," *Russkie vedomosti*, no. 97 (April 10, 1905).

53. A. I. Sokolova, "Vstrechi i znakomstva," *Istorichesky vestnik*, CXXIV (1911), 126.

54. This account is taken from a report in *Moskovskie vedomosti*, no. 19 (January 21, 1875). I am indebted to Richard F. Gustafson for a summary of the article's contents.

55. Boris Almazov, "Aleksey Feofilaktovich Pisemsky i ego dvadtsatipyatiletnyaya literaturnaya deyatelnost," *Russky arkhiv*, no. 4 (1875) ; see also *Sochineniya B. N. Almazova*, III, 401-425.

56. Letter of October 12-15, 1876, to Turgenev, *Pisma*, p. 335.

57. Letter of January 6, 1877, to F. N. Berg, *Pisma*, p. 340.

58. In a letter of October 31, 1876, Pisemsky informed N. I. Zuev that he had produced the first part of a novel. *Pisma*, p. 337. For more details on the novel's creation and aspects of the finished product, see the notes to Pisemsky, *Sochineniya v devyati tomakh*, VII, 419-426.

59. Letter of March 10, 1877, to M. O. Mikeshin, *Pisma*, p. 347.

60. Letter of February 23, 1877, to M. O. Mikeshin, *Pisma*, pp. 342-343.

61. B. P. Kozmin, "Pisemsky i Gertsen: k istorii ikh vzaimootnosheniy," *Zvenya*, no. 8 (1950), pp. 103-151.

62. Letter of April 25, 1878, from Turgenev to Pisemsky, in Turgenev, *Polnoe sobranie sochineniy i pisem: Pisma*, XII, bk. 1, p. 316.

63. Letter of June 9, 1878, from Annenkov to Pisemsky, *Nov*, XXIII, no. 20 (August 15, 1888), p. 205.

64. N. M. [N. K. Mikhaylovsky], "Literaturnye zametki," *Otechestvennye zapiski*, CCXXXVIII, no. 5 (May 1878), section "Sovremennoe obozrenie," 146-152.

65. By 1879, for example, Saltykov-Shchedrin had come to think of Pisemsky as not at all reactionary: the radicals of the 1860's, he contended, had not realized how fortunate they were in having to oppose the relatively harmless conservatives of that day instead of the deep-dyed reactionaries of the 1870's. In an amusing letter of December 10, 1879, to Annenkov, Shchedrin expressed his disgust over the sad estate of contemporary Russian letters. Should one even use the same alphabet as certain people now writing, he asked? "And here just the same you write with the very letters used by Tsitovich, you express yourself with the same words used by Suvorin, Markevich and Katkov [Russian conservatives]! Leskov and Melnikov—all these are paragons of virtue, and Pisemsky—Nikita Bezrylov, the same—is simply most pleasant and well-bred company." Saltykov-Shchedrin, *Polnoe sobranie sochineniy*, XIX, 135.

66. Both sentences originally written but then struck out in a letter of January 2, 1878, to M. O. Mikeshin, *Pisma*, p. 374.

67. Letter of March 23, 1878, to I. S. Turgenev, *Pisma*, pp. 380-381.

68. A. I. Kirpichnikov, *Dostoevsky i Pisemsky: opyt sravnitelnoy kharakteristiki* (Odessa, 1894), pp. 69-70.

69. Letter of January 25, 1879, to Victor Derély, *Pisma*, p. 403.

70. Letter of June 1, 1879, to V. G. Avseenko, *Pisma*, p. 409.

71. It has been claimed that Bartenev served as the direct prototype for the novel's hero, Marfin. A. A. Izmaylov, "A. F. Pisemsky," *Ezhemesyachnye literaturnye i populyarno-nauchnye prilozheniya k zhurnalu "Niva,"* no. 11 (November 1909), col. 446. A. N. Pypin's conjecture that Bartenev was the model for the character Batenev may be closer to the truth. A. V. [Pypin], "Literaturnoe obozrenie. F. M. Dostoevsky—A. F. Pisemsky. Nekrolog," *Vestnik Evropy*, no. 3 (March 1881), p. 429. It is probably most accurate to say that Bartenev was used as a prototype in a very general sense for several of the Masonic characters.

72. Letter of December 10, 1878, to Victor Derély, *Pisma*, p. 398.

73. Several manuscripts showing various stages of the novel are kept in different Soviet collections. Since the relationship between historical reality and the fictional world of *The Masons* is complex, a close analysis of the novel's genesis and development would require substantial study. For a discussion of this problem, see A. A. Roshal, "Iz nablyudeniy nad tvorcheskoy istoriey romana A. F. Pisemskogo *Masony*," *Russkaya literatura*, no. 1 (1963), pp. 180-184. George Vernadsky, who has himself made significant contributions to the study of Russian Masonry, has told me that according to family tradition one of his forebears served as the prototype for a character in *The Masons*.

74. Letter of June 1, 1879, to V. G. Avseenko, *Pisma*, p. 409.

75. Letter of August 30, 1879, to S. A. Yuryev, *Pisma*, p. 415.

76. Unsigned review of *The Masons* in *Russky vestnik*, CLI (January 1881), 438-465.

77. Review of *The Masons* in *Otechestvennye zapiski*, CCLIV (January 1881), section "Sovremennoe obozrenie," 77-81.

78. Letter of June 19, 1880, to Derély, *Pisma*, p. 481.

79. Letter of March 31, 1880, to Derély, *Pisma*, p. 457.

80. Letter of November 15, 1880, to F. G. Flerov, *Pisma*, p. 514.

81. P. N. Polevoy, "A. F. Pisemsky, po ego sobstvennym avtobiograficheskim zametkam," *Istorichesky vestnik*, XXXVIII (1889), 294.

82. Letter of January 29, 1881, from Ostrovsky to F. A. Burdin, in Ostrovsky, *Polnoe sobranie sochineniy*, XVI, 9.

83. Letter of February 9, 1881, to Turgenev, *Trudy publichnoy biblioteki SSSR imeni Lenina*, III (Moscow, 1934), 129.

84. The longest and most solid of these comparisons is A. I. Kirpichnikov, *Dostoevsky i Pisemsky: opyt sravnitelnoy kharakteristiki* (Odessa, 1894).

85. M. D. Prygunov et al., eds., *Neizdannye pisma k A. N. Ostrovskomu* (Moscow-Leningrad, 1932), p. 723.

86. A. V. [Pypin], "Literaturnoe obozrenie. F. M. Dostoevsky—A. F. Pisemsky. Nekrolog," pp. 435-436.

87. N. K. Mikhaylovsky, "O Pisemskom i Dostoevskom," *Sochineniya N. K. Mikhaylovskogo* (St. Petersburg, 1897), V, 410-411.

CHAPTER VI

1. [N. A. Nekrasov], "Peterburgskie izvestiya," *Sovremennik* (October 1855); also in N. A. Nekrasov, *Polnoe sobranie sochineniy i pisem* (Moscow, 1950), IX, 571-573.

2. R. E. Steussy, "Pisemskij's Talent as a Novelist," unpub. diss., Harvard University, 1959.

3. Apollon Grigorev, "Russkaya izyashchnaya literatura v 1852 godu," *Moskvityanin*, January 1853, book 1, section V (Kritika i bibliografiya), pp. 27, 28.

4. Letter of April 8, 1871, from Leskov to P. K. Shchebalsky, in N. K. Piksanov and O. V. Tsekhnovitser, eds., *Shestidesyatye gody: materialy po istorii literatury i obshchestvennomu dvizheniyu* (Moscow-Leingrad, 1940), p. 311.

5. Letter of February 5, 1875, from Goncharov to Pisemsky, in I. A. Goncharov, *Sobranie sochineniy* (Moscow, 1955), VIII, 476.

6. D. S. Mirsky, *A History of Russian Literature* (New York, 1949), p. 200.

7. [Nikolay Strakhov], "Neskolko slov o g. Pisemskom po povodu ego sochineniy. Tom I. Izd. Stellovskogo. SPB. 1861 g.," *Vremya*, no. 7 (July 1861), section "Kriticheskoe obozrenie," pp. 14-15.

8. Letter of May 8, 1854, to Maykov, *Pisma*, p. 69.

9. Letter of May 8, 1866, to I. S. Turgenev, *Pisma*, p. 203.

10. Letter of October 1, 1854, to Maykov, *Pisma*, p. 77.

11. A. A. Izmaylov, "A. F. Pisemsky," *Ezhemesyachnye literaturnye i populyarno-nauchnye prilozheniya k zhurnalu "Niva,"* no. 11 (1909), cols. 439-440.

12. A. F. Koni, *Na zhiznennom puti* (St. Petersburg, 1913), II, 136. In

this instance Pisemsky was referring specifically to characters in *Former Falcons*.

13. Letter of November 4, 1877, to F. I. Buslaev, *Pisma*, p. 366.

14. Letter of October 1, 1854, to A. N. Maykov, *Pisma*, p. 77.

15. Letter of July 26, 1855, to A. N. Ostrovsky, *Pisma*, p. 82.

16. Letter of November 4, 1877, to Buslaev, *Pisma*, p. 366.

17. Petr Veynberg, "Literaturnye spektakli (Iz moikh vospominaniy)," *Ezhegodnik imperatorskikh teatrov*, season 1893-1894, Appendices, bk. 3 (St. Petersburg, 1895), pp. 99-100.

18. The word is used, for example, by Koni, *Na zhiznennom puti*, II, 130, and M. M. Gin, "Sobranie sochineniy A. F. Pisemskogo," *Voprosy literatury*, no. 10 (October 1960), p. 214.

19. A. A. Urban, "Iz nablyudeniy nad stanovleniem realizma v tvorchestve A. F. Pisemskogo," *Uchenye zapiski Leningradskogo gosudarstvennogo pedagogicheskogo instituta imeni Gertsena*, no. 219 (1961), p. 149.

20. Letter of May 8, 1867, to P. A. Valuev, *Pisma*, p. 217.

21. Letter of April 19, 1877, to Turgenev, *Pisma*, pp. 350-351.

22. M. A. Antonovich, "Sovremennaya esteticheskaya teoriya" (1865), *Literaturno-kriticheskie stati* (Moscow-Leningrad, 1961), pp. 218-219.

23. N. Shchedrin, "Peterburgskie teatry," *Sovremennik* (November 1863); also in M. E. Saltykov-Shchedrin, *Polnoe sobranie sochineniy* (Moscow, 1937), V, 173-175.

24. N. S. Leskov, *Sobranie sochineniy* (Moscow, 1957), VI, 641-643.

25. Grigorev, "Russkaya izyashchnaya literatura v 1852 godu," p. 31.

26. [Strakhov], "Neskolko slov o g. Pisemskom," p. 15.

27. Letter of November 4, 1877, to Buslaev, *Pisma*, pp. 364-366.

28. Letter of February 7, 1876, to Turgenev, *Pisma*, pp. 330-331.

29. Letter of May 1878, to M. O. Mikeshin, *Pisma*, p. 386.

30. Letter of October 29, 1875, to Turgenev, *Pisma*, p. 326.

31. For a detailed discussion, see Deming Brown, "Pisemskij: The Aesthetics of Scepticism," *American Contributions to the Fifth International Congress of Slavists* (The Hague, 1963), II, 7-20.

32. Letter of April 26, 1893, from Chekhov to A. S. Suvorin, in A. P. Chekhov, *Sobranie sochineniy* (Moscow, 1964), XII, 23.

33. Letter of May 14, 1871, from Tolstoy to B. M. Markevich, in A. K. Tolstoy, *Sobranie sochineniy* (Moscow, 1964), IV, 365.

34. [Strakhov], "Neskolko slov o g. Pisemskom," p. 16.

35. Letter of October 19, 1861, from Grigorev to Strakhov, in Apollon Grigorev, *Vospominaniya* (Moscow-Leningrad, 1930), p. 474. Grigorev made this comment for the purpose of denigrating Gogol.

36. See N. I. Prutskov, "Tvorchestvo Pisemskogo 40-50-kh godov i gogolevskoe napravlenie," *Uchenye zapiski Omskogo pedagogicheskogo instituta*, I (1941), 3-54 (the title is not accurate); N. I. Prutskov, *Masterstvo Goncharova-romanista* (Moscow-Leningrad, 1962), pp. 72-75; Peter Ledovoy, "Gogol's Influence on Pisemski's Dramaturgy," unpub. thesis, New York University, 1963. This last work is primarily a straightforward discussion of four of Pisemsky's plays.

37. Prutskov, *Masterstvo Goncharova-romanista*, p. 72.

38. I. V. Kartashova, "Khudozhestvennoe svoeobrazie romana A. F.

Pisemskogo *Tysyacha dush,*" *Uchenye zapiski Kazanskogo gosudarstvennogo universiteta,* vol. 123, no. 8 (1963), pp. 71-72.

39. Cited in the unsigned "A. F. Pisemsky, kak dramaturg," *Ezhegodnik imperatorskikh teatrov,* XVI, season 1905-1906, Appendix, 101.

40. Claude Backvis, "Un témoin négligé d'une grande époque: le romancier Pisemskij," *Revue des études slaves,* XXXII, part 1-4 (1955), 43. Backvis also points out a few interesting parallels in the two men's biographies. For instance, Krylov was the son of an impoverished army officer; after his father's death he had to find employment as a clerk, much like Pisemsky, to help support his family. As adults, both were noted as raconteurs and for their addiction to the pleasures of the table.

Index